Modernity, Nation and Urban-Architectural Form

AF798048

Shireen Jahn Kassim • Norwina
Mohd Nawawi • Mansor Ibrahim
Editors

Modernity, Nation and Urban-Architectural Form

The Dynamics and Dialectics of National Identity vs Regionalism in a Tropical City

palgrave
macmillan

Editors
Shireen Jahn Kassim
International Islamic University Malaysia
Kuala Lumpur, Malaysia

Norwina Mohd Nawawi
International Islamic University Malaysia
Kuala Lumpur, Malaysia

Mansor Ibrahim
International Islamic University Malaysia
Kuala Lumpur, Malaysia

ISBN 978-3-030-09759-2 ISBN 978-3-319-66131-5 (eBook)
https://doi.org/10.1007/978-3-319-66131-5

© The Editor(s) (if applicable) and The Author(s) 2018
Softcover re-print of the Hardcover 1st edition 2018
This work is subject to copyright. All rights are solely and exclusively licensed by the Publisher, whether the whole or part of the material is concerned, specifically the rights of translation, reprinting, reuse of illustrations, recitation, broadcasting, reproduction on microfilms or in any other physical way, and transmission or information storage and retrieval, electronic adaptation, computer software, or by similar or dissimilar methodology now known or hereafter developed.
The use of general descriptive names, registered names, trademarks, service marks, etc. in this publication does not imply, even in the absence of a specific statement, that such names are exempt from the relevant protective laws and regulations and therefore free for general use.
The publisher, the authors and the editors are safe to assume that the advice and information in this book are believed to be true and accurate at the date of publication. Neither the publisher nor the authors or the editors give a warranty, express or implied, with respect to the material contained herein or for any errors or omissions that may have been made. The publisher remains neutral with regard to jurisdictional claims in published maps and institutional affiliations.

Cover illustration: HHakim/Getty and mrdoomits/Getty

Printed on acid-free paper

This Palgrave Macmillan imprint is published by the registered company Springer Nature Switzerland AG
The registered company address is: Gewerbestrasse 11, 6330 Cham, Switzerland

Preface

The book attempts to frame a series of perspectives, writings, debates, and discourses around the issue of 'national' versus 'regional' identity in architectural expression and urban language in a developing tropical Asian city. Through a range of typologies that characterise modern life a series of discussions and frame works of present and past thoughts are framed. In Asia, large buildings with urban and modern functions characterise the rise of urbanisation. The focus is on Malaysia, and the discussions aims to bring to light how physical and symbolic structures can be read against the dynamics of a nation's history and post-colonial trajectory. Malaysia in general, and its capital city Kuala Lumpur in particular, have become an ideal ground for such a confluence and convergence of issues and idealisms. As a young nation with its own vernacular tradition arising from its local geography, it also boasts a unique and multicultural population. Malaysia seems locked in a constant state of negotiation and convergence due to a population of which 53% is comprised of Malay native backgrounds, while Chinese, Indian and other minority races constitute the remaining 47%. The dilemmas that it has weathered since independence are inscribed in its physical landscape, and these deserve attention and study.

During the decades after independence, which was achieved in 1957, the architecture and urban forms of Malaysia's capital city, Kuala

Lumpur, have become a field of exploration and breeding ground of new vocabularies. These represent variants in a continuous attempt at reflecting society's ever-present need for differentiation, a sense of independence and identity. They perhaps constitute an ever-present thread of anxiety, as in many modern nation-states in South East Asia. They are constantly negotiating a stance to appease and unify an increasingly diverse and multicultural population. The vernacular architecture of Malaysia is at times accepted as the fundamental basis of identity in the nation, as it is rooted in the traditions of the Malay world, yet at certain times, there is demand for a 'national' architecture that must somehow transcend 'cultural roots' and reach, capture and 'touch' more universal values and ideals. These must consequently result in forms that can be acceptable to, and appease, all races. The authors hence have attempted to trace past discourses and case studies, and have structured the discourse according to key typologies in urban architecture. It is hoped this framework creates a fresh viewpoint and captures moments in the history of the nation; including thresholds of key forms eras when help shape the nation's independence. These represent a trajectory of maturity, and how architecture and urban elements are physical inscriptions that represent the identity of a people and their collective consciousness.

A multiracial country such as Malaysia is thus constantly faced with the issue of cultural representation and identity. A 'national' architecture must be deemed as one not explicitly making specific and direct reference to the symbols of one race above the other. A recurring debate in Malaysia is how to reach such a consensus as to what constitutes the architectural language of 'Malaysian architecture' that is acceptable and able to represent all races. There have been a range of efforts made by various stakeholders, since independence, to incorporate principles in the development of 'national Malaysian architecture'. This include guidelines that regard Malaysia as an entity that has a neutral tone, although local traditions are multi-cultural and Malay cultural forms remain basic expressions of a range of localities' traditional legacies. Many of Malaysia's national buildings have been inspired by Malay forms, idioms and references. The Malaysian Architectural Policy (MAP), initiated by Malaysian Institute of Architects (PAM) in 2009 towards Malaysian Vision 2020, was an effort to outline the principles of a 'Malaysian architecture'. Some of the guidelines are a result of how, since independence and in only a short span of decades, architects and urban designers have sought to instil or instigate a Malaysian identity. This is done either by alluding to elements of tradition or by syncretising elements of multicultural sources towards a combined representation of national identity.

The context and realities of a multicultural society are challenging. Using broad themes, basic urban typologies of the modern nation, the book presents a discussion of how architectural language has evolved and has been appropriated towards the reinvention of identity through 'regionalism'. The focus on architectural language is a crucial one as it links physical outcomes of urbanism with the ideals, intentions, dilemmas and dichotomies of a multicultural society in the scenario of rapid development in tropical Asia.

The physical nuances of architecture and urban form are thus reflections of these negotiations, and recall a certain idealism. At times, perhaps they indicate different extents of insecurity and immaturity. Yet debates are constantly raging, fuelled by developments in the region and the more global movements of design. The forms are mostly explorations by architects and urbanists and are symptomatic of the perennial search for identity and regional assertion. Some argue that 'local' identity must refer to the vernacular roots of a place, while others posit that a struggle must be forged to reflect a more neutral position in terms of physical expression. This book is thus an attempt to refine and document this unique intersections and junctures through the Malaysian cases that symbolise this debate.

Hence the book summarizes key issues in past theoretical debates, writings, key case studies and discourses that are often linked with threads of modernity. These are distilled as it discusses the means of how the case studies encapsulate theory and practice in the context of the nation. Key points deriving from past writings and case studies are grouped according to major typologies and functions which constitute basic elements of urbanism in a city. The structures are then linked to readings, interpretations and intentions. They reflect the different facets of a tropical city and the social, political dynamics of the creation of this city.

To achieve this, the book is divided into 12 chapters. Chapter 1 presents past theories and developments definitions including review of operational key terms in past discourses and terminologies. As it attempts to summarize key points in past discussions and writings, the framework of Malaysia and its scope and boundaries are clarified. Chapter 2 begins the trajectory of building typologies characteristic of modernity and the modern world beginning with the mosque. As Chapter 1 starts by outlining several key definitions and summarising past theoretical writings, propositions, debates and frameworks, Chapter 2 begins to frame the journey in time, which commences with the colonial era and views the 'eclectic' language of the mosque as part of a nation's initial trajectory of modernity. Several iconic mosques are discussed as reflections of key thresholds in Malaysia's development. Chapter 3 begins the story of the International style of the post-independence era in earnest, and its role in expressing and elevating national projects of the 1960s that ultimately produced tropicalised variations of the International style. The rapid diffusion of the International style was forged during a time when local architects came home from abroad and extended Modernist ideals and trends. Chapter 4 uses the case studies of museums and convention centres as frames of reference to discuss the rise of a more emotive, and idiosyncratic approach to fulfil the need for monumentality in the Asian city. These include references and expressions of cultural traditions from the malay world in Modernist typologies. These typologies are similar due to their size, volumetric form and key spaces – and through these, the world had witnessed how vernacular identity became a means to an end, and the key strategy of monumentalising the vernacular in the Asian city. It represented a more assertive language to reflect identities through inflections in form, space, programme and structure. Chapter 5 highlights the ability of construction expression or tectonics to express a subtler yet powerful form of regionalism and uses the university buildings as a typology, focusing on key structures and tracing the evolution of their changes and developments in architectural stylistic trends in this typology including the years of Islamic renaissance and its hybrid offshoot, the Arab-Islamic expression in public buildings. Chapter 6 begins the discussion of elements of identity in tropical urbanism in Malaysia, focusing on public spaces and their evolution, and highlighting the role of walkways and greenery in outlining a unique identity for urbanism in the tropics. Chapter 7 moves to the specific case of Putrajaya in an attempt at a critical review of both language and the problem of the centre, focusing on the criticism, contestation and debate on the Putrajaya Boulevard, the core centre of the Putrajaya masterplan. Chapter 8 dissects how regional and national identity were conflated in a ubiquitous building type, the high rise, which has become a status symbol in Asia, and of nations worldwide. Chapter 9 highlights the transport hub or 'terminus' typology – train stations and airports – as a way of charting the evolution of key 'landmark' buildings, which are increasing recognised as icons and gateways to Asian regions and cities. Chapter 10 proposes a review of current issues in urbanism for the urban core i.e:the tropical metropolis in which climatic goals are crucial in an overall cultural framework that can contribute towards preserving and creating identities, yet folded into the agenda process of realising sustainable targets for the future. Chapter 11 frames the discussion around 'syncretization' and how it is used as a means of regional and national identity in cites and goes into the ability of syncretism as a means of unifying diverse populations. Chapter 12 concludes by highlighting the key points in the book using broad themes and highlights how urban elements and typologies of the city, contain a summary of issues and insights it is the field in which forms were appropriated towards the reinvention of identity and 'regionalism' in the city.

The issue of identity in architecture is characteristic of any emerging state or society. Conflicts and dichotomies are fraught with agendas and often converge onto the city. Tensions become manifested and inscribed into its physical fabric and structures. A struggle towards an established identity is a struggle that constantly exist on two levels; at one level, regional inflections are formulated as localised forms of internationalised structures which embody the global diffusion of the International style. It is a language embraced by multinational corporations, and as nations were anxious to modernise and portray a progressive stance, the language was embraced due to the prevalence of cast-in situ concrete technology. Gradually, architects fought for a more regional identity through a localisation of these global forms and archetypes. At the second level, there is a continuous search for more assertive emotional symbols which can forge a collective consciousness and idealisms in a nation. Particularly in the post-colonial era, nations have sought to strengthen their independence, and architecture is seen as a tool for consolidating and unifying a disparate population within a post-colonial context of an tropical Asian nation.

Kuala Lumpur, Malaysia

Shireen Jahn Kassim
Norwina Mohd Nawawi
Mansor Ibrahim

Acknowledgements

Our deepest appreciation to the academic members of the Kulliyyah of Architecture and Environmental Design (KAED), International Islamic University Malaysia (IIUM), particularly those which we have had the honour to work with in past years. To the fellow academics and professionals who have contributed to the discussions, a depth of thanks must go particularly to the contributors – our colleagues, Dr Noor Hanita Abdul Majid, from whom we have gained so much; Dr Nurul Syala Abdul Latip, who enlightened us on the issues of urban design; and Dr Nor Zalina Harun, whose grasp of history is priceless. Thanks for your constant presence, input and support, and for putting up with our chasing due to the deadlines. Those academics who have allowed us to co-teach courses alongside them in fields of sustainability, critical theory, cultural history and studio classes, we thank you. All the detailed work, writing and the depth of research would not be possible without the constant support and presence of KAED's postgraduates and research officers, namely Maimunah Abdul Aziz, Mustafa Kamal Bashar, Tengku Anis Qarihah Raja Abdul Kadir, Syed Huzaifah Syed Omar, Shaiful Nadzri Shamsudin, Aiman Afiq and Mohammed Hadi. To our wonderful and dedicated assistants who had to put up with us, Azlina Zekri and the talented visualiser and modeller, Nurhamdi Zulkifli, and Zakwan Zakur, our deep and eternal thanks.

The authors would like to acknowledge the Transdisciplinary Research Fund (TRGS16-03-001-0001- Characterization of Rules of Malay Architectural Language) from Ministry of Higher Education for the support of the research leading to this Publication. Our gratitude goes to the past and present leaders of the faculty who have facilitated our leaves of absence to finish the research and writing, including past and present Deans, Prof. Ar. Dr Abdul Razak Sapian, Prof. Dr Alias Abdullah, Prof. Sr Dr Khairuddin Abdul Rashid, Prof. Dato' Dr Che Musa Che Omar and L Ar. Prof. Emeritus Dr Ismawi Hj Zen for their support and vision. Senior members including Prof. Dr Maisarah and recent support by Prof. Dr Elias Salleh, members of the corporate office and administration, namely Nik Hasnah Nik Mat, Norlida Sabri, Raja Ida and earlier, Nor Aiza, all of whom, at one time or other, we had sought support to manage symposiums and meetings during which we could have space to bring our thoughts together.

We extend our gratitude and acknowledgement to Research Management Center (RMC) and the Ministry of Higher Education without whose support the research would not have been possible. We especially thank the team at RMC, namely the present dean, Prof. Dr Ratnawati Ashraf, and her team, Dr Shahrul Na'im Sidek, Haslina Samsuddin and Nurul Afzan, who facilitated the flow of the funding and educated us on the procedures.

A note of thanks to our past reviewers of PhD studies who are advisors in this field; Prof. David Robson and Prof. Dean Hawkes, former academics at Brighton University and Cardiff University, respectively, who had held to the belief that the cause of cultural revivalism and regionalism is a worthwhile one and instrinsically connected with the agenda of attaining a more sustainable world; we thank you.

To the architecture students whom we have had the honour and privilege of teaching and guiding, you have inadvertently and unconsciously taught us in return, as somehow teaching and conveying, had become to us, the best way of learning and processing our thoughts.

To other illustrious industry members: Ar. Tan Sri Esa Muhammad, Ar. Dato' Hj Hajeedar Abdul Majid, Ar. Nik Arshad Nik Mohamed, Ar. Razin Mahmood, Ar. Mastor Surat; the publisher historian and writer Salma Khoo; colleagues and other academicians of architecture from

IIUM, Dr Aida Kesuma Azmin, Dr Zuraini Denan, Dr NoorAziah Ariffin, thank you for the crucial inputs and debates along the way on identity, culture and climate, thus sharing your belief that the cause of regionalism is indeed intrinsically connected with a more sustainable world.

Thank you to the technical staff of the Faculty of Architecture for their relentless cooperation, and the architecture students to whom we had conveyed what was researched, and who added meaning to the journey through understanding and knowledge of their heritage.

To the commissioning editors of Palgrave Macmillan: Holly Tyler, Joanna O'Neil, Joshua Pitt, Rachel Hurley and Shruthikrishna Ramakrishna, thank you for believing in us – the Palgrave team had perhaps believed in us more than we did ourselves – to the last dot!

Lastly, we should like to express our gratitude to our loving families for bearing with us to the end.

Thank you.

Shireen Jahn Kassim
Norwina Mohd Nawawi
Mansor Ibrahim

2017

Contents

Notes on Contributors

Alias Abdullah graduated with a PhD in Regional and Environmental Design (Specialization in GIS and Spatial Planning & Decision Support System) in 1995 from Kumamoto University, Japan. He is a professor and professional planner and was a former dean at the Kulliyyah of Architecture and Environmental Design and Research Management Centre, International Islamic University Malaysia. His research and consulting experiences in related areas cover more than 200 topics, and he has presented over 200 papers and over 50 books, chapters in books and manuscripts. He has served as editor for various local and international journals related to the built environment. His research interests are within the areas of decision analysis and management, urban analysis and municipality management, disaster management, affordable housing studies, *maqasid alsyariah* and Islamic compliance in urban planning and environment, tourism studies, water environmental studies, and 3D urban simulation and modelling. He is affiliated with various professional bodies, local and international, as a member, and has held such positions as President, Council Member and advisor of the Malaysian Institute of Planners and the Commonwealth Institute of Planners.

Norzalifa Zainal Abidin is an Assistant professor in the Department of Applied Arts and Design at the Kulliyyah of Architecture and Environmental Design, International Islamic University Malaysia (IIUM). Her doctorate studied the link between Islamic Arts and the interior decorative elements in the traditional heritage mosques, while her Bachelors (Honours) and postgraduate diploma in Architecture were obtained at the University of Central England in Birmingham,

United Kingdom. She also received a postgraduate diploma in Islamic Studies from IIUM. She currently teaches and researches on Asian Cultural Heritage, Islamic Arts and Architecture, Space Planning Design and Design Methodology. She was a consultant for a recent large green mosque in Malaysia and is currently active in reactivating the arts of the Orang Asli indigenous people in Malaysia through community engagement projects.

Siti Norzaini Zainal Abidin is a senior lecturer at First City University College where she leads the Master of Design Management program. She is also a co-founder of SNor Interior Design. Her latest contribution, the paper 'Strategic Daylight Visualization for the Green Building Process: Integrating Optimization Into An Airport Terminal Design With Skylights', obtained her the best student paper award for ConVR in December 2016 at Regal Kowloon, Hong Kong organised by The Hong Kong University of Science and Technology. Her research interests include passive design in green building, integrated design process and daylighting in airport design.

Nor Zalina Harun is an associate professor and senior research fellow at the Institute of the Malay World and Civilisation (ATMA) at Universiti Kebangsaan Malaysia. She was Head of the Department of Landscape Architecture and Head of Research for the Faculty of Architecture and Environmental Design at International Islamic University Malaysia from 2013 to 2017 before joining ATMA.

Mansor Ibrahim is a professor and professional planner and was a former dean at the Kulliyyah of Architecture and Environmental Design, International Islamic University Malaysia (IIUM). Before joining IIUM in 2001, he was Deputy Dean (Research and Publication) and Head of Department at the University Technology Malaysia. His research and consulting experiences in related areas cover more than 150 topics, and he has presented over 200 papers and produced over 50 books, chapters in books and manuscripts. He has served as editor for various local and international journals related to the built environment, for example as chief Editor for *Planning Malaysia* of the Malaysian Institute of Planners since 2010 and editor for *Habitat International*. He has been affiliated with various professional bodies, local and international, as a member, and held positions such as Vice President and Council Member of the Malaysian Institute of Planners since 2000, Affiliate Member of the New Zealand Planning Institute (NZPI) since 1977, Member of the International Association for Impact Assessment (IAIA), UNEP Member – Inter. Environmental Tech. Center (Osaka, Japan), Member EIA/EHIA Network

(WHO), Member of the Board of Town Planners, Reg. EIA Consultant (DOE 1 00036), Reg. EIA Consultant (NREB, S'wak), Member of the Malaysian Nature Society, and Member of the International Council of Museums (ICOM).

Zumahiran Kamaruddin completed her PhD thesis on traditional Malay woodcarving at UTM, and served as the Head of Department of Applied Arts at IIUM for five years until 2014. She is known for her research in urban heritage, Malay craftsmanship and Malay architecture, with a focus on timber heritage and carvings. She recently supervised postgraduate studies on Islamic art and heritage.

Shireen Jahn Kassim is an associate professor at the Faculty of Architecture and Environmental Design, International Islamic University Malaysia. As a senior academic and a practitioner, she has been teaching in the areas of tropical architecture, critical regionalism, theory of architecture, sustainable and energy-conscious design, and environmental services for more than two decades. More recently, her research has centered on developing theoretical frameworks for identity expressions, the vernacular for urban typologies, and the development of new forms of computational technology for the process of disseminating architectural heritage. She has written a range of books and various papers on these subject areas. As an advisor to government bodies, she has led an advisory and steering committee coordinated by the Construction Industry Development Board Malaysia (CIDB) and Public Works Department (JKR) for the development, enhancement, and implementation of an integrated carbon-based sustainable building rating assessment system for the tropics, mainly for government and commercial buildings in Malaysia. She sits on the editorial board of Elsevier's peer-reviewed *International Journal of the Sustainable Built Environment* and is a member of the Scientific Committee for the annual International CONVR conference series.

Noor Hanita Abdul Majid is currently an associate professor and Head of the Architecture Department at the Kulliyyah of Architecture and Environmental Design, International Islamic University Malaysia. She studied at the University of Nebraska-Lincoln and received a Bachelors in Architecture and then a Masters in Architecture. She pursued her doctorate at *Universiti Teknologi* Malaysia (UTM). Her research interests cover architectural building design, heritage and conservation, and interior environment design. She has received several awards, for instance Veritas Awards of Excellence. She has produced more than 30 articles and writings in these areas. She can be reached at hanita@iium.edu.my.

Norwina Mohd Nawawi (PhD) is an associate professor, in the Department of Architecture, Kulliyyah of Architecture and Environmental Design (KAED), International Islamic University Malaysia (IIUM). Prior to this, she was with the Public Works Department and the Ministry of Health Malaysia. She is a fellow of the Malaysian Institute of Architects and a representative of the Institute at the Union of International Architect-Public Health Group Work Programme (UIA-PHG), UIA-Architecture for All-Region IV and Committee for Social Responsibility for the Asian Council of Architects (ARCASIA). With her understanding of the gaps and different worldviews throughout Asia, at IIUM she taught and researched, among other areas, the history and theory of architecture in the Asian region.

Elias Salleh is an emeritus professor and professional architect who has served in a range of academic roles in local public universities since 1973, namely in the departments of architecture at UTM, UUM, UPM, and UKM, and is currently a senior professor in IIUM. His PhD focused on the prevalence and environmental performance of tropical urban canyons in the city. He undertook his postgraduate studies in building science at the University of Sydney and a doctorate in energy and environment at the AA Graduate School of Architecture London.

Shaiful Nadzri Shamsudin is currently an architect in practice and runs his own interior design company, SNor Interior Design, in Petaling Jaya, Malaysia. He obtained his first degree from University Sains Malaysia Penang. He continued his studies in Scotland and obtained his Masters in Urban Design from Glasgow School of Art, Mackintosh School of Architecture, University of Glasgow, Scotland. He worked with a Scottish architectural firm, Comprehensive Design Pt Ltd., in Glasgow from 1999 to 2000. In Kuala Lumpur he began his architectural work by joining an established international architectural firm called Jurubena Bertiga International under the mentorship of the famous architect Dato Hj Ar Baharudin Abu Kassim. He then continued working with Atsa Architect Sdn Bhd for 12 years before starting his own practice in 2015.

Nurul Syala Abdul Latip graduated with a Bachelors of Architecture (Hons.) from *Universiti Teknologi* Malaysia (1999) and has a Masters of Built Environment (Sustainable Environment) from the University of New South Wales (2002) and a PhD in Built Environment (Architecture) from the University of Nottingham, UK (2011).

She is currently a senior lecturer in the Department of Architecture, Universiti Sains Islam Malaysia. She has been at the forefront of promoting a more sustainable outlook to urban development, particularly related to urban design and heritage. She is currently involved in urban design advisory works such as development of the Urban Image Guidelines for Jabatan Perancangan Bandar dan Desa Malaysia, Urban Design for Azlan Malaysia Masterplan, the Urban Design guidelines for Bako Sarawak Masterplan Project, the Heritage Trail Masterplan for Kuala Lumpur and the Universal Design Masterplan for Petaling Jaya.

List of Figures

1

The Regional and National Agenda in Urban-Architectural Identity through Conflicts and Conflations

Shireen Jahn Kassim, Norwina Mohd Nawawi, and Mansor Ibrahim

Introduction

Themes and debates surrounding 'regionalism', 'identity', 'modernity' and 'form' are not a new field. Any attempt to compile a discourse on certain perspectives on the issue would necessitate taking another look at the multiple definitions and frameworks that have surrounded such concepts. There have been many valuable writings on such themes, and some of these debates particularly revolve around the field of the 'tropical' or the 'developing' nation. Some of these past writings have also centred around multicultural contexts such as Malaysia, Singapore and Indonesia. One of the earliest explorations in architectural thought in these fields in the context of Malaysia as a developing nation is Ken Yeang's 'Tropical Urban Regionalism – Building in a South East Asian city' (1987) in which Yeang compiles and reviews the richly diverse and multiple sources of 'regionalist' identity in terms of images and devices from the vernacular, colonial and post-colonial architecture in Malaysia. Yeang (1987) identifies and highlights a range of past devices, some from the traditional world of the Malay

S. Jahn Kassim (✉) • N. Mohd Nawawi • M. Ibrahim
International Islamic University Malaysia, Kuala Lumpur, Malaysia

© The Author(s) 2018

S. Jahn Kassim et al. (eds.), *Modernity, Nation and Urban-Architectural Form*,
https://doi.org/10.1007/978-3-319-66131-5_1

vernacular, as having potential for 'adaptation' to the modern city: *'Architecural devices include.. porches, verandahways, raised ventilaed timber floors, pitched roofs, balustraded erraces'* and highlights the purity and classicality of the Malay house forms in responding to the tropical climate, from which essential principles can be derived. Abel (1997) similarly, and in more detail, compiles and traverses a trajectory of historical styles and developments in Malaysia, from the *kampung* (village), to the colonial models of public buildings and to modern attempts of interpreting regional essences in modern forms. Recently, Hagan (2000) and Steele (2002) have further discussed how sustainable architecture and regionalism are part of the same ethos. One must reconcile an emphasis on 'empirical performance' with 'design expression' and visual interest. They suggested that combining aesthetics through cultural expression and concerns with environmental performance criteria is necessary. For practitioners concerned about the aesthetic 'expression' of sustainability, a reconciliation can be found through a return of searching for a formal expression of regional 'culture'.

Modernity

The era of 'modernity' is typically linked with a break or rupture with the past. 'Modernity' is often advocated and viewed as a period in a nation's history when the nation and communities become aware of drastic changes. To forge into a new future, leaders and their populations become infused with a new energy and spurts of idealism. Historically, eras of modernity have been linked with technologically driven phases, due to scientific events or eras. The rise of 'new' forms of technology brought about by advancements in the sciences often brings fresh impetus in design, and new ideas into the built environment, in whatever region, and these were always marked by the gradual birth and energy of new movements in arts, architecture and urban design.

Kahn (2006) describes the nature and specific conditions of modernity with a reference to the Malaysian context:

> *When we seek to narrate Malaysian modernity, the question of such a break immediately presents itself ... It produces an awareness of a multiplicity of breaks and a plurality of the past, including the breaks within modernity itself.*

As a newly formed nation at the cusp of independence, Malaysia was a country that needed to project a certain identity to the world. However, Malaysia was also in the South East Asian region, a region fraught with multiplicity and diversity of cultures and identities. As Kahn (2006) again describes it:

> *The nations of insular and peninsular South East Asia – Indonesia, Philippines, Malaysia and Singapore – are frequently distinguished from those in northern and eastern Asia, by the linguistic, cultural, religious and social diversity of their populations. His diversity, is moreover, seem to pose particular problems for modern states of the region.*
>
> *The successes and failures of different governing regimes in the region are therefore often measured against their varying capacities to 'manage' their diverse populations.*

Hence the undertaking, initiating and commissioning of architecture and urban structures is not only an expression of development and modernisation but a way in which identity and symbols are produced and preserved. In the words of Jones (2011), they become part of the wider discourses of identity and belonging. They breed a critical agenda in relation to the evolving growth and dynamics of an urban language and formal representation that can epitomise a developing nation. The field of architecture and urban language, and the large investment they entail, is never a neutral one and is always fraught with 'positions'. They evolve as society evolves and must be debated to ensure that these structures are somehow effective in representing ideals higher than themselves. The goal of multicultural unity is one of these ideals, along with the struggle and effort to preserve local cultures, through political will and social-religious climate, to reflect the specifics of both the environment and geography.

Modernity and Modernism

While 'modernity' is generally understood as a period in which there were tumultous changes in technology and science that affected society, it has been described as one which signals the beginning of a wide-ranging impact. Global developments center around two significant advancements, that is, the Industrial Revolution in Europe and the era of the Enlightenment. As postulated by Frampton (2007): 'The more rigorously one searchers for the origins of modernity … One tends to project it back, if not to the Renaissance, then to that moment in mid 18th century when a new view of history brought architects to question the Classical canons of Vitruvius.' Modernism, on the other hand, is a much more recent phenomenon, linked to the far-reaching changes occuring in the late 1800s and which continued into the era after the 1900s. Modernism, was formulated, during a time in Europe during which there was a search for the 'new' and there was an injection or a broad push, after two destructive world wars. Two urgent agendas came together: the need to rebuild for the masses and the need to avoid recycling forms of the past. Architects, planners and urbanists wanted to redefine the future in terms of the present, instead of the past. Colquhoun (2001) summarises

> *Modernity is broadly understood as all buildings and works that are conceived, designed and built during an intensive modernization period of a nation or country or region.*

To epitomise the idea of progress, a certain objectivity and functionality must symbolise the new mindset. This aesthetic value was diffused in Asia. At the onset of independence this was expressed in architecture as it was connotative of a new socio-ideological framework. Urban-architectural form is thus not only a means of asserting the new found sense independence, presence and identity across nations, but a means of reaching out beyond its own boundaries and asserting a new consciousness and optimism for the global audience. Modern architecture has carried this sense of optimism in its form and appears as a certain unfinished and constantly evolving project. It is seen as expressing the ability of a people to stake their position in a world that must commemorate their attainment and consolidate the political independence of the nation-state, and to show a certain measure of social and technological attainment.

Yet modernisation is also the harbinger of urbanisation and along with it, a gradual destruction of identity, traditions, idealisms and purpose, as Frampton (2007, preface to 4th edition) describes with insight and force:

> *As we are thrown into the modernizing vortex of the 21st century, since the global production of architecture … far exceeds the critical overview of any single observer … This is greatly exacerbated by the fact that technological modernization has become an irreversible fate … The current triumph of market-driven modernization, which under the aegis of globalized capitalism is virtually devoid of any kind of ameliorative aim.*

Thus modern architecture, for example in a nation such as Malaysia, can be broadly understood as all buildings and built works which are conceived, designed and built during an intensive modernisation period of a nation, country or region. However, it can also be understood as a series of works, whether in architecture, art or urban design, that expresses a society's consciousness of an evolution or their newfound position in the modern world. Modern architecture may begin with the need to commemorate their independence or achievement in terms of social and technological development. Architecture becomes a means of expressing their hopes or the 'spirit of the age'.

Architectural Regionalism: A Global Movement

'Architectural regionalism', is generally described as 'a commitment to finding unique responses to particular places, culture and climates' (Curtis 1986), and as Jahn Kassim and Nawawi (2016) have outlined, even the modernist Le Corbusier had not sought only to regionalise his Modernist forms in into acclimatised variants, but had modernised past forms. Essentially a movement or trend that gathered momentum in developing countries, regionalism must be understood in the context of the increasing dominance of a homogeneous style. The local context basically became the basis of inspiration for differentiation in architecture.

The post-colonial era, also saw forms arising as a critique against the universalising tendencies of modernisation in the region. During this period, there was a subtle destruction of local and regional identities, and architectural regionalism represented a response that had gathered momentum after the achievement of independence in developing countries. In this context, regionalism is an assertion of a people's or nation's identity against those forces of globalisation. The urbanising context of developing countries became the catalyst for a search towards a localised style. Powell and Ozkan (1985) has taxonomised the evolution, of regionalism into several broad strands namely two broad streams or branches: 'the historically-derivative' and 'the historically-transformative'. The historically derivative strand refers to a typological approach using 'vernacular vocabulary' including the 'neovernacular' approach which refers to the application of indigenous techniques in smaller-scale buildings, traditional typologies and forms. Aesthetic expression acrose from an articulation of traditional elements and materials and the use of indigenous labour and craftsmanship. With larger building programmes or typologies, Powell and Ozkan highlight the significance of a more 'transformative' form of regionalism:

> *Rather than an eclectic copying of the past or slick collage of elements from Modernism, history and region (as in post-modernism), regionalism seeks to synthesize a genuine hybrid, a new configuration which may include a remembrance of the past, but transformed or framed in terms of its significance for today.*

Rather than a straightforward process of extracting elements derived directly from the past, transformative regionalism often involves a more indirect interpretation in which traditional forms and patterns are alluded to and reinterpreted into new forms. The approach ranges from a climatic position to regionalism to a more iconic tendency. The climatic approach essentially represents a more rigorous approach to regionalism. It emphasises a predominant strategy of deriving architectural form and expression from an analysis of the locality's climate. As defined by Olgyay in his *Design with Climate: Bioclimatic Approach to Architectural Regionalism* (1963):

> *The design approach is based on a systematic analysis of the climate and landscape of a particular locality and the transformation of these principles into architectural form and expression.*

National Identity

The nation, on the other hand, occupies a space that differs from that of a region. Curtis (1996) highlights how in modern architecture, aspiration towards a regional architecture imply a different set of boundaries to a national architecture.

> *'National' and 'cultural' identities in architecture at times, constitutes different set of boundaries; and that ... The dilemma attached to the problem of public representation were not unique to any society.*

Kahn (2006) describes the 'nation' as a modern construct, a process of disembedding the individual and re-embedding it in a new social structure. Kahn (2006) describes a phenomenon and with respect to Malaysia:

> *Regardless of whether civic nation-building in northwestern Europe was or was not successful ... It is clear that the ethnic-cum-racial pluralization of Malayan society is by no means unique in the history of the modern nation-state.*

In any multicultural society, the challenges of representation become acute, as architecture can make or break the consciousness of a people as one nation, as it has the opportunity to act as a uniting symbol, including representing a distinct historical moment. The premise of this book is based on the belief that for relatively large structures, or urban development in independent nations, and in the midst of the search for an inclusive modality of expression and language, at different times and in various degrees of intensity, two conflating and occasionally conflicting forces and dynamics occur: the regionalising force or tendency and, at a higher level, the symbolic agenda or pressure. On the surface these two may seem synonymous, they are two different forms of ideations. As highlighted in his reading of Ken Yeang's bioclimatic architecture, Alan Balfour (1994) succinctly describes the conditions faced by a post-colonial nation and the conflations of regional versus national identity intentions in form and language. In the preface of his book, he observes Ken Yeang's bioclimatic skyscrapers, and views them against the background of momentous political, cultural and economic changes in a post-colonial nation:

> *The evolution of Yeang's architecture is embedded in the emergence of Malaysia as a distinct culture. One hundred years and more of imposed and quite alien reality would make the task of establishing the cultural voice of Malaysia after British rule more complex … The restoration of a regional and national identity after a century of British rule had specific targets: how to negate the presence of the British past; how to inflect architecture with modernist reason while detaching it from Europe's tendency for symbolic abstraction; how to frame an architectural language which, while showing an understanding of traditional values, would express the economic ambitions of the new nation.*

Notes on the Historical Context of Malaysia

In the late 1700s, what began as a British trading post in Penang evolved into a colonial outpost by the early 1800s, and ended with the independence of Malaysia in 1957. By this time, Malaysia was a nation comprising a multicultural population. In the late nineteenth century the British had control over the Straits Settlements of Penang, *Melaka* and Singapore, and extended their power and influence outwards in order to create a safe environment to facilitate increased trade, movement of people and goods, commerce and cultural changes. Hence the rates of migration following colonisation had increased rapidly, accommodated by the rise of new infrastructure of railways and roads. There was a fast infusion and integration of Chinese and Indian communities for labour purposes, particularly in the tin mining and rubber plantation industries. This was followed by a rapid boom in the plantations, which continued to drive large-scale immigration of Chinese populations and labourers from the Indian subcontinents.

Other local factors play a role in the variations found in the Malaysian urban landscape. For example, due to historical factors, Kedah, Kelantan and Terengganu historically have a different cultural and historical heritage from ancient times and whose cultural traditions were slightly different from the rest of the peninsula. Mountain ranges and dense jungles separated the eastern and western regions and this influenced the growth of the multicultural population and its effect on policies and enduring economic prosperity.

Independence was achieved in 1957 and the formation of Malaysia, including Sabah, Sarawak and North Borneo, was achieved in 1963. Malaysia is essentially a plural community that was shaped during centuries of cultural cross-currents and consolidations. During the 1800s, the country saw the administration of the British slowly establish itself for the purpose of servicing the developing colonial economy. Hence during the nineteenth century there was an increasing mix of the dominant ethnic groups in the overall population, and Chinese and Indian immigration was seen as crucial to the mining and commodity-based economic machinery of the British colonialists. Modern Malaysia by the twenty-first century became a melting pot and amalgamation of cultures and a multifaith and multicultural population. Historically, the large-scale importation and settlement of Chinese and Indian labourers was to create an economic engine in order to manage a profitable colony by the British and advance its economic base. Malaysia then grew into a multinational cosmopolitan society and a fast-developing economy in the decades after gaining independence.

Essentially Malaysia is a grouping of 14 states, with an almost equally distributed mix of Malay and non-Malay – predominantly Chinese and Indian – populations. As a former colony of the British Empire, Malaysia, as a nation, thus bears evident traces of its colonial past and its leaders perhaps retain traumatic memories of a nation under subjugation. Gaining independence in 1957 not only brought a disparate nation together, but simultaneously catapulted the nation into a global capitalist network and economy. Located at the crossroads between India and China, Malaysia was previously a meeting point and centre of ancient kingdoms such as Srivijaya and *Melaka*. It assimilated many cultures and belief systems from its traders and merchants travelling between East and West along the Spice Route from as early as the ninth century AD. From a belief system in animism, through to Hinduism and then Islam, its population grew from the Malays as the main ethnic group of the country, to a conglomeration of other Malaysian ethnic groups made up of other races such as Chinese, Indians, indigenous minorities and expatriates.

The experience of colonisation, and its end, signalled a defining era that brought about rapid social, economic and cultural changes. The time before and after this crucial threshold was marked by definitive changes, including in the urban and physical dynamics of the region's history. Before colonisation, traditional ways, forms and systems predominated. After the colonial era, the gates of change opened flooding the space with influences and ideas that uprooted traditional ways. Local communities and societies became reorganised, and remoulded into new national entities with definable boundaries. The periods before and after European colonisation were starkly coloured by the changes in the economic engine including industrialisation. The period before colonisation, as in many South East Asian histories and historiographies, is often referred to as 'preindustrial'.

Asian evolution can be described as a series of 'blocks' or episodes during which the region evolved and attained certain thresholds of technological and cultural development. Modernity may differ from era to era, and nation to nation, from one geographical boundary to another. Modernism plays out in different styles at different speeds. In the context of newly independent nations modernism was seen as a pragmatic tool for nation building and was a progressive symbol. Its architectural language had rhetorical content to spur the national spirit and patriotism of the people. Styles of the 'advanced' West and Modern architecture were seen as modern and progressive. In the 1970s, this very image of science and technology were diffused by the media's propagation channels. This, including the space race, had been spurred by those images of the first landing of a man on the moon and fed into the consumption of a new aesthetic style.

Malaysian Nationalism from the 1960s Onwards

The attainment of independence for Malaysia in 1957 was followed by the 1960s and 1970's era of technological optimism. The rise of Modernism and the International style throughout the world was swept along by this spirit, that of technoefficiency, forged with an idealism that advocated and believed in a complete departure from the past. Globally the idea of functionalism and technological determinism was part and parcel of the rebuilding of Western cities, and by the 1960s Modernism, had converged in the urgency of building in Asia after the two destructive world wars.

Initially the diffusion of this style coincided with an era of growth and optimism due to the newly attained independence, and urban centres were marked by the pervasive International style which not only signified progress, but was associated with the more progressive and advanced values of the Western world and the reflections of a better era of social justice and civic life. In Asia, the shift towards a pluralist society can especially be found in nations where sociocultural developments, including spatial and social patterns, were left by the departing Colonials. Malaysia, previously under the control of colonial powers, saw it as imperative not only to consolidate its identity, but to unite a national community divided by different religions, cultures, languages and past traditions.

National Identity

The idea of a nation is generally understood as a group of people who are tied together by a common land, geography, boundary or place of birth. In the past, national identity had been utilised, remodelled and rephrased in order to guide towards a common path and a reorientation of policies and plans. National identity can be defined as a subset of regional identity, and is represented by forms that stir the consciousness and memory of populations.

Historically, nation-states have long utilised the power of landmark buildings. These edifices to weave a narrative and consolidate a collective consciousness and memory in order to embed ties of loyalty and nationalism. The idea of unity is thus repeatedly expressed in urban and architectural forms. As the new economy fed into the changes, the sociopolitical structures had ultimately shaped the developments in urban form and structures. Typically spurred by a sense of euphoria, optimism for the nation steps across a new threshold of life; buildings and forms with national identity are particularly intense in their design and visual imagery. Jones (2011) gives an apt description of the role of architecture in national identity formation:

> *Architecture was central to the cultural self-understanding of nation states, in this period – it provided an opportunity for emerging states, to give material form, to their political power … Architecture can be framed as a part of a broader repertoire of cultural symbols.*
>
> *States have long used landmark buildings, to supplement a historical narrative of collective memory when seeking bonds of loyalty. … the role of architects, in designing such monumental, national buildings in imposing national styles through particularistic cultural references was beset by tensions, and while the period was one of explicit and creative 'flagging' innovation and experimentation proliferated.*

With respect to Malaysia, Kahn (2006) describes the nation-state as an outcome of the colonial era, with its own sets of boundaries and social structures:

> *The apparent uniqueness of Colonial Malaya dissolves once we recognise that social modernization initially disembeds people from their social and spatial contexts, it then reembeds them in a new spatial order.*

Kien's (2007) 'Building Merdeka' is one of the few attempts to highlight the ideas and intentions that lay behind the making of several iconic structures immediately after Independence. His analysis usefully creates a continuum of landmarks to symbols the Merdeka Stadium, Merdeka Park, University Malaya, Dewan Bahasa dan Pustaka, Stadium Negara, Muzium Negara, Parliament House, Masjid Negara, Subang Airport and the National Monument. Within the first decade after 1957 ten national architectural projects were commissioned and constructed in and around Kuala Lumpur and the historical contexts, considerations and processes leading to their design and realisation were studied in depth. Abdullah (2014) highlighted how the Modernist structures constructed during early Independence were a form of Malaysian heritage. Although many of these buildings have aged and a few have been destroyed, they constituted a unique localised form of architecture that captures an emotive and euphoric moment in the nation's history. He documents a list of

Modernist structures with surreal and astounding photography to show the exciting forms and expressions of Modern architecture embodying nationalistic sentiments from the 1960s to the 1970s.

In terms of theoretical discourses and premises, Yeang (1984) theorises of the 'Malaysian' identity focused on the critical, which should not be merely 'the straightforward transposition of vernacular elements to a modern type-form', but must be 'a process that involves a deeper analysis of general principles'. Yeang elevates the critical position of 'climate' as a main premise and determinant of architectural form. A synthesis between 'climate' and 'culture' as a distinctive form of Malaysian architecture suited to the modern world can thus emerge, muses Yeang.

> *Our architecture should be dissimilar from that being done elsewhere if not but simply by the obvious differences in the local climate and in the complex overlay of the cultural, physical and economic conditions that differ between each locality. This emergent architecture should be critically vernacular and one that can be identifiable and be regarded as the Malaysian architecture.*

Yeang (1984) thus highlights how 'climate' must be championed due to its sustainable and ecological consequences and its value-neutral position. Climatic form was a proposition that would satisfy the need to negotiate between the different races in multicultural Malaysia. To design with climate, a sieving function of the building form and envelope must be worked on and secondary and supporting elements then infused with elements that evoked a location's architectural heritage.

The incorporation of the various cultures and their symbols is seen as secondary to climate as a determinant, but the integration of the tropical landscape and ecology into the urban environment is equally important. Yeang (1984) makes the connection between the 'critical vernacular' with the idea of 'operative metaphors', where elements are selected and designed not merely as aesthetic elements but on the basis of their function.

> *There must be more than just a sense of style. The incorporation of cultural factors and local lifestyle patterns in design should have their own internal justification and consistency and must function operatively with the building's function and system. The use of symbolic cultural aspects in design should have an operative feature besides the aesthetic.*

The dilemmas and tensions that beset a physical representation of a plural society is experienced in Malaysia and as in other countries, any attempt to articulate a language must somehow represent a multicultural ideal, are generally described by Jones (2011):

> *The role of architects is designing such monumental, national buildings, in imposing national strategies through particularistic culturalistic references was beset with tension, and while the period was one of explicit and creative flagging, innovation and experimentation proliferated.*

The earlier years of nation building saw a constant push towards negotiation and convergence. Some argue that 'local' identity must refer to the vernacular roots of a place, whereas others posit that a struggle must be waged to grow from a more neutral position in terms of physical expression. This book is an attempt to highlight examples of this unique intersection and the Malaysian cases that symbolise this juncture and debate.

Critical Regionalism

The term 'critical regionalism' was first coined by Professor Alexander Tzonis and Lliane Le Faivre in their joint article 'The Grid and the Pathway – An Introduction to the Work of Dimitris and Susana Antonakakis' (1981). Their writings and theories on critical regionalism developed in opposition to Modernist positions and forms. They saw Modernist trends – raging during the 1960s and 1970s – as a universalising tendency which threatened to dominate urban centres in various regions of the world. Without prescribing specific architectural rules to critical regionalism, they assert that by way of a general definition, it upholds individual and local architectonic features against more abstract and universal ones. In addition, however, regionalism bears the mark of ambiguity. They viewed the position of critical regionalism as a 'critique' of Modernism and the International style, which they describe as 'machine-like', 'functional' and 'rational'. They argue that these ideas and theories are 'mechanistic' and should be 'complemented by a more comprehensive approach'. They elucidate their position of criticality as one which is 'a more humanistic phase in the mechanization of design. ... A new conceptual and institutional framework in which to gain identity, recognition and currency' (1984). Although they propose a position as a response to globalisation, the intention is still to be a part of the Modern movement.

Discourses on critical regionalism which emerged during the 1980s cannot be separated from developments in the post-Modernist movement during the 1980s, and its impact on architectural theory and design. Essentially post-Modernism – which began in the 1960s and continued until the 1980s and arose as a response to the homogeneity of the urbanising condition – had sought to reintegrate history and interest in modern buildings and cities.

Larson (1995) suggests that the critical approach was meant 'to develop an architectural language and an architecture discourse that transcended the demands of the client or merely pleasing the public'. The position of the 'critical' had risen as a reaction to the post-Modernist position which was increasingly seen as a tendency towards image-making and mere visual variety in architecture. This approach advocated a return to the use of Classical and Neotraditional motifs as part of a reaction against the dominant but weakening paradigm of Modernism, but at times degenerated into mere façade dressing. The exaggeration of Classical elements had once become the favorite dress of new high-rise offices and new urban developments in the West. Ghirardo (1996) summarises:

> *During the late 1970s and early 1980s, structures scripted with recognizable historical motifs, such as Johnson/Burgee's AT&T Building in New York (1978–1984) or Grave's Portland Building, were held to carry meaning simply by virtue of their appropriation of recognizable historical symbols.*

The overall intention was to protect against or pose an armature to the post-Modernist tendency of degenerating into a language focused on the derivation and accentuation of the 'superficial'. The 'superficial' in this context meant the tendency for expression to merely be applied to the surface without any involvement or articulation of space and form. The ethics and aesthetics of Modernism must be armed against and saved from what was seen as the 'risk' and 'onslaught' of certain tendencies in post-Modernism, hence a 'critical' position in regionalism would be a position that could distance itself from the post-Modernist position, which was at times undifferentiated from stylistic tendencies and forms of kitsch or populist architecture.

Frampton (1983) describes the conditions underlying the development of critical regionalism which to him were also part of the new necessity for symbols:

> *Among the pre-conditions for the emergence of regional expression is not only sufficient prosperity, but also some kind of anti-centrist sentiment – an aspiration for some kind of cultural, economic and political independence.*

Frampton (1980) had earlier sought to extend the idea of sustaining modern architecture as a 'critical' practice. The aim was to protect modern architecture from what he saw as an onslaught of mere façade dressing or exaggeration of forms into icons. Principles were outlined, including an expression of topography and tectonics. Frampton (1999) later evolved this as a tectonic approach to architecture, in his seminal *Studies in Tectonic Culture* (2001): *'[I]n which the critical position was expanded to an expression of architecture through tectonic descriptions and constructional aesthetic rather than for "sculptural" modalities and representing a certain meaning that it carries.'*

Hence Frampton sought to protect Modernism from the excesses of post-Modernism through critical regionalism and by positing regionalism within the pure tenets of Modernism. The 'critical' was a reintegration of regionalist tendencies into Modernism. A deeper analysis of the layers of cultural traditions must be initiated and then fused into forms based on a modern and universal language. This position advocated the synthesising of forms related to universal civilisation with elements derived indirectly from the peculiarities of a particular place, and it was clear that critical regionalism was still viewed as being part of Modernism:

> *While it is critical of modernization, nonetheless it still refuses to abandon the emancipatory and progressive aspects of the modern architectural legacy. The fundamental strategy of critical regionalism is to mediate the impact of universal*

> *civilization with elements derived indirectly from the peculiarities of a particular place.* (Frampton 1983)

Tzonis and Le Faivre (1981) had also differentiated their critical regionalist stance with an essentially Modernist stance and that of 'picturesque regionalism' and 'romantic regionalism' which, as described by Tzonis and Le Faivre (1981), were linked to 'nationalist ethos and sentimental underpinnings'. A main ingredient of critical regionalist architecture – according to them (1990) – was that it should not only contain a less sentimental approach to tradition, but also include the notion of 'defamiliarisation'. From an architectural design point of view, critical function is achieved by bringing about the special cognitive aesthetic effect on the viewer which is known as defamiliarisation.

> *Defamiliarisation is at the heart of what distinguishes critical regionalism from other forms of regionalism. These ideas include strategies that involve the organisation of forms and spaces within the building which support human interaction and can function as climatic conduits or places for social interaction of building users, rather than the direct application of traditional forms and elements on established built forms. They include the forms and organisation of spaces such as those based on pedestrian circulation patterns, public use and vertical access.*

Criticality Versus Kitsch

'Kitsch' architecture, refers to the literal copying of forms and patterns derived from the local context. Known also as 'pastiche', this tendency can be related to a certain level of immaturity in coping with the rapid rate of socioeconomic change. It can also be seen as an outcome of insufficient depth in resolving the paradoxical synthesis of modernisation and tradition and a certain level of impatience with the demands of thorough understanding. Yeang (1984) describes kitsch as cosmetic and cut-and-paste language, whereas Ghirardo (1996) attributes the language of post-Modernist architecture to a certain level of kitsch.

Hagan (2001) observes how prominent architect Renzo Piano, in articulating his position of regional design for the Tjibaou Center for the native Karnaks in New Caledonia, had consciously sought to steer away from 'kitsch' by emphasising the role of natural ventilation and passive design in directing the outcome of the building form. Yet to create a landmark and a powerful silhouette, Karnak traditional forms were also given equal attention as the driver of architectural expression.

Hagan (2001: p 160) describes:

> *The result is a design that, once cued, may remind the Kanaks of their own minimal built culture, but in no way seeks to imitate it. Piano was adamant about avoiding the slightest hint of kitsch, what he does is imitate the Karnaks own response to climate, working with, rather than against it.*

The term 'critical vernacular' advocated by Ken Yeang in the late 1970s and early 1980s, was also a reaction to kitsch. The issue of regional identity was actively being discussed amongst architects and politicians in the 1980s. These decades witnessed rapid development within Malaysia, inspiring a series of seminars and various discussions amongst architects, planners and the government on what essentially constituted national identity. In his writings Yeang had articulated a critique of the current views on 'national' architecture which, according to him, attempted to retrieve identity directly through the straightforward copying of traditional elements such as the Malay roof rather than a 'critical' approach.

In his article 'Architecture in Malaysia: In Praise of Innovation' (1977), Yeang attempts to outline a more universal notion of a Malaysian national 'style', stating (due to his aversion to any 'direct transposition' of vernacular elements and forms) that 'a Malaysian architecture should be a result of a deeper immersion in principles of context such as climate and culture rather than simply transposing a vernacular roof-form onto a modern building type'. He argues that climate can form the basis of a more universal principle to counter the 'direct transposition' of tradition which represents an 'intellectual cul-de-sac'. This amounted to 'the use of cultural motifs' for a 'cosmetic effect'. According to Yeang (1984):

> *The idea of a contemporary Malaysian architecture that is at the same time compatible with modern societal needs and yet vernacular is an attractive idea … it is a design question that cannot be solved simply by transposing local historical and traditional elements into a modern architectural situation.*

In the chapter 'Regionalist Design Intentions', Yeang (1987) summarises his ideas on architectural regionalism:

> *Architectural regionalism is an evolving enquiry which has as its aim an authentic built environment. ... In order to avoid the prior assignment of a fixed style or the presumption of an inevitable set of preconceived forms and devices to a design programme, we might start with a systemic view of the attributes of the building enclosure that is independent of locational influences so that it can adequately serve as a general armature for regionalist design.*

Tropical Criticality

Chang (2016) outlines a similar position and ethos to Yeang's in his discussion of the position of criticality of Singapore's Tay Kheng Soon and Lim Chong Keat. The conditions of Singapore are similar to those of Malaysia after colonisation, which he describes by referring to the position of two architects in Singapore:

> *For Tay and Lim, independence meant not a reactionary rejection of Eurocentric modernity or a retreat into parochial nationalism through, for example, the triumphalist assertion of the supremacy of one's national traditions and cultures. Instead, they saw the relevance and liberating dimensions of modernity, selectively embracing it ... their embrace did not mean wholesale acceptance,* ***but partial embrace mixed with critical interrogation ... one that was, and perhaps still is, fraught with tensions, and even contradictions.***

Tay's (1990) writings on the theoretical premise for the tropical language of modern Asia put forward his ideas on the use of 'line, edge, mesh and shade' to achieve the 'soft-edged aesthetic' representative of the tropical Asian context. These ideas can be related to particular elements in the Mesiniaga envelope design. Tay (1990) summarises his position:

> *Because of the equitable climate, building enclosures in the tropics need not be absolute limiting barriers. The aesthetic character of the enclosure system must be of infinite variability. ... Tropical aesthetics needs to imply shade, shelter, shadow and profile. The articulating visual language should therefore be preoccupied by shadow and light gradations and transitions.*

Such articulations include envelope design and elevational characteristics of global forms. Although these can be derived from local patterns, including traditional motifs, as these differentiate expression, they must be fused with climatic form in order to give an imprint of tropicality rather than merely adornment of the surface and elevation of the building form. This is one way in which regional identity and its strategies inscribe a localised expression on the city, rather than the Modernist mute, blank or simplified elevations.

Such a position includes regional inflections ranging from enhancing façade systems with surface patterns or forms to formal devices that are sculpted or incised into global forms in the expressive dynamics. In modern cities where the old has given way to the new, there is a kind of significance of stand-alone structures. The approach recalls different shades of cultural criticality, and the agenda is to assert long-range continuities across the length of time in a nation's past and future. Not only must cultural allusions persist in these structures, but global type-forms must be regionalised and coloured with identity.

Globalisation and Regionalism

Globalisation had integrated Malaysia into the vast global economy, and subsequently drastic changes were made to its urban landscape. The 1960s and 1970s were wrought with tendencies of the International style stemming from a need to express progress and the demands of nationhood. Both regional and national identity in architecture and urbanism became a kind of resistance to what Frampton (1981) calls 'an architecture of consumption', a resistance to being swept into the tide of globalisation and its stylistic trends. A post-colonial nation's moments of independence particularly stir the imagination of its people and the artistic strength of a population is emboldened by the visions of a progressive future. In both cases, national identity is conflated with the regionalisation of a modern typology encapsulated in surmounting a modern structure with an identifiable roof and recognisable grammar and silhouette. Malay roofs remain one of the recognisable elements in using an urban vocabulary to elevate an essentially modern construction into an expression of both Malay regional identity and a national identity.

Kusno (2000) interestingly observes how regionalism has attempted to differentiate global type-forms, including the high-rise, through processes of localisation. The process of globalisation is endemic in South East Asian urban centres due to the regional experience and the era of Modernism and the International style. Later, this spurred a reaction to the homogenisation of the urban landscape.

This represents a process of architectural 'localisation', a cultural negotiation of the authority of the International style wherein the ultimate alignment is established only when the latter no longer exercises absolute dominance. The technique of incorporating climatic modifiers into what is essentially a Modernist structure presupposes an ultimate rejoining of the 'tropical' with the 'modern' and the reidentification of the latter with the former.

Kusno (2000) includes high-rise 'climatic' strategies as attempts at 'differentiating' façade forms through 'inflecting' a global typeform into 'incisions' and 'elements' of identity. The regionalisation of the global high-rise as a type began in the 1980s, and was born out of a reaction to the stultifying effects of the International style in the 1960s and 1970s. The homogeneity of the International style became a reminder of the inflows of capital and the global economy and their voracious impact on urban cities, and were responsible for erasing any traces of tradition. Asian nations were communities which had opened their doors to foreign enterprises, and Malaysia was not immune to their global reach and this diffusion.

The Use of 'Typology' in Analysing Identity

Argan (1963) observes a 'type' as '... formed through a process of reducing a complex of formal variants to a common root form'. More importantly, he insightfully concludes that:

'... the working out of every architectural project has a typological aspect; whether it is that the architect consciously follows the 'type' or wants to depart from it'.

Thus, although throughout pre-modern history reference to the 'type' or typology has been linked to 'an ideal form', in the era of modernity, the 'type' is often linked to a particular function, due to the complexity of functions of the modern world. Hence, the term 'typologies' is then used for builidings that house different key functions which at times are characterised by a certain shape or form. When a shape or form is repeatedly used for certain functions, the typology or 'type' becomes iconic or symbolic of that function. Colquhoun (2001) has highlighted how, in the years after Modernism, innovation was achieved by a mental process that included the use and projection of a typology in the mind of the designer. It was this mental basis of typology which became a springboard for understanding new horizons of expressive form and language. As Carlo Argan (1963) describes in *On the Typology of Architecture*:

> *If the 'type' is a schema and grid and the schema inevitably embodies a moment of rigidity or inertia, the presence of such a schema need[s] to be explained in the context of an artist['s] creative process. This leads one back to the ... relation between artistic creation and historical experience, since it is from historical experience that type is always reduced.*

According to Colquhoun (2001), identity is thus a process of differentiation or a departure from an existing convention. 'In [a] nation's early years, overall forms of modernity with their all-important modern functions are not challenged as they arise of the constructional technology and the need to efficiently use space.' Then envelope and façade systems become more regionally and geometrically differentiated through sunshading systems and expressions of climatic protection from the intense sun or the movement based on geographical sunpaths. Le Corbusier's brise-soleil was essentially a principle that he subsumed under his International style to give meaning and universality to his extension of façade systems as projections and egg crate systems in order to articulate a Modern response to geographical differences. In dry regions, the *mashrabiyya* was advocated, whereas in hot tropical regions such as India and other countries, extended eaves, colonnades and louvres became a palette to locally colour the language and interpret these as regional modern buildings used to adorn modern typologies throughout the world according to the geography and climate.

The Malay Identity

The notion of and focus on Malay identity has re-emerged again after its heyday in the 1980s, during which the Malay cultural forms were evoked and interpreted as a cultural basis for design for various civic structures and commercial buildings of the modern city in Malaysia. It was a time when there was a conflation between the return to history as expression, as part of the movement of post-Modernism, which included a broad push toward regionalism, and the focus on 'identity was underway throughout the world, and particularly intense during periods in which newly independent nations became more economically dynamic, such as Malaysia in the 1980s.' As Ahmad Nizam (2016) observes:

> *The 1980s was the last decade of the identity fever pitch amongs big time archittects in Malaysia. Symbolism and nationalistic pride became almost an obsession at a time when the country began to take the world stage as an economic tiger of South East Asia, as highrise buildings flood the skyline of Kuala Lumpur. the Bank Bumiputra Tower, Putra World Trade center and the Naional library … had some Malay culture metaphors, transposed into modern buildings, while the Menara Maybank and the LUTH tower by Hijjas Kasturi associates followed abstract interpretations of well-known cultural forms …*

In a similar vein, Ken Yeang (2016) insightfully explores the meaning of identity as a basis for design and attempts to unearth the multifarious meanings of the past in designing with 'identity'. By questioning its basis, and compiling past definitions and predispositions, he suggests a more systematic outlook that could pave a path to the future of designing with identity, in which modernity must be reconciled with place and tradition, and local and global concepts must be synthesised and emerge with a more ecological outlook for the built environment and for the planet. While layering the principles of deriving formal expressions of 'identity' through more fundamental principles such as 'systemic design', 'genius loci' and 'abstracttion', rather than emotive foundations, Yeang interestingly highlights the significance of the Malay identity in extracting an architectural language of 'place'. As he remarks:

> *The fundamental premise here is that every place is different and that every place has something unique and valuable to offer. … 'Connection' means a sense of belonging, as a living experience with people and land, and with an understtnading of the cultural patterns and processes in time and space.* ***Creating a sense of place here could mean the subtle incorporation and respect of the local endemic (Malay) context of the place. Every locality has a deep cultural history as well as a more recent history … (emphasis added)***

While 'Malay' identity has been used as a cultural trope in the context of modernisation in Malaysia in recent decades, the definition of Malay as a region itself has a much longer historical evolution. The definition of the 'Malay' region is significantly wider than any national boundary or meaning and has generally covered boundaries such as southern Cambodia, southern Philippines and even southern Thailand. The use of Malay as a language in past history covers an even wider geographical area to encompass East Africa and Polynesian islands. Reid (2004), for example, relates that the notions of 'nation' and 'national identity' are relatively new phenomena in the Asian world, and modern history links the Malay identity to Malaysia and Indonesia. Yet Reid describes the culture and people historically as a region that connects 'a host of courts around the Straits of *Melaka*, from Deli and Langkat in north east Sumatera to Pontianak and Brunei in Borneo'. He defines such royal centres as linked with the 'classical' Malay court literature, which once emanated and evolved from the vestiges of the fifteenth century *Melaka* Sultanate that was disseminated after *Melaka* fell to the Portuguese in 1511. Hence the Malay culture and civilisation were universally connected as one region. The Anglo Dutch Treaty of 1824 had massive repercussions in the region, when the Dutch secured British settlements such as Bengkulu and Sumatera, in exchange for ceding control of their lands in the Malay Peninsula and Dutch India. Historical circumstances made them two nations, as summarised aptly by Andaya and Andaya (2001), which highlights how the unique geographic region was then separated by an event in history. The 1824 agreement represents a turning point in the shaping of modern Malaysia, for the division of the Malay along the *Melaka* Straits laid the basis for the contemporary boundary with Indonesia. Setting aside centuries of history with no qualms, the Riau-Johor kingdom was irrevocably divided and the cultural unity of east coast Sumatra and the Peninsula arbitrarily severed. Ties between individuals and communities remained close, but the division into 'Dutch' and 'British' meant the easy movement of Malay leadership back and forth between the Peninsula and east coast Sumatra was now a thing of the past. In a moving letter, the Bendahara of Pahang expressed Malay bewilderment at arrangements by which 'foreigners in distant capitals had parted father from son, brother and friend from friend'. The unprecedented political division also affected academic scholarship as a new generation of British 'orientalists' concentrated on collecting and compiling Malay texts associated with the Peninsula, leaving the study of Malay culture in Sumatra and southwest and southeast Borneo to their Dutch counterparts.

Multiculturalism

The reality of multiculturalism is another phenomenon that emerged in multiple forms, before and after British occupation. While conventionally one links the British administration with the racial breakdown and definition of communities as a form of spatial and occupationally defined segregation, which persists to this day, Milner (2011) observes that such multiracial pluralism was already part of the Malay world, long before the colonialists' arrival. According to Milner (2011, p. 240):

> *A prominent feature of modern Malaysia which would seem to be at least parly z product odf the heritage of ideas from the age of the 'kerajaan' (Sultanates) is the 'plural' society. This concept – of two or more communities living 'side by side, yet without mingling, in one political unit' – has often been seen by scholaras as characterising wellthe strucure of modern Malaysia, and tends to be attributed mos of all, to development occuring under Colonial rule ... I would suggest the fundamentals of a plural society structure – were put in place well before the Colonial era ... a situation where foreign enterpreneurs enjoyed an advantage.*

It is only in more recent modern times, after Independence, that the populace seems to be in constant need of reminders of peace and stability, and that coexistence and cooperation must always be negotiated. It seems that its ephemerality and fragility must be strengthened with reassurance and reminders through a set of central and national symbols and monumental reminders. Beginning in 1962, these architectural-scale efforts included in the adornment of Modern structures murals in which the mural artists needed to develop and address their artistic compositions within elements of multicultural communities. Murals such as those used in the National Museum and National Stadium (Stadium Negara) featured a figurative composition derived from multiracial representatives. Fundamentally, the intention was to capture and express a national narrative of representing the three dominant ethnic groups in Malaysia (i.e. Malay, Chinese and Indian) as images composed and organised in visual communication with each other.

During the early years after Independence, national projects would often include such multicultural dimensions in terms of imageries and idealisations. Cultural and artistic congresses were convened to bring together a discourse and debate on how to forge the disparate cultures into a nation and, ultimately, into a single cultural identity. The path was towards a unified national identity, but the goal was perhaps idealistic. However, architecture and urban form were part of the strategic media to infuse the psyche of the population with a notion of a multicultural identity in the years after Malaysia achieved independence in 1957. The year 1971 witnessed the organisation of the Malaysian National Cultural Congress which initiated a clarion call to realign artistic practices with the core of the national cultural agenda. Exhibitions were organised by the National Art Gallery. The plastic arts in the earlier years after Independence had the symbolic potential to converge towards a unifying form of expression for all Malaysians, with the aim of transcending various cultural barriers.

A national identity is needed in the early years of a nation, based on attempts to find meaning and identity in a kind of collective expression. Regionalism demonstrates the central preoccupation of emerging societies to imbue their structures with meaning. Jones (2011, p. 64) elucidates:

> *Questions about the political construction of collective identities and the cultural legitimization of power find a clear focus in those objects of state-led architecture that are framed as symbols of national identities. Such state-led*

projects are active attempts to contribute to the cultural construction and consolidation of communities such as the nation.

Hence architecture and urban design either become instruments of the ultimate goal of social unification or a means of asserting the nation in a competitive global space, and design becomes a means of distinguishing itself from others. Yet historically architecture and urban form have often been used as a form of unification. In an earlier era, specific 'syncretic forms were derived from the fusion of cultural symbols and vocabularies and such a notion of fusion at times gave rise to a new form of visual culture which saw disparate traditions merge into a single entity and affecting dress stylisations, artisic works and architectural form.' Such assimilation is a recurring pehnemenon across geogeaphy, cultures and eras. Syncretism will be discussed later in the book.

National identity can be defined as a phenomenon that harnessed regional forms and became embroiled with the movement of regionalisation which had intensified in the years after the reign of Modernism, and resulted in certain buildings becoming scuplted as objects of symbolic content and iconography. The power of forms and shapes in the built environment is perrennial and is constantly harnessed to mobilise a population. A nation-state needs symbols, and at times ethnicity is used explicitly, thereby encouraging more intense ethno-nationalism. The history of urban-architectural form in Souh East Asian tropical cities can be defined as oscillating between a more universal and broad definition of national identity, with shared neutral symbols, and another that swerves towards a more ethnic basis to naionalism, which tends to marginalise those outside a core culture. As Reid (2004, p. 3) insightfully summates: '*Malaysia expressed this dilemna most acutely*', and all nationalisms of South East Asia will experience various versions of this dilemna, in which an ethnic-based identity must gravitate towards a more civic one. The post-colonial evolution of urban-architectural form shows us how important the realm of symbols is when they are appreciated and harnessed for their distinctive silhouette, shape, imagery, emotiveness and unifying capabilities. In many cases, they seem to be a thread or glue that unifies communities, if only momentarily, with a sense of common purpose in order to fuse energies in a concerted action.

Debates are still being played out in the stream of constant change in the trajectory of modernity and the dynamics of a multicultural polity and population. Particularly in the post-colonial era, nations such as Malaysia are part of a group of dynamically evolving economies, yet as smaller nations they have seen their expression of independence as invested in the language, vocabulary and interpretation of architecture and urban form, hence such forms remain crucial as devices, historical expressions and tools for consolidating and unifying a disparate population within a post-colonial context. Such characteristic struggles, negotiations and tensions are played out across Asia, including in tropical cities, yet they have become a character of developed nations as the multicultural dimension of such populations becomes more evident and apparent with the growth of ethnic minorities. It is these dynamic tensions and osciallations that are inscribed in the language of buildings and urban forms, and thus a study of such past forms is crucial to the forging of a more inclusive and sustainable future.

References

Abdullah, A. (2014). In A. N. Arifin (Ed.), *The living machines: Malaysia's modern architectural heritage*. Kuala Lumpur: Pertubuhan Arkitek Malaysia.

Abel, C. (1997). *Eco-development, technology and regionalism in architecture and identity*. Butterworth/Heinemann: Architectural Press.

Andaya, B. W., & Andaya, L. Y. (2001). *A history of Malaysia*. London: Palgrave.

Argan, C. (1963). On the typology of architecture. *Architectural Design, 33*(12), 564–565.

Balfour, A. (1994). Introduction. In K. Yeang (Ed.), *Bioclimatic skyscrapers*. London: Artemis Publishers.

Carlo, A. G. (1963, December). *Architectural design no. 33* (pp. 564–565) (trans: Rykwert, J.).

Chang, J. H. (2016). *A genealogy of tropical architecture: Colonial networks, nature and technoscience*. New York: Routledge, published in the Architext Series of Routledge.

Colquhoun, A. (2001). *Modern architecture*. Oxford, UK: Oxford University Press, 2002.

Curtis, W. J. R. (1986). Towards authentic regionalism. *MIMAR, 19*, 18–67.

Curtis, W. J. R. (1996). Modernity, tradition and identity in the developing world. In W. J. R. Curtis (Ed.), *Modern architecture since 1900*. London: Phaidon Press.

Frampton, K. (1981). *Modern architecture. A critical history*. London: Thames and Hudson 1985. (First edition 1980).

Frampton, K. (1983). Modern architecture and critical regionalism. *Transactions of Royal Institute of British Architects, 2*(3), 15–25.

Frampton, K. (1999, August). Seven points for the millennium: An untimely manifesto. *Architectural Record, 15*, 76–80.

Ghirardo, D. (1996). *Architecture after modernism*. New York: Thames and Hudson.

Hagan, S. (2000). *Taking shape: A new contract between architecture and nature*. Oxford: Butterworth – Heinemann.

Hagan, S. (2001). *Taking shape – A new contrast between nature and architecture*. Buterworth Heinemann. Malaysia.

Jahn Kassim, P. S., & Nawawi, N. M. (2016, September). Allusions to Mughal urban forms, in the monumentality of Chandigarh's capitol complex. *Journal of Architecture and Urbanism* (Vol. 40). Routledge/Taylor and Francis Group.

Jones, P. (2011). *The sociology of architecture: Constructing identities*. Liverpool: Liverpool University Press.

Kahn, J. S. (2006). *Other Malays (2006)-Nationalism and cosmopolitanism in the modern Malay world*. Singapore: Nias Press.

Kien, L. C. (2007). In L. C. Kien (Ed.), *Building Merdeka: Independence architecture in Kuala Lumpur 1957–1966*. Kuala Lumpur: Gallery Petronas.

Kusno, A. (2000). Imagining regionalism, re-fashioning orientalism: Some current architectural discourses in South East Asia. *Journal of South East Asian Architecture, 4*, 45–61.

Larson, M. S. (1995). *Behind the postmodern facade; Architectural change in late twentieth-century America*. Berkeley: University of California Press 1993.

Milner, A. (2011). *The Malays*. Malden: Wiley Blackwell.

Olgyay, V. (1963). *Design with climate: Bioclimatic approach to architectural regionalism*. Princeton: Princeton Architectural Press.

Ozkan, S. (1985). Introduction – Regionalism within modernism. In R. Powell (Ed.), *Regionalism in architecture*. Singapore: Concept Media/The Aga Khan Award for Architecture.

Reid, A. (2004). Understanding Melayu (Malay) as a source of diverse modern identities. In T. P. Barnard (Ed.), *Contesting Malayness, – Malay identiy across boundaries*. Singapore: NUS Press.

Tay Kheng Soon. (1990). The architectural aesthetic of tropicality. In R. Powell (Ed.), *Line, edge and shade: The search for a design language in tropical Asia: Tay Kheng Soon and Arkitek Tenggara*. Singapore: Page One Publishing.

Tzonis, A., & Le Faivre, L. (1981). The grid and the pathway – An introduction to the work of Dimitris and Susana Antonakakis, with prolegomena to a history of the culture of modern Greek architecture. *Architecture in Greece, 15*, 164–179.

Yeang, K. (1984). Notes for a critical vernacular in contemporary Malaysian architecture. *UIA International Architect, 6*, 16–17. London.

Yeang, K. (1987). *Tropical urban regionalism: building in a South-East Asian city*. Singapore: Mimar Publications.

Yeang, K. (2016, December). Architecture and identity. *Architecture Malaysia magazine* "Architecture of identity", *28*(6), 62–65.

2

The Mosque in a Multicultural Context: Modernity, Hybridity and Eclecticism

Norwina Mohd Nawawi, Shireen Jahn Kassim, and Mansor Ibrahim

Introduction

As a symbolic structure, mosque architecture is not only defined by its spiritual function, but by its capacity as 'signification'. Particularly in the case of state-sponsored mosques, mosques are structures no longer conceptualised and constructed merely as spaces for worship, representing and facilitating socio-religious acts and obligations, but often are formed as significant symbols. For the modern state, or nation, the mosque has become a means of mass communication and a bearer of meaning to the general public. National mosques in particular are not only symbols, but can be configured to represent and embody a nation's aspirations, identity and ideals. Holod and Khan (1997) suggest: 'As a type, the mosque is ubiquitous, and at once old and very new. It is a culture-bound place of worship, representing local and regional architectural traditions, and a trans- or supra-regional expression of a contemporaneity which has acquired a pan-islamic, worldwide character. This quintessential Muslim

N. Mohd Nawawi (✉) • S. Jahn Kassim • M. Ibrahim
International Islamic University Malaysia, Kuala Lumpur, Malaysia

© The Author(s) 2018

S. Jahn Kassim et al. (eds.), *Modernity, Nation and Urban-Architectural Form*,
https://doi.org/10.1007/978-3-319-66131-5_2

symbol provides a way of viewing the mechanisms of representation of state and authority within the nations … and self-identity within it as well as outside it.' Yet in terms of language, the mosque straddles between local expression and a global export, diffused from its origins in the Middle East. Attempts to depart from its Arab-Islamic language, in terms of form, have been known to be met with resistance. Just as Modernism and its language became a symbol of 'progressiveness' in the 1960s, the essential dome-and-arch language has become synonymous with spirituality in Islam. Past efforts have however attempted to go beyond the 'eclectic' 'dome-and-arch' stereotype in order to explore a new symbolic language representing emotional responses that convey the hopes of a multicultural society. Modernity brings a fresh outlook to mosques as an urban type-form, in that mosques are seen as not only a form with spiritual functions, but forms that are able to penetrate the subconscious and generate positive perceptions of national identity in the people, including the meaning of inclusivity in a multicultural nation.

Form

Mosque form can perhaps be best understood through the theory of semiotics as propounded by Umberto Eco, the novelist and semiotician, who asserts that architectural form and language are a kind of semiotic system of signification (Eco 1972), and that elements of buildings can have an impact on human emotion, consciousness and perception. His studies assert that architecture, being a form of mass communication, has evolved a range of 'architectural styles' that are linked to their symbolic dimension, each with a connotative ability to communicate. In his 'Function and Sign: Semiotics of Architecture', Eco defines form as the result of two juxtaposed intentions, which can be distinguished as 'the primary function' – architecture as a functional object – and its secondary function – architecure as a symbol. Spatially, mosque forms arise from simple requirements: space extends from the spiritual act of praying in the direction of the Qibla (Mecca), along with the need to extend the congregational line of prayer perpendicular to the line of Qibla. Bougas (1992), for example, relates how the very first mosque in Malaya, devoid of symbolic intentions, was basically and essentially a rectangular form, a reflection of the vernacular of the region. Community spaces simple, encircle this central and functional space. Jahn Kassim and Nawawi (2016), in their essay 'Masjid in Modernity: Form, Space and Syntax', highlight another function which determines the three-dimensional form of the mosque, in that the act of prayer itself is directed to the heavens, and hence space, whether capped by a pyramidial roof or dome, 'implodes' towards the heavens and has a vertical as well as horizontal axis. Hence a conventional mosque is generally centrally configured, having the largest and highest volume centrally located, while the minaret, in an urban context often represents a marker rather than having any actual function. The supportive spaces encircle this primary space, which is the main function of this building type. Its secondary function, that is, the symbolic, changes with changes in time and geography, and in the patron of the mosque itself.

Pevsner (1976) admits: 'Every building creates associations in the mind of the beholder, whether the architect wanted it or not.' Broadbent (1978) also suggests, 'at any time, a building can be signifier, signified or referent. A building exists as signifier in its site but as signified by photographs and diagrams.' Hence the symbolic functions of mosques, particularly state-sponsored mosques, at times overwhelm their primary function. Eco (1972) suggests, at times primary functions can be minimised, while 'secondary functions' are exagerrated. Holod and Khan (1997) also suggest that as the mosque moves into an era of modernity, 'Long-held notions of "otherness" must now be gradually replaced by more pluralistic, inclusive formulations of new societies and a new world order for the twenty-first century'. Large mosques in Malaysia have vocabularies that carry meaning as they fuse functional, religious and public spaces, as a combined vocabulary that contains certain connotations and whose meanings can be suggested to the public not only as 'spiritual' functional spaces but as symbolic structures.

The Colonial Era

Nasution (2014) describes in relation to Malaysia: 'By the second half of the nineteenth century, the nature of British Colonial rule in Asia had changed in fundamental ways ... In the "new imperialism" mode of the late Victorian era, the British began to formulate a more comprehensive ideology of the empire … Lord Napier, the British governor of Madras from 1866 to 1872, had commented that the arch and the dome, were the "most beautiful, most scientific and most economical" ways of covering large spaces.' The Indo-Saracenic style was part of what Nasution (2014) describes as, though 'initiated in India, the ideas, repertoires and symbols of domination, was also introduced in Malaya'.

Eclecticism, in urban-architectural form, is generally known as an approach or movement, originating in the nineteenth and twentieth centuries, in which designers would draw from several stylistic trends or vocabularies for a single composition. Eclecticism can include elements of two styles from a single culture or country, or fuse two vastly different vocabularies from both 'East' and 'West'. While colonial-based eclectic Indo-Saracenic stylisations are appreciated as a valuable heritage in urban centres and are used as a vibrant language at the present time, during the nineteenth century the language itself was a bearer of meaning and was said to have 'expressional character'. Hence while such language presently symbolises a landmark of worship and a link with a universal Islamic community, during the colonial era the state-sponsored mosque, and its eclectic expression, was part of the colonial cultural hegemony, as stated by Crinson (1996): the 'act of building in a foreign country often indicates permanent intent. The building might be an authentication of real colonial power or the symbolic vessel of intended power.' The language of eclecticism recalls the once global reach of British imperialism. The overuse of this language in public and administrative buildings has elicited some criticism and concern in this multicultural nation. An example is the highly Arabic stylised buildings of Putrajaya which have evoked criticism and even dismay. Putrajaya's administrative precinct is known for the Arab-Islamic urban forms of its various civic buildings, which are interspersed with modern hotels, shopping centres and commercial buildings. The Putra mosque or Pink mosque, has been recognised as a central node for the new urban population of the city and increasingly a tourist attraction as well, and is almost universally regarded as a symbol. The use of eclectic language in other administrative and public buildings has brought a certain amount of criticism of the predominance of Arab-Islamic references in the administrative structures of the capital, rather than the local language of architecture.

As Crinson (1996) describes: 'In Britain, a theorised and occasionally doctrinal eclecticism and revivalism formed the climate of debate in architecture.' Crinson further describes: 'These were the products not only of acute historical awareness, and **of a search for the modern**, but also of a new found belief that the designer had the power to select and manipulate the storehouse of historical material.' Hence it was an era with increasing obsession with sources that represented the 'Orient'. More and more materials began to be available for the, designer's palette from the 1800s onwards. The rise of gifted eclectic architects included thinkers such as Owen Jones and Robert Hay; further fuelled the new fusion of the Victorian and Islamic architectural vocabulary. The Arab-Islamic style began as an offshoot of Orientalism through which colonialists intended to formulate a stylistic departure from the conventional classical expressions of imperial power. Eclecticism became a form of expression of the colonial presence, its formal alliances and symbolic identity in lands under imperial control. Globally, from the nineteenth century onwards, eclecticism began to be associated with a combination of Arab-Islamic grammar these concoctions were the vocabulary of a new style that came to express the colonial presence in its far-facing polities.

The Legacy of Eclecticism

The definition of eclecticism in mosques can thus be traced back to the Victorians during the eighteenth and nineteenth centuries who viewed Islam and Islamic lands in terms of its own art, religion and geography. Victorian eclecticism was the product of a juxtaposition of conditions, a rising level of 'historical awareness' among the colonialists. They were in a constant search for the 'modern', and the need for its expressive language. Forms also reflected a degree of 'civil' or public architecture, as described by Crinson (1996), the Neo-colonial forms that expressed 'an architecture of civility'. Eclecticism came into popular practice in colonised regions during the late nineteenth century, as architects sought styles that would allow them to retain previous historic precedent, yet create 'not-seen-before' new designs. Past styles, extracted from various documentations of new 'Oriental' lands, were treated as a palette of design vocabulary within which elements were almost like catalogues of ideas and range of grammar. The ability to mix and combine these grammar was part of the creativity of eclectic architects, and the approach allowed for expressive freedom to create from multicultural sources of inspiration. To the architects practising in newly founded cities, this represent a form of freedom and modernisation. In colonial regions, architecture was seen to center for a specific audience, comprising of those with different racial and religious leanings. Urban-Architectural forms must respond to a different set of ideas and aspirations. Victorian classicism was seen as having a degree of variety and flexibility. Crinson (1996) describes the motivations of the colonialist:

> *[It] was in seeking to analyse the character of those arts, and in erecting buuldings in which the orient was associated, these Victorians tested their eclectic theories to the limit ... Rather than follow a single mode of the British imperial style such the classical paradigm encased in the Neo Classical style, the British saw architecture as a means of reconciliation ... a tool to replace force with civility and govermentality.*

The Ubudiyyah Mosque (Fig. 2.1) was an outcome of an eclectic intention which became one of the nation's acclaumed heritage structures. Presently regarded as one of Malaysia's most beautiful mosques by visitors and locals alike, it was built and completed in 1913 by Arthur Benison Hubback, then known as the Indo-Saracenic style, which has to the present day is seen as a legacy of the past glories of the Islamic civilisation.

The popularity of the eclectic style has extended to the present day in state mosques such as the Putra Mosque, Putrajaya. The language of the dome and arch style, has a particularly long association with the Arab-Islamic origins of Islam itself. Its range of vocabularies and grammars are infused with the historical significance surmounting a spiritual space. The nature of the dome has made it a popular and 'must-have' item, particularly as part of the language of large national mosques (Eisen 2015). Political forces play a significant role in the prevalence of this stereotypical form and the scale of a mosque determined its consequence treatment, form and language (Othman et al. 2007).

Fig. 2.1 The Ubudiyyah Mosque, 1911, Kuala Kangsar

Marking the Centre: The Masjid Jamek, Kuala Lumpur

Strategically located at the confluence of the Klang and Gombak rivers, Masjid Jamek is an example of an eclectic mosque of the colonial period which has become a recognisable landmark and accepted icon amongst the population. The Masjid Jamek is still known for the intensity of history that surrounds its site.

Funded through donations from the Malay community and partly financed by the British Government, the construction of the Jamek mosque was completed in 1909. The opening ceremony was officiated by the then-reigning Sultan of Selangor, Sir Alauddin Sulaiman Shah, the fifth Sultan. The site was previously shadowed by and nestled beneath a canopy of shady coconut trees; however, it is no longer, and historically the decimation of the coconut trees was a loss to the site, leaving only photos reflect the history and nostalgia.

The language of the Masjid Jamek is emblematic of the eclectic Indo-Saracenic style. Its architectural grammar evaded the pure rules and vocabulary of the Mughal language while fusing and recombining Mughal elements with extensions of the Gothic and Romanesque traditions alongside nuances from the Andalusian vocabulary of Islamic Spain. The mosque form itself is dominated and controlled by its two main minarets, constructed with bands of red bricks and cream blocks known as 'bandages'. Three onion-shaped white domes surmount its form and cover the prayer hall. There is a rhythmic linear arrangement of cusped arches stylised in a composition evoking the 'blood and bandages' stylisations of the minaret with its distinctive contrasting dual-colour expression. The shape of its arches reminds the viewer of its essentially Gothic origins, which have been hybridised with the pointed arches characteristic of Moorish-Islamic architecture. It is this known eclectic combination of Moorish and Mughal elements with the Gothic, with its distinguished pointed arches, onion-shaped domes, spires, dome-shaped canopies, multiple minarets and horseshoe-shaped arches, that characterises the innovative eclectic mosque styling of colonial Malaya (Fig. 2.2).

Fig. 2.2 Forms of the Indo-Saracenic style – Masjid Jamek, Kuala Lumpur

The architect and designer is again Arthur Benison Hubback, who was the composer of this hybrid style, and it was, perhaps, his degree of openness and innovation that came to characterise many of his architectural works, including significant buildings in the nation's colonial government centre. The buildings were designed to fulfil the spatial demands of a British-local bureaucracy. Hubback demonstrated a predisposition towards nineteenth-century eclectic historicism, and later, his buildings significantly shaped the architectural landscape of Kuala Lumpur. The impact of his senior engineer, the then State Engineer C. E. Spooner, was considerable, and both gravitated towards a preference for the Indo-Saracenic style with a Mughal-based vocabulary fused with elements of Byzantine, Romanesque and Gothic elements. This stylistic tendency is similar to that of other British imperial architects working worldwide, thus establishing a 'new' kind of architectural language known now as the Indo-Saracenic style.

Modernity in Different Eras

Modernity can be defined as a certain threshold or time frame of a society as it journeys through distinctive stages of change. Certain conditions cause certain inevitable upheavals in a society or nation, with the attendant physical outcomes and ideas. Yet modernity in a society or nation is not linked to a particular time or decade, but can be argued to constitute 'modern' trajectories or thresholds that shift with different eras. The stylistic evolution of mosque architecture in Malaysia can be linked to such changes; its language and expression reflect certain stages in the development and the evolution of Malaysia as a nation. The Malay feudal era before the colonial era can be termed the traditional phase or the pre-colonial era, whereas the age of modernity can be defined as three distinct periods of Malaysia's history: the era of British colonisation, the era after Independence, that is, from the 1960s and the era of industrialisation from the 1980s. Each can be claimed or described as initiating or spurring eras that represented different forms of 'newness' as it signalled the nation was a particular threshold of change. These brought on the development and flowering of different stylisations which were linked to the search for the a new Divergent differences in ideas and expression, including differences in urban-architectural language and expression were sought after.

In general, the British period in Malaysia ushered a new set of influences include an urban language of architecture, recalling Neoclassical, Victorian and Georgian stylistic trends. These are now found in the heritage districts of Penang, *Melaka* and Kuala Lumpur and other forms of architecture in the Straits Settlement. During the nineteenth and twentieth centuries, the British saw themselves as harbingers of 'change', 'progress' and modernisation in Malaya. In Britain itself, the discourse in Arab-Islamic architecture emerged in the 1830s from the various travels and documentation of British residents and travellers to the East due to the search for the 'new'.

Britain itself, during the eighteenth century, had adopted the eclectic element of Arab-Islamic architecture in administrative buildings as a search for the 'new'. To the British, the Arab-Islamic vocabulary became a kind of stylistic trend linked to the mysterious Oriental lands and thus became one of the new styles of the era. British colonial architects who were not predisposed to the regurgitation of Classical styles were known to be predisposed to Oriental language. It was seen as a new style, bringing fresh change and creative experimentation. The changes reflected in present language of the urban fabric and the imposition of what was how known as Orientalism or the Oriental style of design and architecture because a terminology later associated with it.

From the eighteenth century onwards, Britain saw itself as having a mission and a central role in modernising a society that was initially perceived to be a 'backward' country. To British architects practising in the colonial outposts, Islamic eclecticism was a form of physical expression of urban-based modernity it presented an alternative to the dominant and prevailing design language of the day, Neoclassicism. It was at times seen as a Victorian-based eclectic amalgam of Arabic and Gothic elements that were associated with, and seen as, the 'agents of change'. As Crinson (1996) highlights, the intent of an Arab-Islamic architectural vocabulary, from being associated with historicism, was intended to 'conjure an image of newness'. Modernity was, in fact, a claim to justify the Indo-Saracenic stylistic dressings which was a radicall change from the existing, Neoclassical language and its recycled idioms.

Under certain conditions, the adoption of the hybrid Arab-Islamic or the Oriental style was seen as forward-looking. The Arab-Islamic style was, in such cases, perceived as an enlightened style in form and language which sought to avoid historicism altogether and to design without reference to, or the intrusion of, the past. It was thus an attempt, as Crinson (1996) asserts, 'to create a myth in which the British presence was depoliticised and losing its contingent fabricated quality'. The syncretic Mughal-English language with its pointed, cusp-like arches and the bulbous onion domes was thus a language utilised to project an image of modernity and of 'benevolent presence'. Crinson (1996) summarises that the eclectic style allowed the colonialists:

> *to conciliate with the opinions of the Islamic populace. Hence, there was a subtlety to which the language of the arch was articulated in showing affiliations*

to both the local 'periphery' context and the British centre. As time passes, the richly layered hybridism inherent in Gothic and Mughal, and Indo-Saracenic style with ogee arches vibrant banding of walls created its iconic standing and became the identity of the nation-state, Malaya.

Post-Colonial Eclecticism

In the post-colonial era, there was a different set of intentions. The formal architectural language of mosque architecture throughout the world, in the post-colonial context, was linked to the need to be part of a global identity or community of Islam. As such, past vocabularies that are utilised to express such meaning and relationships converge stereotypically on domes, arches and *muqarnas* with calligraphy and arabesque decorative elements (Othman and Zainal-Abidin 2011). Mosque design, features, forms and elements were governed by such dominant vocabulary and are almost always discussed as conceptualisations, processes and thoughts related to the Arab-Islamic origins of Islam. In the case of Malaysia in the late 1990s, it was seen as part of an anti-colonial sentiment. It is argued that such a symbolic representation persisted with the conventions of domes, arches and geometric patterns were part and parcel of the 'Islamic' form that was an anti-theses to the 'Western' form.

Some of the most highly acclaimed mosques in Malaysia are those from the late colonial era, ranging from eclectic mosques such as the Masjid Zahir (Alor Setar), Masjid Ubudiyyah (Kuala Kangsar) and Masjid Sultan (Singapore) were part of a different era. Modern mosques such as Masjid Negara and Masjid Wilayah were regarded as denoting statehood, or seen as national icons. In colonial times, to adorn the mosque with Arab-Islamic language was a calculated style aimed at representing the imperial presence and reflecting a conciliatory and unifying gesture to the population. Today, the style is used to demonstrate a kind of globalised Islamic identity and a rejection of a memory of British imperialism.

The Putra Mosque, Putrajaya: A Case Study

The Putra Mosque was completed in 1999 and became operational in 2000, is a case in point. The Putra Mosque was formulated as an architecture that calls to mind the past glory of Islam. It is the apotheosis of the Islamic expression in the Putrajaya administrative center. Islamic architecture was an instrument of state to exemplify one' s standing as a leader of an Islamic nation. The Mosque was built as part of Putrajaya's masterplan to signify its relevance to the industrialisation era and increase Malaysia's leadership amongst Islamic nations. Hence its eclectic stylings were aimed at reflecting a form of national identity and imagery. Named after Malaysia's first prime minister, Tunku Abdul Rahman Putra Al-Haj, it exudes the distinct language of Persian-Islamic eclecticism, deriving its vocabulary and expression from Persian-Islamic history, primarily the Safavid period, with allusions to Malaysian, Persian and Arab-Islamic influences (Utaberta 2012). Located at the new administrative city of Putrajaya, and designed by a Malaysian architect, Nik Mohammed Nik Mahmood, the mosque's 116-metre minaret and other parts of the mosque were influenced by the Sheik Omar mosque in Baghdad and the King Hassan mosque in Casablanca, Morocco.

The rose-tinted cladding has endowed the mosque with the nickname 'the Pink mosque'. The ornamentations, as per Persian-Islamic building, using the revivalism approach, provide a counter-balance to the sombre *chengal* Malay woodwork on the entryways, windows and boards. The main prayer hall has a 36-metre-diameter principal vault. The mosque complex can accommodate over 10,000 worshippers, and the courtyard that stretches between the main prayer hall and the main entrance may be used to hold an additional 5000 people for prayers. The arabesque at the dome was designed based on the domes of the Safavid architecture of Isfahan, Iran and the domes of Egypt. Decorative Malay carvings of *chengal* wood provide a local flavour to the otherwise foreign architecture in the interior (Fig. 2.3).

Fig. 2.3 The Putra Mosque, Putrajaya, completed 1999

Hybridity as Form and Language

Yet some reject a total embrace of this 'global' language, which is a form of homogeneity. There is a certain difference between the position of eclecticism and hybridity. While in general, eclecticism is a form or a subset of a hybrid approach, hybridity, in terms of style, can represent a more subtle localised approach. In contrast, eclecticism is generally associated with an assertive forms of grammar or language. Hybridity, it is argued, can take the form of a more subtle infusion of a cultural form, and local climatic strategies. Hence while eclecticism is the combination of two or more sources of historical style in an equal manner, hybridity may involve the seamless fusing of a locality's climatic form and any externally sourced cultural elements. It then constitutes a new style altogether, particularly with other considerations of form such as climate. An overall synthesis then occurs through a balanced synchronisation of climate and cultural allusions. Representing a typical hybridity in the twentieth century is a modest mosque (originally a *surau*), the Surau Precinct 8, designed by Malaysian architect Hajeedar Abd Majid in Putrajaya, which can be described as a 'pure' hybrid that avoided the trappings of state-sponsored iconography. In this instance, the global preoccupation with Arab-Islamic form in the mosque is essentially tropicalised to fit its context. The architect solely sought to capture a locally-rooted yet global language in architecture, combining the subtle infusion of tropicality with the familiar composition of Arab-Islamic language. Open-air tropical Asian principles are fused in the overall stylisation. This recalls the vibrancy of Arab-Islamic style, yet no element is seen as iconography. The eventual form, is a localised form of a global 'Islamic' type-form. A hybrid language and form emerges without the trappings of a conscious iconography. The form is totally inspired by the need to link with the global identity of Islam while maintaining a rooted form it expresses the tropical specifics of the location. This hybridity can be defined by the ultimate localisation of a global Islamic language. A similar hybridity can be observed in the older heritage mosques of *Melaka*, such as the Tengkera and Kampung Hulu mosques located in urban centres which evolved through centuries. In both mosques, there is a distinctive fusion of Malay, Chinese and Arab-Islamic elements and vocabulary, yet the overall form recalls the archetypical roots of the 'tropical verandah' with colonnaded styles recalling the region (see also Nawawi et al. 2016).

From afar, the Arab-Islamic elements of style predominate, yet on closer inspection its form is not a box but is pierced with an openeness. Recesses that capture the dynamics of the tropical environment reflect how a more acclimatised envelope can soften the iconic language. This unique juncture is achieved through a syncretic approach of infusing essentially a cube-and-dome Arab-Islamic form with tropical acclimatisation. In Surian Presint 8, the humble scale of the brief allowed its PAM Gold Medalist architect, Ar. Hajeedar, to express a purity of expression yet focus of elevational form and a contemplative spiritual enclave. The architect sought not only to depart from the 'eclectic' Middle Eastern language but to embrace local values and the memory of Malay traditions. Initially, the architect wanted to create the ideal-type *surau* and was drawn to the notion of cubes and a simple equal-sided cubic form reminiscent of the Kaaba in Mecca. A symmetrical square-based plan emerged but was subsequently transformed into a hybrid typology of an enclosed dome-shaped ceiling, a conventional form. The form is then pierced with openings on all sides. What are typically walls open into the extensive greenery and a surrounding reflecting pool. The envelope is installed with large latticed shading devices or awnings to protect the interior space from rain and to filter daylight. The allusion to Malay traditions is palpable, evoking a sense of the past and the regimented rhythm of columns and the use of water and greenery around the mosque recall spiritual overtones.

The interior connects with the exterior and incorporates the fresh and lush greenery environment of a traditional *kampung* ambience. The masonry structure is punctuated with large openings and enveloped in a calm oasis. The interior evokes the columnar wood-based structures of the Malay world, while at the same time recalling the column-rich halls of the Alhambra mosques in Granada, Spain. Malay values are expressed with the design elements and construction systems that are embodied in an interplay of form, columns, pilasters and verandah.

Departure from Conventions

Regionalising the 'Modern'

The 1960s represented an era of optimism and idealism in Asia. This brought about a predisposition or aesthetic movement that symbolised society's embrace of technology, including the idea that scientific progress and precision is crucial as to the 'new' and 'progressive'. The debate is now the underlying formative ideas reflected mosques as public buildings, and demonstrating their spiritual function can be able to elicit and penetrate the psyche of the masses to symbolise such progress and 'forward thinking'. Just as in the Modernist and post-Modernist eras, architects are caught in a dichotomy of choice between 'imitation' and 'invention'. As Broadbent (1978) observes, 'we all share a social contract as to the conventional form', and the sense of progress is reflected in the need for a departure from the 'convention'.

The Masjid Negara: Fusing National Identity and Tropicality

After Independence, Malaysia was anxious to assert its national identity, and its public buildings were part of this 'anxiety'. A universal outlook and identity was sought in public structures that would also serve as symbols. One recalls the prevailing trends movements of the era, i.e. the diffusion of the International style which the public associated with progressiveness and universality. The National Mosque, or Masjid Negara, was crafted to satisfy such a need to assert an embrace progressiveness, a spirit of nationalism and a will to depart from eclectic conventions all in one. Located in Kuala Lumpur, it was designed for a capacity of 15,000 people and is situated among 13 acres (53,000 m^2) of gardens. Its original structure was designed by a three-person architectural team from the Malaysian Public Works Department (PWD): one is a British architect named Howard Ashley, and the other two are Malaysian architects, Hisham Albakri and Baharuddin Kassim.

Constituted in 1965, its form was meant to represent the progressive aspirations of a newly independent Malaysia, yet it was linked with symbols of modernity. Its form is International, with its minaret and roof appearing to be the only vertical elements which grow from a horizontal 'floating' base and the interlocking nature of the cubic volumes. Its signature element is the folded umbrella roof, a 16-pointed-star concrete folded roof that caps the prayer wall and is accompanied by a 73-foot-high minaret evoking a closed umbrella. The umbrella or parasol is synonymous with a consistent principle in the tropics: the idea of shade from the intense heat and rain. The iconography is expressed and articulated conspicuously: the main roof is reminiscent of the open Malaysian umbrella, and the minaret recalls a folded one.

Construction-wise, the folded plates were structurally needed to achieve the larger spans required for the main prayer hall. Reflecting pools and fountains were then interspersed throughout the compound. It was on 5 March 1958 that the chief ministers of the 11 states in the Federation of Malaya proposed to name the national mosque 'Masjid Tunku Abdul Rahman Putra Al-Haj', in recognition of Tunku's efforts in uniting the country towards Independence. The Tunku had then refused this honour, and had proposed to name it 'Masjid Negara' – National Mosque, in a spirit of thanks for the peaceful attainment of the country's independence without bloodshed.

Its main architect, Dato Baharuddin Kassim, recalled how he was given the opportunity to implement his ideas as he was commissioned by the then Prime Minister, Tun Abdul Razak, together with the PWD-based British architect Howard Ashley. Ar Baharuddin was trained in London and his sources of precedents were books and photographs in London. Masjid Negara was an amalgamation of national symbols while still maintaining a link to a global language that represented state-of-the-art technology and modernity. An awareness of the critical function of public structures and civic architecture is a medium of uniting a disparate multicultural population, an emphasis on climatic strategies in 'neutral forms' and any references to external cultures and their forces. The parasol-like local umbrella was used as an analogical element for its dominant roof form, rather than the conventional dome roof, and it celebrates both identity and inclusivity. The extended pavilions that invite airflow and breeze speak volumes of the intentions of its patrons to seek conflation between identity and modernity, unification and democratic synthesis. Its dynamic intersections of almost 'hovering' planes in the form of rectilinear pavilions, interspersed with still pools of water, evoke and recall the centripetal organisation and elements of Barcelona's famed Pavilion by Mies Van Der Rohe but reworked into a dynamic intersection of the open-air tropical verandahs alluding to the *anjung* of the traditional houses of the Malay world (Fig. 2.4).

In terms of identity, the iconography of the opened and closed umbrella is used not only to express the national position, but to seek in principle to depart totally from the memory of Indo-Saracenic forms and eclectic Arab-Islamic vocabulary of the colonical era. The roof caps a basic form, which can only be described as Modernist as it consists of an interlocking cubic volume, and this recalls planes brought together in a centripetal form, which itself recalls the pinwheel language of Modern architecture,

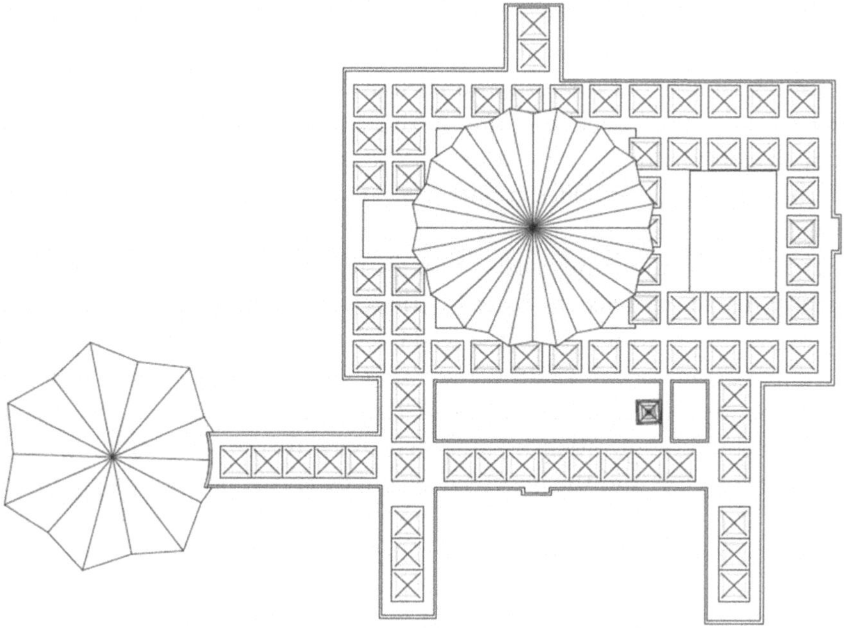

Fig. 2.4 Masjid Negara – layout plan showing extensions of the 'tropical pavilion'

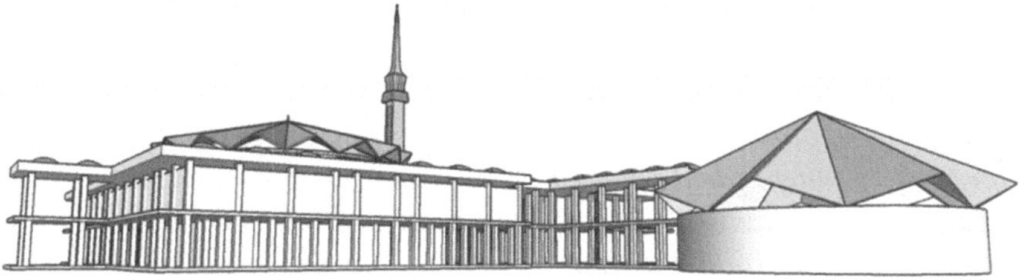

Fig. 2.5 The Masjid Negara – the predominance of a columnar open air design and the reference to the iconic Malay umbrella in its roof – the main roof recalls the open umbrella, while the minaret recalls the 'closed' umbrella form

extending from a centre from which spaces and planes dynamically flow into or away from each other (Holod and Khan 1997). The spaces seem randomly organised, yet on closer inspection there is an internal principle of growth – not unlike a centrifugal or tree-like extension of spaces from a central core (Fig. 2.5).

The overall language is a concrete aesthetic of hovering planes and intersecting slabs characteristic of the International style of the time, and its influence in a mosque of national significance is representative of the anxiety and aim of appearing progressive and avant-garde. The departure from an overwhelming dome must also be an icon that can be accepted by all ethnic groups, and hence at once appear and function as a unifying tool while capturing a certain euphoric moment.

The local parasol umbrella – though referencing Malay traditions – became an analogical element, rather than an iconography or form related to any race or even religion. The Malay element was proposed in lieu of the conventional Arab-Islamic roof or dome. It included Malay references, yet its exclusions in terms of language ensured that the overall result celebrated both identity and inclusivity. At the same time, the language of columns and the intersecting and extended pavilions were interspersed with pools and invited airflow and breeze, recalling the climatic regionalism of tropical design. The emphasis on function and climate, although expressed in a language of austerity and volume, reflected the intentions of its patrons to seek conflation between identity and modernity, unification and democratic synthesis.

The public impact of the design is evident in tourists' comments (Jahn Kassim et al. 2016) which demonstrate the success of its message in the medium of architecture is clear, for example: '*A nice Structure … I am non-Muslim, so only I entered in mosque but I was impressed by bold and modern approach in reinforced concrete, symbolic of the aspirations of a then newly independent Malaysia*' (Tourist from India, extracted from reviews on Trip Advisor); '*Nice pious place. … This mosque is different and does not have Arabic/Mughal influence. That way much different from other mosques as it does not have typical domes or minarets*' (Tourist from India); '*Uniquely Beautiful Non-Arab Mosque. This mosque has a different style of architecture to it and it is worth seeing. The roofing is similar to that of other religious temples in that it appears folded, different from that of dome-shaped Arab mosques … there are many doorways and openings to admire its beauty to the nice aesthetics of carpet, walls, and ceiling … Enjoy the nice design outside with all the pillars and pools of water*' (Tourist from New York); '*The mosque is modern and unique, fitting for the aspirations Malaysia has as a nation.*'

Masjid Negara thus became known for its ability to engender a universal response and acceptance in a multicultural society due to its universal appeal. Its form and language are seen as able to communicate a universal message rather than being merely a mosque as a representation of the Islamic community. This achievement is attested to in statements by The Centre for Modern Architecture Studies in Southeast Asia – MASSA (2001) that it is unique in gaining recognition for its architectural message of inclusion and its imagery that signifies the sociocultural cohesion of various cultures and communities. It demonstrates the emergence of a new nationhood which can spur new forms of architecture based on a certain combination of euphoria and nationalism, where under certain conditions, it can give rise to new forms.

The neutrality of its language became an advantage. This is verified and attested by tourists and visitors who have commented (Jahn Kassim et al. 2016) on how they are able to 'read' not only the symbolic gesture of a new Malaysia, but the image of 'progress' and modernity, along with the 'aspirations' of a new nation. The critical language syncretises climate, symbol and tectonics and avoids any cut-and-paste of surmounting Malay roof forms on structures. Instead, the tropical sense of form is nurtured from the rows and rows of columnar spaces which interlock elements of water, pools and fountains, that not only elicit tropical comfort with minimum air-conditioning, but reverberate a general feeling of peace and spiritual well-being. The overall design creates an uncluttered and simple design with no copying of the past but more in the spirit of its principles which are embodied in the form. Comments gleaned from the local intelligentsia include, amongst others, those by Yong, L.L. (2001) in the MASSA Monograph which clearly encapsulate the achievements of its form:

> *The construction of Masjid Negara is one of the most important events in Malaysian modern architecture history. It was built 40 years ago, yet its modern approach is still relevant in the context of today's' social-cultural and modern environment in the country. Its architecture emphasised functional aspects as well as the spirit of time and place. It does not imitate the Middle*

Eastern and Indian mosque architecture that was commonly practiced during the colonial period to symbolise the Islamic religion, It has been identified as an International-style building that does not convey any architectural references towards any ethnic or cultural values of any particular race; it reflects the effort and contribution of every level in a multireligious and multiracial Malaysia.

Modernising the Vernacular

The local form of the Asian Nusantara region is essentially linked to in a timber-based pyramidal form (Ahmad et al. 2013) based on the post-and-beam system of construction. The Masjid Nat Tanjung or Surau Aur at Aur village, Saiburi District, Pattani, Thailand, is one of the oldest indigenous forms of the Malay mosque, built over 359 years ago at a village called Bendang Jung. It is essentially made of wood, with a step-roofed structure. This evidence indirectly supports the contention that Pattani was perhaps one of the first Malay kingdoms on the Peninsula to embrace Islam (Bougas 1992). There is also evidence that early Pattani Muslims adapted their domestic forms in constructing their first mosque. The mosque has a gable end with a three-tiered roof known as the *pemeleh* roof. The roof form was a natural outcome of the simple system of a wood structure with indigenous connections. The prayer hall is a simple rectangular structure following the external form, measuring eight metres by five metres. As domestic architecture, its rear and annexes resemble the local traditional house layout. The highly steeped roof that breaks into three layers with two sloping ventilation panels forms a system completely in tune with the environment. The oldest mosque in Malaysia – the Masjid Kampung Laut – is believed to have been built during the fourteenth century, and recalls the *waqaf* or place of rest, a timber pavilion found in the Nusantara region. In the original mosque, the entire language is derived from a wood-based tectonic, consisting of the columns and hanging column joints as well as detailing typical of traditional Malay woodcarving. Its main pyramidal roof is supported by secondary pillars whereas the four primary central columns, called *saka guru* or *soko guru*, support the topmost pyramidal roof tier. The columns supporting the lower middle roof and the sides of the square space remain in a symmetrical arrangement with the structures.

A Modernist interpretation of tradition is embodied in the UTEM (*Universiti Teknikal Melaka*) mosque, built in 2007 and officially opened in 2011, in Durian Tunggal, *Melaka* which basically represents the transmutation of the traditional timber language into a modern concrete aesthetic. Following a brief that called for expression of the identity of *Melaka* as a state, the architects were driven by the need to express a Modernist version of the pyramid form yet create a departure from the curved (almost Chinese influenced) roof forms on its predecessor, the Masjid Al-Adzim of *Melaka*. Other than the distinctive vertical and horizontal members, elements and pilasters were brought into play to allude to a Modernist outlook yet reflect the Malay timber and tectonic-based language, and it is infused with Chinese motifs and references throughout its decorative elements and interior language. Façade treatments evoking columns and openings are tectonically expressed through proportioned pilasters and window frames which project from the window wall, alluding to the post-and-beam and louvred language of tradition. Traditions are transmuted into its modern concretised version, including a proportional interpretation of the tiered pyramidal form.

Malaysia as a nation became a more active member of the global economy in the 1960s (after Independence) and in the 1990s, during the era of the 'Asian Tiger' economies and industrialisation. As urbanisation escalates and industrialisation continues to propel changes, the central dichotomy is always how to express the future yet still retain a hold on one's values and traditions. Forms must be expressed in a language which not only signifies a break with the past but evokes an optimism about the future and a conscious embrace of the new and the objective. Physical expression and vocabulary, amongst others, seek to root their form in traditional values, yet must have a communicative ability to be acceptable to a multicultural mass and population with differences in faith and culture. Two case studies represent the possibility of designing the mosque not as a product of convention, but arising from aspirations outside this convention and at times drawing inspiration from the modern urban context (Fig. 2.6).

Fig. 2.6 The UTEM mosque, *Melaka*

The Mizan Mosque, Putrajaya: Industrialisation and Islamisation

Designed to symbolise a period when Malaysia had a single-minded focus on industrialisation, the Tuanku Mizan Abidin Mosque, better known as the 'Steel Mosque', represented a return to key elements of the 'dome-arch' eclectic form yet interpreted in terms of modernity. Built on a site at the end of Putrajaya Boulevard, this mosque constitutes a kind of crowning apotheosis of the industrialising ambition of the new capital of Putrajaya. It encapsulates the nation's attempts to signify a new image – that of progressive Islam – into the modern world. Malaysia's industrialised era spurred as an avant-garde expression of Islamic architecture.

Conceived in 2004 and completed by 2009, during the era of Malaysia's industrialisation, it boasts a structurally explicit language of the mosque, while the exposed series of arches and explicit use of steel and glass express the image of industrialisation. The end of the boulevard is signalled by an elevated bridge or urban promenade that links the urban visitor or worker to the Masjid Mizan. At the end of the boulevard, just before the massive lake, lies this mosque representing a new industrial aesthetic of fused elements of coated and stainless steel. A steel dome surmounts an essentially multivolume cubic structure and is enveloped by a curved grille façade whose checquered patterning can be appreciated from afar. The dome, the curved walls and the glass *mihrab* wall were stylised to encapsulate industrialisation by evoking the idea of transparency. Constructed from anti-reflective glass and supported by a cable-net structural system, the glass pieces are held together by fine stainless steel cables. Internal space has an almost austere expression, enveloping the human scale within the multistorey heightening of the central prayer hall, recalling the ethos of 'space filled with light and air' underlying its design concept of 'breezy, moderation and transparency' (Fig. 2.7).

The mosque's steel facade is 7.7 metres wide and it has an up to 8.3-metre-long rise and curved silhouette with grilles that reference the rational cubic patterns of Mondrian. The dome is almost a steel version of the folded structures of Masjid Negara but translated into a curved dome; its metallic, shimmering, even monochrome, light-grey appearance is meant to depart from the eclectic bulbous form of the Islamic dome. The search for a new expression and language of the dome is given a new twist. The folded surfaces have diamond plates made of steel elements causing a play of form and light in the sun, producing a crystalline and shimmering surface as sunlight is reflected in an angular and dynamic dance, which changes depending on the time of day, recalling the expressionist crystalline tendencies of the Expressionist stream in Modernism.

Conclusions

In the context of Malaysia and its evolution from the colonial era to post-Independence, the symbolic 'language' of the mosque has overwhelmed its basic form. In particular, the production of national or state-sponsored

Fig. 2.7 Interior of the Mizan or the 'steel mosque'

mosques and their architecture has become a largely cultural and ideological effort. The form and its intentions themselves extend beyond the functions of the communal and the spiritual. Sociocultural forces and the work of individuals asserted themselves in these forms. Their language, expressed meanings beyond function, into a certain ideological and sociopolitical message. The symbolic role of the mosque carries a legitimising power and hence it will continue to attract large investments and resource allocations. It is also a representative and symbol of the global link to Islam and functionally, a mosque is simple in its spatial requirements, yet the spectrum of its iconic form is a reflection of how it is harnessed as a symbol that reflects the traditional 'rhetorical' functions of architecture.

Through centuries, the mosque has undergone a vibrant evolution in form and expression. Yet as the world journeys into the twenty-first century, one must question the need to regurgitate eclecticism. A more inclusive and cosmopolitan meaning must be carried forward as a means of community building. In Malaysia, forms and language of its mosques have oscillated between provinciality and universality, with cases of success drawn by a universal acceptance by its role as a symbol. In the case of Masjid Negara, its overall synthesis and form seem to appeal to a multicultural nation; the mosque become a symbolic structure and a means of unity by revealing a more 'open' and reformist spirit, a challenge to conventions. Its courage in departing from convention brought about a thoughtful layering of cultural and climatic principles translated into the spatial demands of mosque form. In Masjid Negara, instead of reverting to the conventional eclectic and Arabised forms, the International style is localised. A regionalism here is elevated into a national icon, via metaphors and tropical references, and ground-breaking intentions. The chapter highlights that in a multicultural society, it is possible to harness such forces of culture and climatic sensibilities into fusing Modernity, to and Islamic architecture. A mosque, though a religious typology, is able physically commemorate a distinct historical moment in time, recalling the youthful spirit of a new nation, yet it is also to express the idealisms of a community, in need of an identity.

References

Ahmad, A. Z., Mat Zin, A., & Arbi, E. (2013). Typology of interior architecture for traditional mosques in Peninsular Malaysia from 1700–1900 AD. *Journal Al-Tamaddun Bil, 8*(2), 89–100.

Bougas, W. (1992). Surau Aur: Patani oldest Mosque. *Archipel, 43*(1), 89–112.

Broadbent, G. (1978). A plain man's guide to the theory of signs in architecture. *Architectural Design, 49*(8/9).

Crinson, M. (1996). *Empire building – Orientalism and Victorian architecture*. London/New York: Routledge Publishers.

De Botton, A. (2006). *The architecture of happiness*. London, UK: Hamish Hamilton Publishers.

Eco, U. (1972). Introduction to a semiotics of iconic signs. *Versus, 2*, 1–15.

Eisen, A. (2015). Mosque, dome, minaret: Ahmadiyya architecture in Germany since 2000 Minnesota State University. *Mankato International Journal of Islamic Architecture, 4*(1). Intellect Ltd.

Holod, R., & Khan, H. (1997). *The mosque and the modern world – Architects, patrons and design since the 1950s*. London: Thames and Hudson Ltd.

Jahn Kassim, S., & Nawawi, N. (2016). The Masjid in modernity – Form, space and syntax. In *Dimensions of Masjid architecture – Perspectives and writings in theory and design*. Kuala Lumpur: Kulliyyah of Architecture and Environmental Design, IIUM.

Khoo, S. N. (2014). *The Chulia in Penang*. Penang: ARECA Books.

Othman, R., Inangda, N., & Ahmad, Y. (2007). A typological study of mosque internal spatial arrangement: A case study on Malaysian mosques (1700–2007). *Journal of Design and the Built Environment, 4*(1), 41–54.

Othman, R., & Zainal-Abidin, Z. J. (2011). The importance of Islamic art in mosque interior. *Procedia Engineering, 20*, 105–109. https://doi.org/10.1016/j.proeng.2011.11.144.

Pevsner, N. (1976). *A history of building types*. London: Thames and Hudson.

Ruskin, J. (1851). *Stones of Venice*. London, UK: Kemlscott Press edition.

Utaberta, N. (2012). Contemporary architecture of Islamic societies between globalization and tradition. In Chief editor (Ed.), *International research book* (2nd ed.). Malang: PenerbitUIN.

Yong, L. L. (2001). *Masjid Negara: The national Mosque*. Petaling Jaya: MASSA Monograph.

3

Public Buildings of Early Independence: Conflations of Regionalism and National Identity

Shireen Jahn Kassim and Norwina Mohd Nawawi

Introduction

The formation of a new nation after independence catapults a community of people onto the global stage. As it struggles to assert its identity, urban and architectural form become part of this search. Emblems such as monuments, flags and cultural artefacts, become harnessed as symbols to unite and drive a new future.

Similarly when Malaysia was formed in 1963, the nation had to embark on an active and intense period of development, including the construction of key institutions and government buildings to mark its status as an independent country. At the same time, the 1950s and 1960s coincided with the global diffusion of the International style. In many parts of the world, including India and South America, the founding of new nationhood coincided with the diffusion of the International style. The clean lines and minimalist image of this style concurred with the need to erase the past, to 'start with a clean slate'. It was a new style to

S. Jahn Kassim (✉) • N. Mohd Nawawi
International Islamic University Malaysia, Kuala Lumpur, Malaysia

© The Author(s) 2018

S. Jahn Kassim et al. (eds.), *Modernity, Nation and Urban-Architectural Form*,
https://doi.org/10.1007/978-3-319-66131-5_3

express an optimism about the future through a language with a 'neutral', 'universalist' and 'progressive' appeal.

Agents of diffusion, such as foreign-educated local architects and British architects who were still part of the local proffession & industry and their services, became the sought-after skills of a growing city. They were actively sought as participants in design competitions. Mursib and Rasdi (2016, pp. 17–18) point to new Modernist architects had been active change during the 'Pre-independence' year just before 1957 – referring to architectural firms which already gain a foothold before Independence, such as Palmer and Turner, Booty and Edwards, Iverssen and Van Sitteren, and Swan and McClaren. Mursib and Rasdi (2016) also highlight that the sudden departure of colonialist create a situation when local experts were few and far between. Yet there were pioneering locally grown practices such as the Malayan Architecs Co-partnership (MAC), which became widely known for some of its pioneering tropical Modernist designs. It established itself as one of the advocates of a tropicalised International style. The style was further advanced by the tropical schools of AA (The Architectural Association School of Architecture) and the writings of tropical science advocates such as Koenigsberger. The 'neutrality' of the language itself came to be seen as a uniting factor in a search for symbols that were both palable & universal in a newly minted nation.

The International style projected a progressive image of a new nation, and the universal appeal of the language to a multicultural populace. It carried the overtones of a visionary yet utopian-based idealism that symbolised a total rupture from the past. It was also economical to build, because the use of standard elements and the modularity of concrete and steel technologies were the construction method. In Asia and elsewhere throughout this era, the image of new technologies such as the motorcar and the jet engine, and engineering feats such as the Eiffel Tower and long-span steel bridges, became emblemetic of how the Western world, was a standard-bearer. Building form must also be modelled on the desire for efficiency, modularity and precision. In multicultural Malaysia, there was another factor, a heightened appeal for a new form and a language that was essentially devoid of racial and provincial overtones. Urban-architectural forms must serve as tools for unification, rather than forming ethnic narratives. The notion of a national collective must drive a national supra-cultural consciousness. 'National identity' became the motto that reigned during the period of formation of the nation-state, and was characterised by a kind of euphoria of the 1950s and 1960s. The form and language of tropical Modernism immediately became a symbol of independence from colonisation, denoting a certain freedom and a break from a nation's past. Kusno (2000) observes the link between urban-architectural form and a process linked to the regionalisation, or localisation of a generic type-form:

> *This represents a process of architectural 'localisation' – a cultural negotiation of the authority of the 'international style' that the ultimate alignment is established only when the latter is deprived of exercising an absolute dominance. The technique of incorporating climatic modifiers into what is essentially a modernist structure presupposes an ultimate rejoining of the 'tropical' with the 'modern' and the re-identification of the latter to the former.*

With respect to post-independence Malaysia, Azaiddy Abdullah (2014) in his overview in 'The Living Machines' sums up the context of the profusion of the International style: '*By the 1950s, the Modernist … philosophy had taken the world by storm. Far flung places in the Far East, even the depths of the African continent, and the tip of South America were all gripped by the Modernist fever, … many governments around the world weere adopting the relatively quick, economical, sturdy and robust Modernis buildings, …*' The rise of a new language – basically a language of clean verticality and horizontality, was climatically adapted they form the tastes of the newly formed elite i.e. the upper middle class populations of newly formed nations. Its image was linked to new taste, that of the rationality of science and the idealism of technology. The image of science and precision was the ulimate ethos of functionalism and new vocabulary from which architects, artists and urbanists can replace the old 'eclectic' forms. Professionals became anxious to develop a new 'aesthetic' based on the potentialities of a new 'revolution' in design. These form a meta-narrative of rupture with the past, and embody a new 'objectivity'. These were argued to reflect the 'common' man, the 'rights of the individual' and social agendas and programmes. The new position was that of 'objectivity' or '*Sachlichkeit*' – from which two major trends based on the mechanical and organic analogies had grown, yet from which, after several decades, the mechanistic or 'machine'-based view became predominant.

In the West, the 'machine' became the paradigm – and the model of mechanics became an eventual esthetic response to the Industrial Revolution. These tendencies resulted in designs based on surfaces sectioned via right angles, and groupings of panels vertically and horizontally. Eventually this gave rise to a 'cult of the right angle' in which novel designs were drawn from rudimentary geometric forms.

Ockman (1997) usefully describes how the ideals of Modernism began as a 'principle' in the West – which later became an 'aesthetic'. *'Modern architecture stopped being an American import and became an export. … The abstract, laconic façade and highly refined glass and steel facades of the international harbored no explicit critical messages. … The architects of the post-war International style aspired less to avant garde heroics than to integration within the mainstream of capitalist production.'* When Modernism in 1920s Europe had shifted from the ideals of social reform to an aesthetic style, architects were eager to re-align their agenda with the imperatives of American capitalism. The successes of industrialisation in America resulted in avant-garde architects 'accommodating' the idealism of the Bauhaus and early Modernism to the pragmatism of global capitalism. Ockman further relates: *'The glass house of the 1920s, repository of modernist culture's most utopian hopes, was transformed into a fully embodied expression of advanced capitalism, corporate bureaucracy and big business. Post-war modern architecture absorbed the ethos of capitalism, disciplining it and giving it an aesthetic form.'* Hence the trends observed in tropical cities of the newly independent nations of South East Asia reflected a newly formed social structure and the presence of global capital within these previously tradition-bound societies. Gradually, the International style became more than just the dressing for multinational commercial complexes. In new nations Public and administrative buildings was seen as a symbol of progressiveness. Its primarily orthogonal and geometric character aligned with the modularity and cast-in situ methods of construction.

For a new nation, the future meant treading into the unknown. The International style expressed three values: progress, democracy and a sense of belonging into the progressive future. This is well summarised in

Ford's introductory chapter 'Artefacts of Industrialization' (Ford 1996 First Edition 2003, p. 2 and p. 21), which he highlights how the International style became a language embraced by so many nations during the 1960s. Its adoption and diffusion was particularly by emerging nations throughout the era:

> *These issues (of the International style) – of what constituted an appropriate economy of material and the importance of achieving a stability that was not only real but perceptible. The ideal constructional principles of the 20th century conformed to the idealized theories of the 19th century which were:*
>
> *1) The doctrine of material efficiency, in which the best structure is that which uses the minimum material to enclose maximum space.*
>
> *1. The doctrine substantiates that structure equals architecture. That is to demonstrate that if a form was the result of the structure, and if that structure must be made clear that there is no alternative but to make what is not structure transparent, i.e. glass th[e]n that structure is itself the architecture.*
>
> *2. The doctrine of transparency suggested that if architecture was to reduce to skin and bones, it was imperative that the curtain wall appears just that, a curtain.*
>
> *3. The doctrine of monolithic construction.*
>
> *4. The doctrine of standardisation of architecture lies in architecture as a result of the industry. To be industrialised, its components must be reduced to a limited number of standard parts and mass produce[d].*
>
> *5. The cult of the everyday.*

In India was, a similar threhold was being expressed and the Modernist language offered the possibility of a 'clean slate' for the nation and a new beginning. Acclaimed architects such as Le Corbusier, found enthusiastic patrons for a style that represented egalitarianism, symbolised freedom a clean beginning from its own past. As Jahn Kassim and Nawawi (2016) describe in relation to the aesthetic intentions of the Capitol of Chandigarh, India:

> The Capitol was envisioned as a series of
> monuments and plazas whose form and urban patterns
> would allude to, but never directly express, existing
> devices and patterns..rom India's traditions
> Corbusier's predilection for the abstract and the dynamic

> in terms of composition would come into play
> and such forms of the past, would become suggest to a
> new expression and give birth to a new vocabulary. The
> city was envisioned as a language of extended portico
> elements, extensive shading, deep recesses and lightwashed
> walls. More significantly, it contained forms
> that were articulated towards a monumentality that
> represented a new India. Corbusier envisioned that
> such forms and symbols would then overthrow existing
> preconceptions and forge new icons from the collective
> past .... almost
> every line and form drawn was inherently a fusion
> between Modernist leanings and traditional forms distilled
> from the context. The architect's own ... affinity with the artistic streams
> of Modernism
> would play its role in ensuring that form would synthesise
> into an entirely new sense of 'order'.

In the context of independence from colonial 'masters', Modernism replaced the legacy of the old with a new 'slate' signalling the threshold to a new era. As Jameson (2002) observes, cited by Kahn (2012):

> *The process also recalls Frederic Jameson's observation that all modernist narratives must give rise to the consciousness of a break or rupture with the past, a consciousness that gives way in turn to the awareness of that past as a period in itself.* (Jameson 2002, p. 24)

Modernity in Malaysia, became a harbinger of new values – progress, democracy, freedom – and a new architectural language. Though this reflected its 'parental' origins in the West, but inspired a series of regionalisations of the global language and style which came to be characterised by a 'cultural' diffusion from the West. Attempts to 'regionalise' the International style also included formal climatic elements such as Le Corbusier's brise-soleil and the use of 'parasols'. Le Corbusier was inspired by the Moroccan clusters and Arab *mashrabiyyas* and had translated these into a concrete frame vocabulary in Modernist blocks and cities throughout the world. Tzonis and Le Faivre (2001, p. 35) summarise this phenomenon in terms of regional expression during the early post-colonial period as follows:

> *It freed tropical architecture of the region from narrow constraints of the bungalow, suitable for small-scale buildings only, and allowed it to adapt to larger scale urban projects such as extensive housing projects, banks, schools and commercial buildings.*

Tropicalisation and National Identity

The impact and infusion of the International style in Malaysia's early years of nationhood is best described by Abdullah (2014):

> *With the onslaught of social upheaval and the oil crisis of the 60a and 70s,many governments around the world were adopting the relatively quick, economical, sturdy n robust modernist buildings that were easy to construct and maintain yet still able tobe infused with strong regionalist and nationalistic metaphors. Modernist arcg was not only born out of economic necessity but alsoas away for people to create architecture tht expressed the idea of freedom from, Colonialism.*

The early Independence buildings of Malaysia, exuded the same zest as those works of Le Corbusier in Nehru's India, India sought to express a new beginning for the nation, through symbols for the people freed from the encumbrance of colonialism. Le Corbusier's forms and plazas of ancient origins, and the orchestration of tropical variants of the *pilotis* and the brise-soleil, became a language that sought to erase any semblances of colonial memory. The absence of any reference to past tradition was tantamount to rejecting the past and its value systems. In retrospect, both Malaysia's spate of early Modernism and India's Chandigarh complexes expressed the euphoria of the moment, coupled with the desire to embrace the idea of newness and progress. Another factor at play, is, the role of Malaya-based British architects and of British-trained local architects, and the role of the mass media in glamourising the minimalist style as a mark of advanced economies. As stated by Khairuddin and Yong (2012), *when a nation which grew from a loose composite of agricultural communities progresses towards a modern industrialised state, the construction of a national culture is necessary for such post-colonial phases. National or federal buildings are vital visual signs towards which a public gaze or imagination gravitated. As federal works, although architecture and building were seen both as functional and expressive, it inherently exudes actuality of purpose and the confidence commensurate with the times.*

The Parliament Complex, Kuala Lumpur

A Parliament complex must negotiate between the language of the times, and elements that represent a multicultural and multireligious population. The task was given to a senior architect at the Public Works Department, William Ivor Shipley, who was known for his preoccupation not only with the potentials of standardisation & modularity, but with ideas of Expressionism. The Malaysian Parliament complex (Fig. 3.1) was completed in 1963, but in the 1950s, Ivor Shipley, who worked

Fig. 3.1 The Parliament building, Kuala Lumpur

as a Selangor state architect, travelled to Penang and had a meeting with Konrad Wachsmann (1901–1980), a German architect who had studied with the German expressionist architect Hans Poelzig in Potsdam.

Hans Poelzig was known for his expressionist leanings during a time when Germany and the rest of Europe were actively searching for a new *Sachlichkeit* as a new way of designing without reference to past ideas. Poelzig, like many of the more avant-garde architects, belonged to the more expressionist stream in Germany during the early 1900s, who was exploring new forms derived from the purity of nature's forms and structures. Expressionism was a stream within a European movement from 1910 to 1925 and brought together architects such as Taut and Mendelssohn. They believed that Europe was at the dawn of a new age. There must be a search for a new style in public buildings. They did not favour the more rationalist industrial aesthetic of the Bauhaus. In search of a new style, they sought inspiration from the structures & processes of nature mirroring growth and repetition. Inspired by the stalactites and stalagmites of caves and hills, Poelzig then synthesised Modernist ideas with such crystalline yet cavernous forms is 5000-seat indoor theatre in 1919 in Berlin (as Frampton 2007) was formed:

> *after the war ... a year later. He announced his affinity with artists of the Glass chain. In his SalzburgFestpielhaus project, where his newly invented pendentive motif was piled up into an imageimage of proportions. In his Istanbul project of 1917, these arched forms were assembled in such a way so as to create a ziggurat form whose interior was a prismatic cavern made up entirely of pendentive elements ... the Schauspielhaus for Reinhardt was Poelzig's last fully Expressionist work ...*

Wachsmann, who had once worked for one of Europe's Christoph & Unmack, in 1925, became familiar with a pre-fabricated wood system of construction before immigrating to the United States in 1941 and establishing a partnership with Walter Gropius. After the end of World War II, Wachsmann's design for a 'wedge connector' was used to build a prefabricated building element. In 1949, Wachsmann began his teaching career in Chicago; in 1964, he was in Los Angeles, where he taught architecture for a decade at the University of Southern California School of Architecture. He was known for continuing to develop and espouse the use of standardised building systems.

Shipley was known to be influenced by Wachsmann's ideas about modularity in timber construction. During those key discussions, a brief for a new centre of administration for a new country representing a major national construction programme for the growing multicultural population must have inspired and preoccupied its architects with the excitement of the 'new'. The challenge of a universal language of unification to symbolise the nation's nascent identity must be economically, technically and technologically feasible. The standardisation and modularisation of design and building processes were the facilitative principles. These diffused Modern movement principles guided Shipley and allowed him and his team, to some extent, to build buildings with industrialised parts as well as modularisation of processes. Thus costs were controlled and at the same time architectural statements were allowed to establish a significant symbolic masterplan. Both the design and the system of construction must also be capable of integrating new building products and systems, as well as efforts to translate and install them locally and cost-effectively into the Malaysian environment. This process became an industrialised aesthetic and process, akin to the movement in Europe, that was communicated by Wachsmann through Shipley and thus embedded in the architectural symbol of Malaysia's independence.

Regional identity became the basis of national identity; the aim was a recognisable departure from the homogeneous façade through localised sun-shading louvres developed as tropical protective devices. These recall the influence of the essence of Poelzig's luminous stalagmites, yet at the same time, their pointed elements allude to the roof finials of Malay traditional house forms or the scales of the tropical pineapple fruit. The influence of Modernism and Expressionism are undeniable, and these were broad stylistic and constructional streams in Europe which had permeated other countries. The Parliament House became acclaimed for its universal appeal to a diverse community. Even today its architecture is seen as an emblem that can unite a population, and the realisation of a significant and crucial symbol of a nation which can be executed during challenging times.

Some still identify its forms with allusions to Malay local forms. The articulation of the steeply serrated pitched roof of the Dewan Rakyat is not according to Kien (2015) a reference to local forms. The roof was originally formed as a pleated shell with a five-sided section but was later refined into a more triangular one. These had led to claims of its references to the steeply pitched 'Malay House Roof' form although it was not originally intended as such.

Its internal space provision for future expansion saw its accommodation of Malaysia when 11 states became 14 (and then 13). Shipley was also known to have experimented with formal ideas on an eight-bay and three-dimensional grid linear layout standard office block that expedited construction and planning. Over 200 office buildings of similar design were eventually constructed nationwide. Expanding on his grid measurements, Shipley articulated spaces around the functional arrangements required to accommodate both the Dewan Senat (Senate hall) and the Dewan Rakyat in the podium block. Separating processes of the Parliament from the governmental establishment, offices were laid out and contained within the 18-storey tower, a structure that projected through the masterplan and reticulated a façade of Neoexpressionist stalactite-like forms yet recalled the roots of tropical traditions in its function as a climatic armature and protection from the intense sun. Construction with pre-cast terrazzo cladding panels became its signature. The symbol had become an enduring one for Malaysia, and was accepted by the multicultural population at the national level. It was even acclaimed as an 'architecture of democracy', whose external language did not give precedence to any race.

Although the Parliament building embodies an essentially climatic position, its sunshading resonates to references to a tropical fruit form. The pointed pitched form of the Senate hall still recalls the steep-pitched forms of Malay architecture. These references to cultural imagery ensured a broad universal appeal to different racial sections of the population. It embodies the capacity of architecture to function as 'signification' and of meaning to different audiences while negotiating symbolic meaning to a diverse population. The overall language can be international; nuances and gestures as inflected tropicalised forms can still communicate a critical message, hence fulfilling architecture's role as mass communication and bearer of meaning to a multicultural mass and general public.

Such forms can be defined as tropical and regional inflections of an imported style, yet they convey universal meaning to the population. This meaning and message of inclusivity is contained in neutral language generated by the absence of parochialism and thus experienced even today as a part of national identity. The language of such public structures has become a determining and productive field through which social meaning is constructed, experienced and interpreted. These elements can be read in terms of their intentions and messages at the time, yet in hindsight, they capture the era and the meaning they had for different communities.

The Angkasapuri Building

The Angkasapuri building was built from 1968 to 1972. Designed by NJ Pappas and Associates, a local firm, the eight-storey building has similar overtones of a climatic tropicalisation tinged with expressions of cultural iconography. The building is essentially a rectangular multistorey form clad with pointed forms of shading devices reflecting a pineapple skin. The entrance podium is roofed with a folded concrete structure, a contemporary expression of the steep-pitched Malay roof. To promote patriotism amongst the multiethnic Malaysians, not only was the position of a climatic regionalism adopted, but murals with paintings that reflected the coexistence of various cultures and religions in one nation were included. In 1964, to commemorate the formation of Malaysia in 1963 as well as to symbolise the consolidation of the new nation, prominent architect Kington Loo designed the Sarawak State Assembly Building, in which the imagery of the steep-pithced forms of the Malay vernacular was combined with elements of modularity characerisitic of the concree aesthetics of tropical Modernism. The juxtaposition similarly brought together façade and columnar structures into a standardised and modular type approach, yet inflected with reference to Malay forms that are also based on Sarawakian architecture. The pointed forms of the local architecture roof shapes and finials were combined with the columnar spaces of the entrance podium in order to create a modern abstraction of a regionalised style, which was ingenously synthesised, to embody an inflexion towards the region, while still retaining a celebration of an architecture of modularity of concrete elements and roof shells.

Acclimatising the 'Box'

Regionalisation through acclimatisation was seen as a necessary strategy to synthesise modernity and tropicalisation. Instigated by theories and publications from the AA tropical school, and advocates such as Koenigsberger and Le Corbusier, the notion of a tropical architecture quickly found a footing in developing nations. It was both scientific and progressive at the same time. The use of louvres, filtering façades, extended eaves and verandah protrusions became not only an aesthetic of a tropical language grounded in the 'progressive' International style, but was a conflation of both 'rationalising' the style through a scientific basis in climatic design and 'regionalising' the language through a tropical adaptation of a global style. There was an easy capacity of the International language to extend its vocabulary to respond to the dynamics of the climate including sun path and daylight. Evoking identity in a global type-form was essentially a climatic adaptation involving the addition of louvres and filtering elements and the amelioration of heat and sunlight in the internal spaces. Façade shading became fused with geometries that became optimised to the prevailing sun path. They represent climatic strategies were part and parcel of the regionalisation of the International style which witnessed the judicious positioning and dimensioning of climatic devices. The rationalisation of climatic design would elevate the 'machine for living' or the 'box' to a localised form.

A major government project with International neutral forms but localised with climatic inflections was the Kuala Lumpur General Hospital (KLGH) project by Wells and Joyce, built in 1966. The KLGH, as it is now known, was perhaps the epitome of a Modernist complex of a young country embarking on a new journey of identity and statehood.

Built into the natural terrain of its 150-acre site, the spaces in the hospital are characterised by the use of many levels linked by ramps.

It became a national reference as a centre of excellence for tropical diseases, and what was designed as a space for 900 beds was later expanded to accommodate over 3000 beds with inbuilt flexibility of spatial provision. Throughout the interior, there are nooks and corners providing shade, and modules and meeting places for staff and patients. Each section to connected to another, at a certain distance from wherever one parks as there is no adequate visitors' parking area, with the exception of the limited spaces under the ward blocks near the Emergency Department. A new parking block has been constructed across the Modernist 'narrow-plan' maternity block. Oriented north and south, the series of rectangular blocks housing wards, clinics and diagnostic areas are linked by winding, sometimes bridged and shady, corridors with gentle ramps to other floors and pocket gardens and intermittent balconies as places and spaces for reflection. All the wards are separated into bays with low walls in between to facilitate natural ventilation, with the exception of the limited first-class and two- to four-bed second-class wards as rooms. All waiting areas in the hospital are naturally ventilated. Louvred glass windows command the inner façade of the buildings, with window curtains and privacy curtain tracks for each patient being added later in the wards, along with the concrete soffit with exposed building services which were trendy elements at that time.

Although the whole hospital was distinctively orthogonal and finished originally with a natural off-form greyish concrete, colours were then used to accentuate identity and the medical and surgical disciplines. Each block was custom designed to suit the specific function first. Areas that are nonclinical, although rich and flamboyant in design expression, are still naturally ventilated. Being geographically located in the tropics, and inspired by Le Corbusier's precedent designs, the language used to articulate the whole sprawling hospital was distinctively a tropicalisation of Modernism. Identity was the reason for provision of extended eaves, deep fenestration, profusion rhythm of sun-shading fins and the proliferation of *pilotis* composed through raised levels and walkways. These enriched blocks of homogeneous forms were made from off-form concrete and took over eight years, from 1966 to 1974, to complete.

Cultural Inflections of the 'Modern'

In mathematics, an inflection point is the point on a curve at which the gradient of the tangent, that is, the curvature, changes sign (Bell et al. 2014). Contours are generic curves, but inflections are points where curves change direction. Previously, these terms were used as descriptors in mathematics, linguistics and architecture/engineering (Jahn Kassim 2002).

As Kuala Lumpur grew into a new metropolitan centre, buildings in the International style sprouted in the new urban landscape, mostly expressed in concrete technology, yet inflected with tropical acclimatisation. The open-air corridors, the louvres and egg-crate shading devices and extended porticos were elements that are climatically judicious, and these became environmentally conscious 'green' features of their time. Yet when contrasted with the 'glass boxes' that emerged in the industrial boom of the 1990s, such concrete structures are linked to difficulties in maintenance due to incidences of mould infestations in the humid environment. The orthogonal forms of the maternity block of KLGH, for example, are reminiscent of the brise-soleil and brute forms of Le Corbusier's Unité d'Habitation. In retrospect, can be read as the outcome of the force of cultural diffusion of the West, due to a vacuum created by newly developed urban centres.

Yet as one moves away from the cultural centre of 'modernity' in Kuala Lumpur, iconic buildings begin to be 'inflected' with references to tradition. Such forms were abstracted and integrated with tropical Modernism. In buildings which do not involve a rigorous spatial programming, a more flexible approach involves abstractions of local forms. Yet in all cases, there is a persistent principle of 'designing for light and air' as promulgated by Corbusier as one of the essences of a Modern style. At times, these cultural allusions are stronger and others, references are more subtle. The Seremban State mosque, for example, was designed based on an open floor plan, with nine parasol roof forms, nine conical buttresses and nine towers – synthesised in one composition. The roof consists of a hyperbolic concave concrete shell, meant to allude to the curvature of the Minangkabau roof. There is a generous admission of daylight and a similarly generous provision of verandah, which ameliorates heat and diffuses the light as it surrounds the main hall. The Sarawak State Secretariat Legislative Assembly Complex, designed by Kington Loo in 1964, could almost be read as an extension and evolution of the Parliament Complex in Kuala Lumpur (at the time the Parliament was one of the largest projects in South East Asia). It resonates with similar pointed forms of the local steep roofs and yet recalls the pointed shading devices of the Parliament façade. What sets them apart is the different interpretations of an abstract, steeply pitched roof form. While there was no clear agreement on the origins of the steeply pitched forms of the Dewan Rakyat complex in Parliament, there is a clear reference to local traditions in this complex.

A Universal Language

These buildings, many of which have aged due to the humidity of the tropics, have been criticised for their homogeneity and propensity to poor maintenance due to extensive mould growth. They symbolise a time of optimism and their very neutrality and reductionist approach to expression have made them 'impartial' symbols, irrespective of race, of 'Modern style buildings'. The style is hailed, even today, as 'Merdeka [freedom] architecture', referring to what it embodied, an architecture for all. It had become a symbol and a style of 'the state of merdeka' a newly formed community and people who had to work out quickly how to coexist and work together without conspicuously privileging one race above the other. As simultaneously embodying a departure from the past, it was able to embody aspirations towards the future. The Modernist neutral style was a palatable language, the 'clean slate' needed to fuse a new multiethnic society. It became representative of a new beginning of a nation that strove to depart from the feudalistic past and post-colonial structures. These forms became neutral elements for unification. They were not only economical to construct but successful to capture and form a narrative that embodied that search for unity and identity. Localisation of this style – afforded by the tropicalisation of formal gestures of International style – became forms that infused the nation with the idealism of multiculturalism. Yet some lament how today it still serves as a reminder of colonisation. The International style was represented by the 'educated' elite and hence was readily adopted by various nations in the developing world. To the general masses, particularly the Western-educated elite, saw the style as a new idea and a mark of civilisation and advancement. Despite its noble intentions, many would eventually, in time, react to these 'efficient' yet 'austere' forms as a reminder of a legacy of colonisation. Its legacy in the overwhelming homogeneity and uniformity of growing cities are but reminders in the urban landscapes of these cities and their localities.

Conclusions

Modernity was a certain number of thresholds where a society or a civilisation becomes aware of drastic changes in their history. These may instigate optimistic conditions in the people's psyche as they find themselves entering a new chapter of the nation or a new horizon into the unknown (Curtis 1996). As individual and independent entities, nations become collectively aware that they must establish their identity at this crucial juncture in their history. Modernism and the International style became a means of symbolising a 'clean slate', yet their homogeneous language no longer holds sway over present trends. For some, the Modernist style still recalls a nostalgia, history and memories of the optimism of a new nation. A multiracial country such as Malaysia constantly faces the issue of cultural representation of its identity. A 'national' architecture must be deemed not to make specific/direct reference to the symbols of one race above another. A recurring debate in Malaysia is how to reach such consensus on what constitutes an architectural language of 'Malaysian architecture' that is acceptable to and represents all races. There have been efforts made by various stakeholders since Independence to incorporate in the development of 'national Malaysian architecture' guidelines that regard Malaysians in a neutral tone, although the Malay traditions have been deemed acceptable, as Malay cultural forms remain the localities' traditional legacies. Many national buildings have been inspired by Malay forms, idioms and references. The Malaysian Architectural Policy (MAP), initiated by Malaysian Institute of Architects (PAM) in 2009 towards Malaysian vision 2020, was such an effort. It was to provide the nation with a common framework that can be used to propagate the ideas of innovation in the design and the aesthetics of buildings in keeping with the natural heritage. It was to promote architecture as a symbolic utility, according to the level of importance of the building's purpose and function.

Many have lamented the bland and almost mute forms of architecture and its digression from traditions, that would eventually bring on its demise. It expressed a discordance with humanity's natural propensity to tradition, as Watkin (2000, p. 561) summarises on how its represented a position of ambivalence: 'Reaction was bound to come against an architecture with such polemical lack of reference to historical traditions, … mouldings, ornaments, symmetry and warmth had been abandoned in favor of glass walls and drab, irrerievally stained concrete.' He also made reference to the fact that these buildings essentially symbolise functionalism, rather than being made to perform functionally. Broadbent (1978) attests that the functionalist buildings of the 1920s are in fact very poor in function. For example, Le Corbusier's Villa Savoye, the epitome of the Modern movement, was prone to flooding and overheating and thus was actually poor in function but is a magnificent symbol of the 1920s. Thus, like it or not, all buildings symbolise or 'carry' meaning.

Hence, as Saussure (1959) famously deduced, linguistic system can be seen as tools to organise communicative systems such as those governing the built environment. His study highlighted how buildings can be structured according to language and carry semantic meanings like language. These iconic buildings had sought stark rupture with references to the past. The era signalled a time when Modernist style had a kind of stranglehold on the imagination and values of the middle class and had formulated the aesthetic sense of a new nation.

Not only was the regionalisation of a global style accepted by a new nation-state, it signalled a time when the image of progress and technical efficiency coincided with the ease of assembly of such standardised elements. They were essentially the tropicalised diffusion of the vision of modernism, in which the domesticated house is suddenly transformed into 'machines for living'. Though this austerity instigated a movement, it is the very neutrality of language that lends itself readily to its being subsumed by economic expediency. It became a reminder of placelessness and emblems of the coolly competent and cosmopolitan individual. As the following chapters will show, it is the essentially restrained and mute language that gave rise to form with a more sculptural quality and iconography in later years.

References

Abdullah, A. (2014). *The living machines – Malaysia's modern architectural heritage*, published by Persatuan Akitek Malaysia (PAM).

Bell, J., Sampasivam, S., McGovern, D. P., Meso, A. I., & Kingdom, F. A. A. (2014). Contour inflections are adaptable features. *Journal of Vision, 14*(7), 2–2.

Broadbent, G. (1978, July–August). A plain man's guide to the theory of signs in architecture. *Architectural Design, 47*(7–8), 474–482.

Curtis, W. (1996). *Modern Architecture since the 1900s*. London, UK: Phaidon Press.

Ford, E. R. (1196). *The details of modern architecture, volume 2: 1928–1988*.

Jahn Kassim, P. S. (2002). The 'curves of nature' – The organic inflections of modern regionalism in an urbanising context. *WIT Transactions on Ecology and the Environment, 57*.

Jahn Kassim, P. S., & Nawawi, N. M. (2016, September). Allusions to Mughal urban forms, in the monumentality of Chandigarh's capitol complex. *Journal of Architecture and Urbanism,* 40. Routledge: Taylor and Francis Group.

Kiean, L. C. (2007). In C. K. Lai (Ed.), *Building Merdeka: Independence architecture in Kuala Lumpur, 1957–1966*. Kuala Lumpur: Galeri Petronas. issn: 9789839738612.

Kusno, A. (2000). *Behind the postcolonial: Architecture, urban space and political cultures in Indonesia (Architext)* (1st ed.). London/New York: Routledge Francis Group.

Mursib, G., Rasdi, T. (2016). Regionalisme dalam Seni Bina Malaysia: Era Moden, Pascamoden dan Global Penulis: Gurupiah Mursib dan Mohd. Tajuddin Mohd. Rasdi Dewan Bahasa dan Pustaka.

Ockman, J. (1997). Towards a normative architecture. In S. Harris & D. Berke (Eds.), *Architecture of the everyday*. Okay: Princeton Architectural Press.

Tzonis, A., & Le Faivre, L. (2001). Tropical critical regionalism – Introductory comments. In A. Tzonis & L. Le Faivre (Eds.), *Tropical architecture – Critical regionalism in the age of globalisation*. London: Wiley Academy.

Watkin, D. (2000). Karl Frederich Schinkel. In *A history of western architecture* (3rd ed.). London: Laurence King Publishing.

4

Monumentalising the Vernacular: Criticality, Culture and Identity of the City

Noor Hanita Abdul Majid and Shireen Jahn Kassim

Introduction

In post-colonial societies, the years after independence saw the emerging need to infuse growing cities with landmarks of identity. In the case of Malaysia, the search for cultural symbols is conflated with the need for universal emblems for a multicultural population. The simultaneous search for symbols and universally accepted landmarks initiated a degree of anxiety towards the creation and reception of meaning in built form. Urban-architectural forms were articulated in a vocabulary that could be read by all as part of a collective effort to demonstrate a testament to a nation's ability – through form – to communicate, tacitly, certain national and inclusive ideals. Certain forms of public architecture, in a multicultural society, became the focus of emblemetic language that

N. H. A. Majid (✉)
Department of Architecture, Kulliyyah of Architecture and Environmental Design, International Islamic University Malaysia, Kuala Lumpur, Malaysia

S. Jahn Kassim
International Islamic University Malaysia, Kuala Lumpur, Malaysia

© The Author(s) 2018

S. Jahn Kassim et al. (eds.), *Modernity, Nation and Urban-Architectural Form*,
https://doi.org/10.1007/978-3-319-66131-5_4

must emphasise an identity through references to 'culture' as a representation of the nation, yet at the same time, must negotiate a universally accepted position through both 'form' and 'facade' references in order to garner majority acceptance amongst the public. Urban-architectural forms become part and parcel of the 'rhetoric' of national plans, yet these forms also signal a gradual collapse of vernacular lifestyles and the restructuring of a new, post-colonial society, that would later evolve into a rapidly developing nation.

A new nation arising from such a colonial past is in search of an identity that symbolises progress from its past, as well as a 'rupture' from its colonised era. Past forms, which refer to traditions and heritage, presented themselves as a means by which such a language could be elevated to expressive forms. The 'vernacular' presented an arsenal of ideas, thus enabling a link to be made between 'tradition' and progress. During the 1960s and 1970s, a reference to the vernacular range from artistic nuances to ideals of multiculuralism, and to monumental insertions in the city.

Curtis (2001) refers to 'traditionalism' as a mode or form similar to the romanticisation of the Classical rhetoric of public architecture including the Neoclassical style. The work of Classical-romanticist architects such as Karl Frederich Schinkel in Germany (1781–1841) is a embodies the same ethos and demonstrates how the 'classical system', it essentially 'regionalised' a system to its particular time and place. Schinkel's architecture can be described as a product of an underlying 'tension' related to its time and place, that is, 'during a heightened sense of national identity provoked by Napoleon's occupation of Berlin in the 19th century' (Watkin 2000). Schinkel was concerned with a national architecture that can represent its 'times' and its people. He strove to romanticise the 'rigorous' tendencies of the Classical order in order to produce monuments and large buildings that would be representative of the spirit of the times and its people.

Similar forces were perhaps at work during the crucial decades following Independence in Malaysia. Throughout this post-colonial world, strategies of traditionalism were harnessed to add an emotive content or dimension to what was essentially a rational order. To enhance their civic representation and monumental expression in the midst of urbanising forces, a more intense, symbolic language was needed to endow an urban realm with identity and to create meaning. Yet the challenge was twofold – how could such forms elicit an allusion to place while still resonating a multicultural spirit, yet how could the required emotive dimension be extended while resisting the tendency toward degeneration into kitsch. Hence regionalism must revert to monumental gestures which, as described by Curtis (1996), were efforts to imbue large buildings with a degree of symbolic 'intensity'.

To achieve this, the roots of the Malay indigenous tradition or the 'vernacular' were often harnessed in order to inflect a Modernist programme and archetype with symbolic form. One of the most dominant traits of vernacular architecture of the region is the large, steeply pitched and generously extended tropical roof forms. These range from the curved gables of the northern states of Kelantan and Terengganu to the stately forms of *Melaka* and Johor. The idiosyncratic variation of forms of Malay roof across the Malay states, for example, had inspired a series of monumental forms in the city. The chapter attempts to chronologically present a path by which such models evolved from a muted regionalised aesthetic to a more assertive language using a more global language.

The Malay Vernacular

Historically, Malays do not identify themselves as a homogeneous entity but as multivariate groupings and communities whose artisans, carpenters, builders and craftsmen have identified themselves more with the peculiarities of their own community, village, state or national boundaries. There have been innumerable peculiarities of architecture and artisanal works that were not merely the work of Malay artisans and artists of traditional times, but had been crossbred with other artisanal traditions into syncretic forms that possessed a high degree of flavour and peculiarities which are inherently growths and offshoots of the immediate locality or soil from which they sprang. There is an idiomatic impact of such social communities, and these are outcomes of a network of local and regional identities that gave rise to a spectrum and efflorescence of artistic flavours, predispositions and stylistic tendencies that emerge from its cultural geography.

The Malay artisans have unconsciously evolved their own identity and reflected these in physical expression of their arts and architecture. In a way, they are responsible for giving physical form to the mute hopes, visions and unconscious sentiments of the local people, hence Malay vernacular architecture has been summarised as arising from an emotional bond reflecting collective consciousness of the region. Though an evolved process, these gradually converge into traits of national character and identity. The *Awan Larat* or 'moving clouds' is an example, it occurs endlessly in Malay craftsmenship, they physically appear to be the same shape, yet when observed and studied close they unveil their idiosyncrasies. They appear as communal signatures and recalls the dynamics on facades of culture and nature as one. Closer inspection shows the same archetypes reworked in many ways. They are then fused with many other shapes and compositions such as diamond motifs, large flowers, different varieties of flowers and plants and climbing creepers. At times, these are extended to a lavish degree of decoration that is contrasted with the generic simplicity and formal compositions of the tectonic structures of large typologies such as palaces.

In terms of overall form, Malay architecture represents a type of which modern variations have evolved. The Malay vernacular house, for example, is an archetype varying across the region. Its degree of openness differ by which the Malays as a culture and people have absorbed and fused the influences of cultures from other neighbouring communities and races.

Argan (1963) usefully observes how 'type' is part of the thinking and working processes of designers. However, rather than associating type with typology or with certain functions, 'type' according to Argan was 'always deduced from a series of instances. … The birth of a "type" is therefore dependent on the existence of a series of buildings having between them an obvious formal and functional analogy'.

Hence Malay vernacular architecture, including the quintessential Malay house, and its monumental counterpart, the Malay palace, is a 'type' or an 'archetype' whose form elevate Modernist structures to cultural forms. From the 1960s to the present day, the formal and spatial characteristics of house and palace have been used as a model for the design of museums, cultural centres, offices, universities and even commercial restaurants and eateries. An interesting case study is the A & W restaurant in Petaling Jaya, built in the early 1970s by Malaysian Architects Co Partnership (MAC); according to Lillian Tay (2000), 'This first drive-in restaurant translates the pitched roof and gable of the vernacular Malay house into a new commercial building type. The concrete A-frame structure is strongly expressed in line with its Modernist approach.'

The northern and southern variations of 'type' demonstrate the diffusion of neighbouring language are seen in the Kedah, Kelantan and further states to the south such as Negeri Sembilan and Johor which have their nuanced identities from which to derive vocabularies that could reflect the influences of the Riau and Minangkabau cultures into their architectural traditions and influences from neighbouring cultures, including Thai and Chinese influences.

Malay society is intrinsically a multilayered, adaptable community. It has a hierarchical character, but also a multinational dimension. The location of West Malaysia, bordering the Straits of *Melaka*, has made it a sort of cultural melting pot, as it has been, from ancient times, the cultural and commercial conduit between East and West. Its geography, physical land forms and surrounding seas have been the cross roads of a dynamic quagmire cultures and traditions. As Tan Sri Mubin Shepard has related in his seminal writings on Malay traditions, it is through historical and mutual cooperation that cultural forces are found and assimilated in works of traditional architecture. 'The Locally domiciled Chinese carpenters worked alongside Malay craftsmen in the construction of large Malay timber building in Terengganu and Kelantan in the 19th century.' From the Malay viewpoint, such coexistence is crucial to the nature of society's dynamics, whether of villages, houses, neighbourhoods and states, or other religions and cultures.

The mapping of Malay forms in contemporary architecture and the built environment has demonstrated that there are essential types which represent root from which variants evolved. This included the modernisation of local forms, which are driven by abstracted expressions that may range from exaggerated forms to Malay artefacts to simple structures surmounted with artefacts and icons such as the *tengkolok*.

A monumentalisation through elements and forms of the Malay vernacular is characterised by the use of an archetype, primarily characterised by the inherent variations of its dominant roof forms. Across the vernacular typologies of the feudal Malay past – house, palace, mosque – the roofs define the Malay form, and it is these traditional forms that have given rise to more complex forms of Modern architecture. Some of these forms adopted from the Malay world have then been developed into elements of a vocabulary of a hybrid syncretic architecture.

Two Cultural Landmarks

The transformative position, and its physical outcomes, can be defined as a 'third' way. This form of 'traditionalism' is an 'emblemetic characterisation of urban form' (Curtis 1996). Mubin Sheppard's request for the National Museum proposal, the nation's first national museum, was to create an 'alternative' to the Modernist position. He refers to the Miesian box and called for a more distinctive cultural form and layering. The Museum Negara must be seen as the search for a third path – neither the Neocolonial style nor International-style Modernism; but a search for the 'monumental' vernacular. The outcome, however, at times can still be argued as putting a Malay roof on a standard box, but it is in architectural details that a more critical stance is celebrated. Yet, the overall impression is still a box.

Cultural centres can be interpreted as structures that to house the arts and artistic works in a nation. These may refer to buildings built either to house a country's traditional artefacts or centres intended to facilitate cultural activities such as the performing arts. Such structures have become a kind of field of expressing tradition in monuments. In the trajectory of modernisation, the vernacular always emerges, with its ability to 'differentiate' a newly emerging city or state. 'Houses' of the arts – whether physical arts or applied arts – are built to create landmarks for the city and at times within an urban enclave that stem from a confluence of the arts and their associated activities and exhibitions of works and artefacts.

By 1971, a new national cultural policy was announced: both arts and the applied arts must focus on a return to cultural roots. This included the search for 'iconic' structures, and this justified the substantial investment in their architectural construction. To carry nationalist ideas, it must also be strongly cultural, though sometimes this would conflict with universal and multicultural references and meanings. The architect or urbanist may seek departures from existing stereotypes, however, they must also not be constrained by a certain style. The International style began to be viewed for its sterility and muteness, though at the time, it represented a multicultural aspirational stance.

Both the Museum Negara (Malaysia's National Museum) and the *Istana Budaya* (Malaysia's centre of performing arts) are examples of monumental insertions in the city that have harnessed the iconography of vernacular form. They point to an interesting evolution of the use of the Malay roof to create landmarks in the city. The Museum Negara, for example (Fig. 4.1), is almost a direct transmutation of the Malay palace form in its sense of axiality, hierarchy and ceremonialism. Yet a horizontal mural is used to counter-balance the emphasis on axiality. The ideals of national unity were embodied in the artistic details of the National Museum's mural composition, similar to the mural adorning the facade of the Dewan Bahasa and Pustaka (DBP) building. Rather than an iconographic three-dimensional form, both harnessed the representational power of two-dimensional art to reflect emotive themes in their mosaic compositions. The work of art has both an emotional and ideological dimension. The idealism is palpable, and a young nation's hopes are composed and crafted into works of public architecture. These became the national icons that can advance the message of a new nation's hopes and aspirations.

The multicultural agenda was paramount in the early years of public architecture in Malaysia, as universal emblems were needed to address a range of audiences and sections of the population. In Malaysia, the agenda of unity and multiculturalism is reflected in debates and negotiations that simmer without spilling over into confrontation, and these include debates on definitions of national identities architecture and urbanism, particularly in urban centers.

In tropical architecture, the roof is a defining element. In the years preceding Independence, surmounting structures with Malay roofs was the first means of imbuing modern buildings with a cultural identity. This device, so easily made to surmount or sit atop modern structures, was sufficient and effective in elevating a utilitarian structure into a national symbol. The steep pitch and clear lines of the roof brings on an evocative silhouette, producing a recurrent visual image in the city. Subsequently, a slew of national landmarks were built based on such formal themes in the dynamic of composition of Malay roofs on which became symbols and landmarks.

Fig. 4.1 The National Museum, Kuala Lumpur

The National Museum was initially conceptualised as a repository of the nation's vernacular arts and traditions. Its overall approach and external form were reportedly requested by its first director general, Tan Sri Mubin Sheppard, who requested the designer forge a third path, an alternative to the Modernist 'box'. This regionalisation, is referring to a more intense form in order to nationalise a 'type' by surmounting it with a steeply pitched Malay roof with the characteristic *tebar layar* roof gable, and the iconic *lipat kajang* (cross finial). It became a modernised scaled-up version of a palace adorned with a *tebar layar* roof form. Its modern façade was given a local expression by adorning it with a rich interplay of Malaysian mural art. The result was a degree of iconographic form recalling a palatial-type configuration. The layout and planning were intended to reflect and evoke a Nusantara palatial structure, with an inherent axiality and symmetry evoking a certain formality and infusing a ceremonial aura in the entire complex.

The *Istana Budaya* in Kuala Lumpur, which opened in 1999, was composed only as a centre of arts and a city landmark, but ultimately to elevate of Kuala Lumpur as a centre of the arts. As a landmark structure in the city, it needed to assume a strong presence. Located in the lush tropical vicinity of the Titiwangsa Park, its monumentalisation of the Malay roof form was meant to invest a symbolic capacity into the city. The dynamic roof form and its associated structure, designed by Malaysian architect Muhammad Kamar Ya'akub, was both 'artefact' and 'architecture'.

Elements evocative of the Malay world that helped elevate 'structure' to monument include layering the form to recall Malay gifts such as the *sirih junjung*. The folds of its roof at oblique angles crown a layered massing in its ramps and plinths, setting this building apart from others. The form displays a focus on roof dynamics surmounting a promenade-like progression of space. The result is a cultural monument or landmark in the city centre with a recognisable presence amidst tropical greenery in the heart of Kuala Lumpur. Internally, and in its entrance, the composition makes reference to the hierarchy of formal Malay spaces as celebrated in Malay palaces (Fig. 4.2).

Cultural identity is infused in the progression of spaces as this is a conscious attempt to recall the hierarchical progression of Malay spaces in palaces. These were harnessed and remodelled for a modern function,

Fig. 4.2 The *Istana Budaya* (Palace of Culture), Kuala Lumpur

that is, the progressive journey and heightened anticipation towards a theatrical event. In terms of spatial articulation, the progression is mainly organised in three main parts: there is a lobby and foyer which are functionally similar to the Malay porch (*serambi*), there is the main auditorium, locally known as *Panggung Sari* which is similar to the 'parent house' (*rumah ibu*), and the main stage and rehearsal area which would be the equivalent of service areas (*rumah dapur*). The staircases (*tangga-tangga*) that lead to the *Panggung Sari* recall the distinction and richness of the curved staircase of the traditional *Melaka* house.

In the case of the National Museum, the more forceful assertion of a 'national identity' is in the murals adorning the frontage. Distinctively adorning its elongated façade is a range of murals, a momentous artwork designed to symbolise the multicultural ideals and capture the vision of inclusivity and common identity seen as crucial in a new nation. A similar strategy is employed in the Dewan Bahasa dan Pustaka building, built in the heyday of the early 1960s, and designed by Y.T. Lee, which, as Lillian Tay (2000) notes is 'an internalstyle building with nuances of monumentality to assert the front facade dedicated toa mural depicting nationalistic themes'. Although the building itself modelled its expression on the Malay vernacular, the mural façade paintings aim to elevate a regional localisation to a nationalising icon and symbol. As described by Jegadeva (2012):

> *Measuring 115 feet by 20 feet on either side of the grand entrance, and to be fabricated in Italian glass mosaic, the design of the murals was decided through an invitational competition. ... A broad, inclusive brief was given.*
>
> *It called for a chronologial depiction of 'Episodes in Malaysian History' to front the History Gallery on the left, and a design to capture the various cultural elements of Malaysian life.*

Jegadeva (2012) goes on to describe why the submission of Cheong Lai Teong won the competition. The representation of national identity had elevated the role of the arts within the framework of expressing the essence of the spirit of community and cultural universality. This embodied an idealism that gripped the nation and captured the imagination of the public:

> *This inclusive version of a national narrative, conveying an idea and image of independent Malaysia that was culturally and racially diverse, with an economic abundance shared by all, was mirrored in other public art works of the period.*
>
> *The new government initiated many such projects, anchored to a narrative specifically aimed at forging a common, unified national identity.*

Four Cultural Icons of the City

The original Dewan Bahasa and Pustaka Building (DBP), is an iconic structure, modelled on a Modernist-styled block. It is distinctive for it mural-based facades. As a symbol of a newly independent era, it recalls how a new nation set off to harness the power of the arts to express a symbolic forms with a reminder of a national narrative. It was a milestone commemorating the early era of Independence. DBP was specifically built to house an agency set up to champion the role of the Malay language. As Jegadeva (2012) summarises: 'The idea of one language to unify the nation's peoples was seen as central to forging this national consciousness.'

The DBP, which in terms of overall form was modelled as a regional, acclimatised expression of the reigning International style, was completed on 31 January 1962. Throughout its years, the DBP as a literary agency had itself produced several outstanding novels from different races and backgrounds, such as the renowned writers Siti Habsah Abdullah, Malardevi Margamuthu and Syed Satahkatulah Bin Mohamed Kalik.

The building was made up of two orthogonal massings, one of which was inflected towards the Malay roof form. The architect, Lee Yoon Thim, included a prominent mosaic façade by a young artist, Ismail Mustam. Jegadeva (2012) goes on to attest:

> *The mosaic, beautifully designed and simply conceived, depicts five Malaysians – of different races- a national community – at the center of the picture plane. They pore over an open book, surrounded by the representatives of different ethnic groups engaged in activities.*
>
> *This expression of inclusiveness, naïve as it may seem today, relies on a narrative within which something as ethnically biased as language could be happily contemplated as a unifying, embracing and nurturing force.*

In this case, the fine arts were harnessed in order to elevate the structure to a national symbol. Stadium Negara, another national icon, was also adorned by murals painted by Yee Chin Ming and Phoon Poh Hong, and also depicted multiracial figurative representations of a new nation.

> *Their narrative depicts representatives of the three dominant ethnic groups, – Malay Chinese, Indian – arranged in intricate proximity to each other, each related to particular economic, social and cultural activities.*

Museums, literary centres and performance arts theatres are typically stand-alone structures. Convention halls and centres are typically inserted into the urban fabric. As a typology, the variations in these public spaces are different expressions, subsequently evolving into prime centres of civic life. They are also economic generators, as cities no longer see these as containers of functions and events, but as integrated plazas, public spaces and promenades. These urban spaces have become the centre of collective urban life. The convention hall, as a type, has evolved from simply a functional space to a mixed development complex. Ghirardo (1996) has termed these 'public space' or the 'space of the collective'. They provide dynamism to cities and urban centres as they grow from confluences of public and private spaces – shops, retail outlets, public plazas and thoroughfares – whose energy radiates into the surrounding existing fabric.

As the Putra World Trade Center (PWTC) is essentially a convention center located in the middle of the city, the need for iconography (due to national identity) had conflated with the regionalist need to depart from a homogenous 'modern' cube-like typology, the use of a Malay roof, with a strong dominant pitch (the curved and steeply pitched Malay-Terengganu roof) had fulfilled both national and regional agendas simultaneously. The 'typology' or 'gridded schema' was essentially a large multivolume structure enclosing a flexible yet multilayer and multivolume space, was essentially a large sprawling complex that could contain and host varied functions including exhibitions, meetings, seminars, expos and conferences. In urbanising centres and new capital cities, these have become urban 'enclaves' and symbolic icons of cities, complete with links to mass transit. As cities grow, convention centres become more and more integrated, designed with hotels, retail shops, food and beverage and entertainment outlets, as a draw for local and international crowds. Their location and urban role enrich the city's activity and the vitality of the urban fabric and contribute to the public sphere, contributes to the broader social, cultural and economic goals and dynamics of a modern nation. The form of the convention centre has reflected its increasingly iconic status and significance. Many cities have been repositioning and rebranding themselves through large-scale investment and master planning, including convention centres, urban design and landmarks.

In Malaysia in the 1970s, the urban population of Kuala Lumpur was undergoing a rapid process of urbanisation. The challenge in evoking identity and tradition is how to abstract culture through devices those elements that are familiar and recognisable to the general populace. These simple exaggerations of traditional archetypes into iconic forms are at times argued as simplistic, yet they are easily recognisable to the public.

The critical ideations of Tzonis and Lefaire (1981) and Yeang (1984), who in the 1980s advocated a critical position, mention forms of monumental vernacular. From the 1980s on, the global movement of regionalism brought with it a resurgence of tradition and place-making rooted in the local impetus to resist the dominance of a global homogeneous style. The aim was also to contribute to the elevation of a city's status and the consolidation of a city's identity through recognisable iconographic urban forms. This new kind of traditionalism later grew into a form of monumentality through the direct and subtle evocation of the vernacular.

The cultural policies of the 1970s were brought on by a general observation that the local Malay traditions were on the verge of disappearing. There was a sense of urgency to elevate the local arts in the face of growing homogeneity and a sense of alienation from the rising urban landscape. The government began to formulate a national cultural policy that was rationalised as being based on the loss of tradition and rootedness that was felt amidst the rising tide of internationalism in urban areas. Artistic works were encouraged to reflect the local identity with which the nation could differentiate itself from other nations globally. The rapid rate of rural to urban migration and the rapid rise of an urbanised population had increasingly made the imagery of the *kampung* house an emotive symbol and a national tool to elicit nostalgia and a longing for the past. Amoroso (2014, p. 8) provides insight into similar conditions and how tradition becomes meaningful:

> *In a period of change, the way things have lately been (and are no more) is thrown into high relief. Once that way no longer exists, it can be named – tradition – and becomes the beautiful thing that once was, longed for all the more when change is rapid and dislocating. As in the Malay case, there often arise movements, to restore, hold fast and return to tradition.*

The convention centre of the PWTC was designed not only as a convention centre but as the national headquarters of UMNO (United Malays National Organisation). The Malay identity was asserted through the Malay iconography of the curved *tebar layar* Terengganu style which not only represented a formal variant of a more common *bumbong panjang* (long roof) roof form, but whose higher and steeper pitch, when compared to the variations of roof styles of other states in Malaysia, would make a more intense iconographic impact through a steeper profile in the city centre. The Malay house form became essentialised into a different variation of its form and rescaled to suit modern functions and the urban context. One is reminded of how designs can be based on preconceived schemas or archetypes, as in the observation by Argan (2001):

> *If the type is a schema or grid and the schema inevitably embodies the moment of rigidity or inertia, the presence of such a schema need to be explained in the context of an artist's creative process. This leads one back naturally to the general problem of the relation between artistic creation and historical experience, since it is from 'historical experience' that the type is always deduced.*

The past historical 'type' of the Malay house, is transformed into its urban counterpart by simply exaggerating this type. It is a sublimation of tradition into an urban monument of its times; in the absence of other symbols or precedents, that can assume the role and value of a symbol in the city.

As a main convention and exhibition centre in Kuala Lumpur; the PWTC also part of a multifunctional integrated mixed development, coupling a large convention centre, adjacent to an existing shopping mall, with a high-rise for the headquarters of a political party. The seed of its intention, which led to its conceptualisation, was planted in 1971, when the nation witnessed a national congress, on 'culture' convened by the government, to bring together the public and private sectors in order to align the cultural agenda with public activities including the arts and artistic works of the nation (Figs. 4.3 and 4.4).

Construction of the PWTC commenced in 1981 and the centre was completed in 1984. Functionally managed also as UMNO (United Malay National Organisation) headquarters, the building was officially opened on 2 September 1985 by then Malaysian Prime Minister Tun Dr Mahathir Mohammad, during the first UMNO General Assembly, and has been a staging area for following UMNO General Assemblies ever since. It is also used for the International Quran Reading Competition

Fig. 4.3 The PWTC

Fig. 4.4 Façade detail, PWTC

every year, in which nations compete in the traditional skill of reading the Quran.

The problem remains that although the roof form was inspired by a template of the Terengganu house and has its recognisable curved *tebar layar* or *pemeleh* form, the aesthetic impact of the intricate motifs inscribed on its massive glass façade of metallic and glass plates (Fig. 4.4), were less intense. Though it recalls the checquered pattern reminiscent of the *'Janda Berhias'*, it can be experienced at eye level. Hence it is less conspicuous to the city users and less apparent to everyday pedestrians principal architect, Datuk Hisham Al Bakri, was commissioned to design not only a convention centre, but also the high-rise office which would have its dual role as the headquarters of UMNO, hence the focus was on the roof forms.

This contrasts perhaps with the more intense expressionism of the Putrajaya International Convention Centre (PICC) in Putrajaya, designed by Hijjas Kasturi Associates. The PICC is located at the opposite end of Putrajaya Boulevard, the focal point of Malaysia's new administrative capital. Hijjas Kasturi has been crucial in the creation of a range of Malaysian symbols, landmarks and modes recalling the decades in which the nation was searching for its identity. In PICC, the structure represents one end that marks the length and axis of the Putrajaya Boulevard and has become part of the intended overall impact. A certain ceremonial form is evoked in such civic spaces. To create the notion of a centre of power, strategies include axiality, formality and symmetry is often used. In contrast to PWTC and Kuala Lumpur City Centre (KLCC), the PICC is more distinctive for its sculptural approach. The complex is a landmark containing seven levels including a plenary hall for 3000, a banqueting hall for 3500 and two large conference halls (capacity 2000). It also has mini-halls, meeting rooms, suites, galleries and supporting services – yet its footprint occupies only three acres of its 51-acre site, leaving the remainder for use as a public park. To achieve this, more than 60% of the spaces are submerged below ground.

The PICC can be viewed as representative of a late Modernist strategy is derived from artefacts of a traditional world yet transformed into iconography for the city. The axial form of Putrajaya Boulevard is brought to a visual crescendo through a complex at the end of a central city promenade.

Based on the shape of the eye of *pending perak* (a silver Malay royal belt buckle), architect Hijjas Kasturi Associates conceived of a convention centre that would at once fulfil the need for locally derived symbols while responding to the local climate of high temperatures and monsoon-driven rain. The structure of the roof was designed similarly to folded origami to alleviate the plain roundness of the structure. From the front view, the building's eaves or wings are lifted at the sides, creating broad overhangs over the raking wall. Most of the walls are made of glass, so natural sunlight can easily illuminate the auditorium through the raked and shaded windows.

Hijjas has consistently expressed his concerns about national identity despite having to respond to specific needs for symbols. Viewed from afar, it does not overtly make any reference to a particular culture, and celebrates the idea of a national inclusiveness but through a monumental yet modern rendition of tradition. Complementing the architecture of this convention centre is the long span, geometrically complex roof structure over the plenary hall and the column-free banquet hall. The latter space can accommodate 3000 delegates, each with an uninterrupted view of the stage, with the conference and main auditorium floors above supported on a sculptural system of radial arms. Surrounding these main spaces, the ancillary accommodation follows a conical geometry with the rings increasing in diameter up the building to provide the larger area needed for the plenary hall itself.

The KLCC convention centre is a similar attachment to the tall KLCC twin tower. Yet its allusion to Malay forms and imagery is less assertive, expressed mutely in the multiple pitched roof of the convention centre. There are references to narrow diamond-shaped elevational treatments of the frontage and back façade. The PICC in Putrajaya is perhaps the most expressionist of the three modes of regionalisation, as its formal composition and expressive strategy arise from a position of constantly searching for a universally accepted symbol of multicultural Malaysia. It can almost be described as a form or position that refuses to be nostalgic yet who looks at tradition through the lens of an essentially Modernist stance. It highlights the entirely public nature of architecture, with architecture being composed as the vision of a sculpture or monument in the city.

However Bunnell (1999) comments:

> *[T]here is the exaggeration of artefacts into monuments and while the emphasis of form is seen as simplistic, it can be seen as pertinent as architecture has become a way of breathing new life into otherwise forgotten objects of tradition.*

The KLCC Convention Centre embraces the Modernist imagery, yet on closer inspection there are subtle references to local forms. There is a vast roof, yet it is composed of a series of pitch profiles with slight protrusions that evoke the idea of the traditional Malay roof forms. The subtle allusions to Malay cultural patterns are seen in the linear striations of its façade systems composed as abstract diamond-like motifs, recalling the *songket* fabric patterns of the Malay world. It is not a direct replication of traditional motifs, yet its striations and sharply pointed patterns subtly recall the *songket* patterns of the past. Its form is unabashedly modern, yet it is not provincial.

Conclusions

The challenge for large public building is how to acquire the appropriate degree and force of urban presence as symbolic monuments, while at the same time, being accessible to public. Identity seem to be forged through explorations and the process of searching, and collective significance of form must continue amidst the pluralism of its populace. The earnest search for traditional expression speaks of the need for monuments in the city that can capture the aspirations of the people through expressive and poetic constructions, nuances and treatments rather than mere iconic assemblages. The Malay vernacular form and traditions are a recurrent and emotive strategy, inspiring monumental forms. The aim is to gravitate any cityscape towards memories and structures of its past. Such traditions must be orchestrated towards public spaces in which cultural traditions must be experienced as allusions and nuances and can be read by the public as genuine elements of memory. To contain elements of civic life, if the reference is too subtle, the form tends to be overwhelmed by the homogenisation of a city. The need for recognisable references and emblems is acute, and to meet this need, traditional forms and devices are utilised as 'typology' or archetypes. Yet the problem remains as to the manner in which they are rescaled, magnified or simplified. Their scale and size must ensure that the presence of such symbols in the city and civic identity is must somehow evoke a memory with cultural references and rootedness. Inspiration can be sought from the landscape, the 'vernacular' and the iconography of national 'arts'. The use of Malay motifs, values and forms must play their role in adorning and elevating modern boxes with the required allusion to cultural identity. The monumental vernacular must steer away from, and navigate through, the tendency to degenerate towards kitsch, by adopting the deeper, more layered critical position. Yet across the eras, there are varying with the degrees of intensity of expression and form in order to create formal variants that can champion cultural a message and meaning. Between the precipitous range of positions from kitsch to criticality, the search is on for a more critical form yet one which does not degenerate into superficial. The Malay culture, is one path, of many, in instilling a collective consciousness and a response to the dilemma of infusing identity at critical junctures of the nation's history.

Reference

Argan, C. (1963). On the typology of architecture. *Architectural Design, 33*(12), 564–565.

Bunnell, T. (1999). Views from above and below: The petronas twin towers and/in contesting visions of development in contemporary Malaysia. *Singapore Journal of Tropical Geography, 20*(1), 1–23.

Curtis, W. J. R. (1996). Modernity, tradition and identity in the developing world. In W. J. R. Curtis (Ed.), *Modern architecture since 1900*. London: Phaidon Press.

Ghirardo, D. (1996). *Architecture after modernism*. New York: Thames and Hudson.

Hancock, J. (1986). Between history and tradition – The use of precedents in design. *Precedent and Invention – The Harvard Architectural Review, 5*, 65–70. Rizzoli International Publications.

Jegadeva, A. (2012). This is where we live: The ongoing search for a national narrative. In N. H. Khairuddin, B. Yong, & T. K. Sabapathy (Eds.), *Imagining identities – Narratives in Malaysian art*. Kuala Lumpur: Rogue Art Publishers.

Tzonis, A., & Le Faivre, L. (1981). The grid and the pathway – An introduction to the work of Dimitris and Susana Antonakakis, with prolegomena to a history of the culture of modern greek architecture. *Architecture in Greece, 15*, 164–179.

Watkin, D. (2000). Karl Frederich Schinkel. In *A history of western architecture* (3rd ed.). London: Laurence King Publishing.

Yeang, K. (1984). Notes for a critical vernacular in contemporary Malaysian architecture. *UIA International Architect, 6*, 16–17. London.

5

Regionalism in University Buildings: Tectonics, Form and Criticality

Shireen Jahn Kassim and Norwina Mohd Nawawi

Introduction

Public universities represent a typology that is built often, on the outside of the core of the city. Their form and language is often harnessed to evoke a collective consciousness of an identity often sited at the fringes of the city. One encounters a more refined and tectonic approach rather than the iconographic or the monumental. Identity-making is more about exploring subtle strategies and these often focus on nuances, inflections and details. As part of a continuous urbanising process and accompanying a nation's maturity, there is an oscillation between the 'emotive' and the 'rationalist' position in form that manifests itself in a range of positions between a climatic approach a monumentalisation of the vernacular style. In the early days of Independence, the pendulum of styles had swung towards the clean and the rational, while as decades move onwards, trend evolved into post-Modernism. One observes how, this romanticist-regionalist position became characterised repeatedly by an exaggeration

S. Jahn Kassim • N. Mohd Nawawi (✉)
International Islamic University Malaysia, Kuala Lumpur, Malaysia

© The Author(s) 2018

S. Jahn Kassim et al. (eds.), *Modernity, Nation and Urban-Architectural Form*,
https://doi.org/10.1007/978-3-319-66131-5_5

or inflation of tradition, artefacts or cultural elements. Naturally, the emotive often reverts to a simplistic strategy of image-making and at times this simplifies into an approach of surmounting modern structures with abstractions of the Malay roof form. In Chap. 1, both regional and national identity formations are described as a series of positions veering into two positions of form, one which represents an essential position that favours emotion, intuition and nostalgia, while the other springs from the position of functionalism and rationality.

A critical approach to regionalism, can also include a 'third' position or path. As the pendulum swings between the highly emotive and the uncompromisingly rational, at times it comes to a state of equilibrium. From the 1970s onwards, the maturity of the nation, including its professionals and its public, began to be reflected in the details of language and form. A more tectonic position began to take root and be explored. This emphasised less on the iconographic or veering towards rationalised tropical boxes, and more towards the details, including column beam connections. External and internal placed details were celebrated in the tradition of rhythm, grammar and façade treatments. The 'tectonic' essentially means an approach pertaining to the expression of construction in general. The approach refers not only to the formal expression of structural components but also to the formal amplification of connections and load pathways. The whole assembly of 'parts' is a poetic manifestation of connections and elements. It is a different approach to the iconographic, in which 'parts' are subservient to form. Giles (1999) interestingly describes, with respect to large building programmes in Malaysia, the often-observed strategy of 'inflation' of artefacts to symbolise localisation.

> *Often in architecture, it would mean little more than putting coloured, funny shaped roofs on otherwise a standard Modernist block. More dignified approaches include scaling up the traditional house roof from or adopting abstracted forms of cultural artifacts. Example of the approach as seen this has been taken to extreme in the design of the National Library, National Theatre … the architects claim to have drawn inspiration from different forms of Malaya headgear.*

The 1950s and 1960s saw the rapid development and urbanisation of cities such as Kuala Lumpur, Singapore, Colombo and Jakarta in this region, simultaneously in search of a more mature approach to regional style. To depart from the romanticist approach to tropicality, there was no universal position on which to base more modern building programmes. Their consequent expression ranged from a tropicalised 'imported' style to a 'modernised' local tropical form. Geoffrey Bawa, known worldwide for his tropical modern vernacular, took a different approach in the Steel Corporation offices of Oruwela, Sri Lanka in 1968. He interpreted the brief through an appropriation of regional form evoked by punched recesses that are varied and expressed in bare concrete.

The 1970s can be described as a time when there was a dichotomy between the two worlds of the rural and urban: vernacular models were used in a position of nostalgia, while more complex briefs and building for urban functions were expressed in the 'functionalist' language and 'rationalist' models from the West. Yet elsewhere throughout the world, Le Corbusier was known to evolve his modular style into a more emotive approach in his search for a more ancient basis to form. His Monasery of La Tourette, near Lyon, for example references a more ancient basis of expression in epitomising such identities. The austerity of the monastic way of life became inspirational and is epitomised his approach to mass, light and textures. It offered the possibility of a poetic concoction of the elements without referring to any past models. His use of bare concrete was part of his search for an ancient type in which plane, volume, heavy mass and light were physical forms that were woven together. It was in the Villa Shodham (1951–1954) that Le Corbusier began to explore the dramatic brise-soleil and raw textures that eventually evolved and became the language of the bruton-brut or what became known as Brutalism. Tropicalisation could be achieved by imbuing the composition with dynamic elements that could express the movement of light and infuse the multiple layering of the walls with the filtration of sun, light and breezes. The regional outcome and apotheosis was perhaps the High Court of Chandigarh (1951–1955), which as described by Curtis (1996) was:

An open sided box wth a sculpted protective roof in the form of a huge sluice, the Parliament Building has the presence of a colossal, grave and dignified ruin. The side of the box was perforated by the repeated shadows of the brise soleil, while the main façade had a scoop shaped portico on lateral piers.

Regionalising the 'Box'

The first few years of regionalising the Modernist language saw how climatic devices, inflected with references to cultural imagery, were used to regionalise the 'box'. On closer inspection, what seem to be overall orthogonal and compact forms reveal the detailed elements that recall intentions of regional identity. These are typically present at corners, in the breathability of walls or in the filtering effect of vertical panels adorning façades, projected as porticos and eaves and central spaces such as atriums. Because university campuses are typically located outside the core of the city, they are not subjected to the same pressure to produce iconography to compete with homogeneous the urbanscape. Identity thus resides in the detailed articulation of constructional elements and of interiors and parts of a building, which may be more significant in their contribution to the dialectics of regionalism and national identity.

The University Malaya's Chancellory Building is often not duly recognised for its regional approach. It rather became a hallmark or an idiom of Brutalism back in the 1960s. Abdullah et al. (2014) succinctly describe the language and expression of its essential form:

> *These exposed concrete wall surface[s] imposed a rusticated look to the building as it stands against the intense tropical sky and weather of Malaysia. … Its façade comprises thick concrete sunbreaker screens that modulate the massive look of [t]he building.*

As a product of the 1970s, the form reflects an era oriented towards a nation's intense ambition to be seen to be on a par with other developed nations. International trends converge into the city and forms became those which are resonant of masters such as Le Corbusier, including the raw and brutalist learnings of modernist designs. Recalling the new Capitol complex of Chandigarh, India, Corbusier was hailed as having produced a refreshing masterpiece of the times, a work that could potentially uproot the prevailing style, yet recalling ancient principles and themes. It was celebrated as a regionalisation of a Modernist archetype in which façades were regionalised to climate as masses 'composed in light', and elements such as louvres and columns were specifically angled to the sun to ensure a constant play of light and shadow on the bare concrete surfaces. Curtis (1996) describes the tropicalised version of the Modernist Brutalist language as (Fig. 5.1) evoking a kind of primal, ancient, relationship between man and nature.

Yet on closer look, elements of regional identity derived from climate and ecology are predominant in the essentially Modernist form. In many cases, the form itself reverts to a purist principle of Modernism, yet somehow able to absorb and commune with the elements of nature in the tropics. There is a regionalisation occurring in the dynamic play of fins and louvres designed to simulate the path of the sun. Form arise from climatic forces from which the architect subjects a global form to values and technological prowess' that essentially define tropicality, such as water, greenery and filter walls. These are designed in response to the tropical climate, including the play projections of podiums and insertions of pathways. It was a time when Le Corbusier's influence had reigned globally and had rippling effect on world-wide public architecture. The same ethos is reflected in

Fig. 5.1 The Chancellory Building, University Malaya

the General Hospital in Kuala Lumpur (which was discussed earlier). The Chancellory reflects how powerful the hold of ideas from the Western world was, as the design was awarded by a jury whose members were part of the British establishment. In the recognisable vocabulary of the Brutalist movement, the articulation of bare concrete exteriors is known as bold and uncomplicated, yet honest. The unfinished concrete exterior reminiscent of the 'avant-garde', became the image of a forward-looking nation with a progressive vision. Its play of massive bulk symbolised a departure from the norm, its neutrality was being hailed as a symbol of its times and a unifying symbol for all.

Designed by architect Kington Loo, the Chancellory was opened for its first convocation ceremony in 1966. The style recalled Le Corbusier's signature low-rise institutional buildings, in which angled shades mean to regionalise a global form. The angular style is sometimes softened with curved staircase elements. Many saw the style as dehumanising, yet it must be remembered that the essence of Brutalism is a range of gestures that sprang from humanitarian ideals. During the 1960s, it symbolised a certain ethos and socialist ideology, including equality and egalitarianism. Concrete was used in bare form as this was seen as a neutral and plastic material. It gave physical form to a collective conscience with socialist leanings. The style was seen by some as synonymous with the values of democracy and the struggle to provide equal rights to all, demonstrating a departure from the past and embodying freedom from colonial structures. It was part of the search for a universal, forward-looking and democratic symbol that would symbolisee the liberating and egalitarian nature of the human spirit. In a tropical city within a newly independent nation, its essential orthogonal character lends itself to a modularity that allows for relative ease and economic advantage in construction. Like for Le Corbusier and the proponents of the Brutalist style, there was an essential notion that architecture must begin 'anew', and symbolise an entity that must rise and shake off the shackles of the past. These forms were seen as neutral, democratic and free from racial overtones, yet expressed simplicity and complexity at the same time. Like Brutalism and its Modernist 'parent', it was an attempt to redefine modern architecture with humanistic values and differentiate its own era from the one preceding it.

While many people currently consider its stylistic expression outdated, at the time it signified an effort to take a neutral stance toward climatic devices. It was an attempt to embody a universal message rather than a culturally-based rhetoric. Today its expression has gone out of style; yet during its own time, it exemplified the 'shock of the new'. It suggested a kind of optimism yet with an aura of inclusivity. Later it was gazetted as a national heritage building.

Many of the 1960s and 1970s buildings reflected the ethos of an International style, yet the Chancellory was singular for its reference to, and direct expression of, Brutalism. It is inflected towards climate, with subtle vernacular references to traditional construction such as the *tanggam*, a method of joints in malay architecture without nails in which beams are wedged into columns to create a firm frame. Such detail are found in many traditional palaces and houses of the Malay world. The concrete elements and constructional exposure of beams recall the character of the vernacular without copying it (Fig. 5.2). *Tanggam* refers to how the beams criss-cross each other at the corners, expressed as intersecting vertical and horizontal elements, and these recall, or can be

Fig. 5.2 The Chancellory Building, University Malaya

referred to as, the essential traditional Malay *tanggam* construction of connected wedges. Though the overall design aspires to an image of the 'progressive' style of the West, there is a celebration of minimalism, rectilinearity and austerity to respond to the ideals of Modernism. Overall, it is in the façade details that one finds, on closer inspection, the localised expression that corresponds to the tropical conditions of a developing city. Aside from the façade articulations, the surroundings are a play of water and green elements which are a studied response to the essences of tropicality (Fig. 5.1). Its language was meant to reflect and embody universal values to all, regardless of race, and hence was widely accepted as the expression of public buildings.

In a tropical nation, the search was on for a more inclusive idea was needed to define the time that celebrated the new and the progressive. Yet within the new, identity was expressed through elements that evoked and recalled mental models of past, and the memory of tradition. The eventual form of various Malaysian universities was thus a result of grappling with – and reconciling – the traditions of the past, yet recasting it in a language expressive of the ambitions of a country in the grip of rapid changes.

Elevating a Hybrid Columnar Language

Nesbitt (1996) summarises the significance of the tectonic approach in the writings of Gregotti:

> *For Vittorio Gregotti, architecure resides in the detail … he laments … detailing demonstrates the attributes, of materials of applications of the laws of construction. It renders design decisions articulate. [A] design also raises the issue of hierarchy, suggesting a relationship between the part and the whole.*

In his seminal 'The Tell-the-Tale Detail', Frascari (1984) echoes the same sentiments, and posits criticality as a necessary position in the use of detail in producing regionalised forms. This is in opposition to Le Corbusier's dictum of 'Plan is the generator of form'. In the framework of critical regionalism, Frascari highlights why details are crucial to the expression of identity:

> '*to indicate the role of details as generators, a role traditionally ascribed to the plan, and to show that technology is the basis for the understanding of the role of details. The construction and conserving of architecture are both in the detail.*
>
> *Columns and details can be regarded as minimal units of signification in the architectural production of meanings.*
>
> *... Dictionaries define detail as a smaller part in a larger whole ... A column is a detail as well as it is a larger whole.*

The administrative building of *Universiti Teknologi* Malaysia (UTM) similarly contains more than just the conspicuous reference to the Malay roof; it represents an approach of regionalising or localising a Modernist form. On closer inspection, while the external vocabulary explores, innovates and applies a variation of the Malay roof, what is more significant is the play of columns, which attempt to modernise and evoke traditions of the Malay vernacular, while at the same time, it departs from its Modernist roots to embrace a uniquely tectonic approach. This approach sees the wall being made up of rhythmic positioning and dimensioning of openings and louvres, and columns treated as varying elements, with secondary and alternate columns creating a series of shadowed recesses and projections. The approach to form is essentially tectonic in order to create a layering of elements, recesses and consequent shadows, a strategy of aligning a modern structure with local Malay vernacular references and resonances.

The Malay vernacular is still a source of form; yet it no longer taken merely as recalling past roof forms, but be interpreting details with new materials. Often, the vernacular is lamented as 'folk architecture' which is lacking in sophistication and vibrancy, yet such vocabulary and nuances can be reformulated into regionalising themes. This administrative complex had transformed the vernacular elements into a concrete aesthetic. Its façade and structural elements are no longer flush, but fragmented, reflecting the louvred and columnar language characteristic of the Classical vernacular forms of the Malay world. The use of attendant roof forms, with their steep pitch, is still present and *pemeleh* fascia boards are also part of the reigning language. The columnar nature of the vernacular is celebrated, in the overt articulation of columns and the characteristic elevated forms of the Malay *kampung* structures. The approach of interspersing thin columns with their thicker counterparts is a rhythm reminiscent of the palatial forms of the past. Extruded vertical element combined with recessed windows bring rhythm and play in the evocation of both tradition and modernity.

By the 1980s, the rise in Islamic conservative trends brought Islamic or Middle Eastern style to the fore. Among the key complexes built during this time was the Dayabumi Complex by Petronas, which celebrated geometry as the motif for their *mashrabiyya* in the façade expression. In an era of reorientation of Malaysian policies towards 'Look East', Malaysia was seen as an active member in the Organisation of Islamic Countries (OIC). The then Deputy Prime Minister of Malaysia, Anuar Ibrahim, was seen as a new professional class of Muslim leaders that represented the movement towards global yet moderate Islam in Malaysia.

In 1990, the fifth Prime Minister of Malaysia, Tun Dr Mahathir Mohamed, laid the foundation stone for the building of the International Islamic University Malaysia (IIUM) campus in Gombak, Kuala Lumpur. The masterplan and site of IIUM as a planned, purpose-built complex reflect a unity of expression and treatment that fused both Arab-Islamic and local nuances of the Malay style as a unified language and a natural physical expression of the university, whose mission and vision in the teaching of Islamic values and knowledge became the focal point in all disciplines. What is different is the entire design of the IIUM complex, which is a reflection of its Arab-Islamic predisposition. The architectural language of columns, rhythmic arches and geometric patterning, refer to global Islam, rather than local references. The physical appearance of the main campus in particular was modelled on styles from the height of Islamic civilisation during the period AD 711–1492, including Spain's Islamic Andalusia, which left a particularly rich heritage of palaces, mosques, and fortresses as the legacy of the Islamic era.

Hajeedar Abdul Majid, architect for the IIUM mosque, recalled his intention to infuse the 'global' Islamic vocabulary and local identity of Malay architecture as the host country and metamorphosise it into a hybrid style. The Kulliyyah or Faculty of Architecture and Environmental Design (KAED) reverted to the local traditions of Malay architecture as its basis. KAED stands out from a dominant Arab-Islamic campus from, due to its *Melaka*-style roof piercing through the massing. A skylight caps a multivolume atrium. Internally, the atrium is designed with regular columns adorned with decorative panels and elements of language that evoke timber elements of Malay palatial architecture, with detailing of stained glass, louvred windows, *belian* roof, references to the local *janda berhias* panels as well as the use of column-bean wedges and column base forms. Throughout the university there is a predominance of courtyards linked by generous walkways with variations of symmetry and shade from arches evoking the tropical entity of the whole development. What differentiates KAED from the rest of the university academic faculty buildings is not only its eventual hybrid Arab–Malay style, but how the interior of its atrium was modelled towards the Malay vernacular. More significantly, key interior design and constructional elements, were expressed in timber. Forms are transmuted into a play of rich hybridity in white concrete and elaborate timber carved panels. The KAED building epitomises how a combined team of university professors and local architects sought to depart from the predominant Arab-Islamic style that management had insisted on and that threaded through the entire campus. Professor Emeritus Dr Ismawi Zen, then project development director, reminisced about how the local team insisted on departing from the norm by introducing a specific Malay identity into the overall form. The volumetric atrium ornamented with Malay ornamental references and even material specifications had insisted on the traditional 'berlian' hardwood. These strategies represent a more tectonic, detailed and even modernist approach to regionalism, as opposed to a merely iconographic or kitsch approach. It goes beyond merely surmounting a modern structure with a Malay roof, and recalls Modernist leanings and the ethos of aligning the interior space with exterior form (Fig. 5.3).

Fig. 5.3 The Kulliyyah of architecture and environmental design (KAED) building in IIUM, internal view – a form of palatial Malay vernacular fused with Arab Islamic form

By the 1990s, the nation's economic policy and thrust was towards industrialisation. The Aga Khan Award winner University of Technology Petronas (UTP) in Tronoh, Perak (designed by the GDP Architects of Malaysia in collaboration with Fosters and Associates) was designed based on a unique tropical form expressed in a sprawling masterplan of individual structures set on a vast site. The overall language reflects an industrialised aesthetic with varied approaches to expression, signifying a phase in Malaysia's evolution into industrialisation. The tropicalised concrete and masonry aesthetic of the 1960s is replaced by a glass and metal aesthetic representative of the globalised era after the 1990s. UTP's Chancellory Complex, a signature building on campus, was a colossal structure 21 metres high representing a large parasol-like structure. The overall circular structure is separated into two crescent-shaped halves. One half accommodates the resource centre, where the crescent shape is filled with a four-storey-high display of books. The building is fronted by a multistorey steel and glass façade through which the library can be viewed from the outside. Its series of academic buildings is generally four storeys high, consisting of laboratories, workshops and supporting teaching facilities such as computer labs, tutorial spaces and technical rooms. Academicians and lecturers are located on the topmost levels of the larger academic buildings which contain the teaching facilities; the pocket buildings contain the lecture theatres, retail facilities and student support. As the centres of student activity, these pockets form a brightly coloured contrast to the control of the academic buildings.

The parasol as a canopy recalls the traditional tropical Malay roof with its large protective function and sweeping dimensions. As a prominent element of the scheme, the sweeping mega canopy roof is held aloft by the tall columns of the rain forest. Surrounded by a natural forest, the canopy suggests a double roof – a roof beneath a roof – protecting the enclosed spaces below from the tropical driving rain and intense sun while allowing cross-ventilating breezes to cool the structure, spaces and occupants. A central unifying promenade serves as a covered pedestrian axis which mirrors the symmetrically organised semicircular forms of the overhead canopy while linking the academic building with the central Chancellory Complex and the student support facilities at the ground level, further integrating a set of individual buildings into one holistic complex.

The entire expression is brought to life in steel and glass materials in the double-curved steel structure roof in essentially two crescent-shaped halves. External elevations are made of curved pre-cast concrete with ceramic tiles, while internal elevations are glazing systems suspended by cables. The tall, slender, steel columns recall the slenderness and columnar character of the traditional raised Malay architecture. The floor deck follows the roof plan to create a floating structure slightly above ground level, and the coloured pre-cast panels supported on steel frames recall the elevated nature of traditional forms of the region.

Conclusion

Symbolically, campus buildings are representative of a certain phases of development and urbanisation and reflect the ideals and hopes of a new nation. The buildings symbolise a nation's attempts to propel it into the technological era. The appropriation of language and vocabulary is part of a challenge on how to express its identity amidst such changes. In tropical cities, new modern universities have conventionally evolved as loose conglomerations of air-conditioned structures sited within large tropical gardens, to ensure an environment of comfort to facilitate learning. Malaysia has recently projected itself as an education hub, and a spate of university colleges, private and public, have been actively constructed. Although identity has been explored and searched for, and has evolved, along the path defined by modernity, the journey for a tropical city is reflected in the progressive evolution in the style of campus buildings within Malaysia, whether they are the Modernist rationalist predispositions of the 1960s or the globalised aesthetic of glass and steel of the 2000s. With the escalating global agenda of sustainability, the ingenuity of local forms has to be combined with principles of sustainability and ecology. The low-rise nature of the university typology allows for such explorative styles and range of ideas in a continuous research towards epitomise the tropical language and a national symbol.

References

Abdullah, A., Hussainn, N. H., Peng, V. N. F., Ariffin, A. N., & Fun, T. L. E. (2014). *The living machines: Malaysia's modern architectural heritage*. Kuala Lumpur: Pertubuhan Arkitek Malaysia in collaboration with Taylor's University, 2015.

Curtis, W. J. R. (1996). Modernity, tradition and Identity in the developing world. In W. J. R. Curtis (Ed.), *Modern architecture since 1900*. London: Phaidon Press.

Frascari, M. (1984). The tell-the-tale detail. In K. Nesbitt (Ed.), *Theorizing a new agenda for architecture, an anthology of architectural theory 1965–1995*. New York: Princeton Architectural Press.

Giles, B. (1999, October). Letter from Kuala Lumpur. *Architecture Review*.

Nesbitt, K. (1996). *Theorizing a new agenda for architecture: An anthology of architectural theory 1965–1995*. New York: Princeton Architectural Press.

6

Tropical Urbanism: Greenery and Walkways in Mediating Identities

Nor Zalina Harun and Alias Abdullah

Introduction

Urbanism is a challenging concept in the South East Asian tropics due to the historical condition, which seems to highlight the lack of urbanism in the histories of the region, with scant models of past cities. Hans Dieter and Korff (2000) observe:

> *Linguistically there is no concept of a city with a [bourgeois] as found in Medieval Europe. Here is a lack of urban institutions … hence my thesis here is 'urbanisation without urbanism (referring to Indonesia)'.*

N. Z. Harun (✉)
Institute of the Malay World and Civilization, Universiti Kebangsaan Malaysia, UKM Bangi, Selangor, Malaysia

A. Abdullah
Department of Urban Regional Planning, Kulliyyah of Architecture and Environmental Design, International Islamic University Malaysia, Kuala Lumpur, Malaysia

© The Author(s) 2018

S. Jahn Kassim et al. (eds.), *Modernity, Nation and Urban-Architectural Form*,
https://doi.org/10.1007/978-3-319-66131-5_6

> *Involution designates a process in which structures, patterns and forms become more and more intricate and complex without reaching a new stage of evolution.*

In a post-colonial nation, despite past attempts to define Asian tropicality in terms of urban design, there is still a gap between theory and practice. Recent townships and masterplans are more often than not based on a spate of templates that focus on imported models rather than reverting to more locally derived models linked to past traditions.

A key executed masterplan example is Putrajaya, which was designed as an 'intelligent garden city' using the model of the garden city derived from planning concepts of the West. It is an example of how from the 1970s city models were based on the rise of the private automobile. As the discussion of the book suggests, such externally sourced ideas may constitute an interference that disturbs the natural evolution of local thoughts into regional identity, nationalism and the vernacular. Putrajaya was the outcome of a time when politicians were anxious to sever ties with the past and build a new city based on a new era of optimism and independence. However, the anxiousness to sever the present from the colonial past led to an embrace of imported models of urbanism instead of resonating in more Asian-rooted urban forms. Interestingly, Forty (2000) observes how architectural trends and movements have always veered toward nature during periods when ideas stagnated. Wang and Heath (2008) also observe the same garden city idea that was used in the national development of Taiwan, which was similarly anxious to distance itself from symbols of China. In its early years, it observed this as a way of asserting its nationalistic identity, and growing its own roots. The overall agenda was to start afresh with a new vision of a new republic and create a new identity for its peoples. They narrate:

> *In the creation of this new government seat, the planners' reference to the British postwar New Town Programme – or its antecedent, the Garden City movement – was rather casual and not remotely conscientious. It goes beyond the scope of this essay to give an account tracing the historical background, professional milieus, and the importation of planning practices from Britain to Taiwan. Likewise, in view of the fact that the origin of the Garden City*

Movement, the subsequent experiments of the concept in the UK and the evolution of worldwide emulations and derivatives in the twentieth century have been popular topics addressed by a significant volume of literature, they are not intended to be encompassed in this essay (Buder 1990; Hall and Ward 1998; Meacham 1998). Yet it may be worth noting that, from its outset, the advent of the Garden City Movement at the turn of the twentieth century was for the purpose of social and economic reform, and it drew inspiration from Ebenezer Howard's seminal texts, especially a reprinted version of his 1902 work Garden Cities of To-Morrow. Howard's vision of a planned city set in the beautiful, unspoiled countryside, was of a self-contained settlement that enabled the nourishment of a self-governing community with residents from all social classes communally holding property ownership. It was genuinely believed that, by means of decentralizing urban development, the dreadful living conditions and urban problems in the overpopulated industrial cities would be resolved.

In Malaysia, there are different forms of traditional patterns and histories of local cities, towns, urban centres and conurbations. Comparison between past and present urban forms highlights the dominance of the more organic nature of local traditions and urban forms, including the differences between traditionally based urban forms, colonial urban forms and the current, more 'nationalistic' forms in cities.

Past City Forms

In South East Asia, past settlements are structured as natural outgrowths from a nucleus; they grow from the centre of a 'seed' into larger conurbations. Through centuries of layering and overlaying of physical development and economic activities, buildings and civilisations are manifested. Miksic et al. (2016) describe South East Asian cities as spatial patterns that have grown organically from the river routes of transport and life. The famous international entrepôt of *Melaka* was a growth that developed organically along sea and river transport routes that were focused on rivers and coastal areas. Ancient cities are known for their organic form, and modern cities can be conceptualised as more sustainable centres if both planned principles and traditional lessons can be fused into a synergy. With the immediate royal courts and the vicinity of the palace and central mosque being the only rationally ordered open spaces within a city in order to evoke the position of ruler, the rest of the city was a natural outgrowth of life itself. Asia has a long history of ancient cities; however, many of these ancient models have characteristics of organic settlement that recall the crucial insights and observations of Alexander (1964) regarding the 'rule' of the timelessness of old cities. His prophetic insights are crucial to a sustainable future and are currently compared to the principle of sustainability in the rise of a new urbanism in line with climate change. Under 'Visions', Alexander (1964) observes a key principle of old cities:

> *The rule requires that the increments arise from a vision of what is needed to heal the existing structure, not from an intellectually formed concept.*
>
> *We have found, in various earlier experiments which preceded the main experiment reported in this book, that the substance of any growth in the city, can be either authentic or not, heartfelt or not. ... We have found that increments of development will not produce wholeness unless they come from a sort of dream-like quality, unless they come from a childlike, almost childish quality of directness, direct concern for life ... in short they are genuinely based on human visions.*

The organic patterns are found throughout Asia and its settlements, as attested by Alex Kerr (2013) in describing Japan:

> *Every country I believe has its typical 'pattern of landscape'. In England the keynote is grass – in town squares, in meadows, and in college quadrangles. In Japan, it is the village cluster. Usually the houses in a Japanese village huddle together in a group, on the flatlands, either in the valley or at the foot of a hill, surrounded by an expanse of rice paddies.*

Similarly in Malaysia, many of its historic settlements are organic huddled villages and appear to share common characteristics in that their existence is always influenced by a river, which often acts as a lifeline and the main artery for transportation for seafarers and fishermen (Ooi 1990). For example, the early Malay villages or clusters can be categorised into three types: (i) settlements developed during the *Melaka*

Sultanate Period, (ii) towns with a fort, and (iii) royal Malay towns. Towns such as Kota Bharu, Kuala Terengganu and Kuching, Alor Setar and Johor Bahru all started as royal settlements (Ooi 1990). Some of these historic settlements, such as *Melaka*, Penang and Klang, developed on the sea coast and became important trading centres, as they were located on international trade routes (Chen 1998). The conquest of many Malay towns including *Melaka* by the Portuguese in 1511 led to a series of European interventions that greatly influenced the nature of the urban settlements. The land use pattern of such settlements appears to be simple and highly functional, with commercial activity located along the primary streets in the form of shophouses, which are normally laid parallel to the river, and residential neighbourhoods of different ethnic groups are located nearby. A fort for defensive purposes is often located near such settlements.

A Colonial Legacy

During the colonial era, most of the streets in towns in Malaysia evolved into well-defined paths laid in the early years of the 1880s following the discovery of tin and the opening of new ports. These streets were narrow and constructed either in an organic, linear or radial layout. The width of the lanes in some instances ranges from 12 to 16 feet, wide enough for a bullock cart used to move goods, rubbish, drinking water and people. The streets were often parallel to the river, constructed without a proper scheme but sufficient to give people various experiences in term of visual quality and urban form, hence offering a clear image for the town. Among the early streets laid in the Kuala Lumpur city centre were Jalan Ampang, Jalan Pudu and Jalan Petaling. These streets became tracks to the mining area located at the tributary of the Gombak and Klang rivers. By the end of the nineteenth century, as the population increased, the streets in the city were widened and well arranged with a large and growing number of food stalls and activities.

These streets were often straight and reasonably wide, based on a grid-iron layout, to facilitate drainage and firefighting services. The strong and visually integrated street edges also became one of the common characteristics of the colonial town in Malaysia. Normally the street ended with the market, which was the most important and liveliest hub of the historic settlements. In some cases, the major streets in such settlements were planted with shade-giving trees that were imported from India, Thailand and Burma (Ismawi 1997). Many of these trees still grace the sides of such major roads, as well as parks and riverbanks of the historic settlements. During the colonial period large squares (*padang*) were provided in such settlements for recreational and ceremonial purposes. The surface of a square is often green and is surrounded on three or four sides by significant administrative buildings and often lined with trees on all sides (Shuhana and Ahmad Bashri 2002). It is generally an important public focal point and centre. In addition, many parks and botanical gardens were also established in these historic settlements (Ismawi 1997). These were generally well-maintained gardens with manicured lawns, providing a surreal look amidst the surrounding dense tropical jungle.

Consequently, features such as open spaces, streets and traditional activities were attributes that gave a city its unique character and provided a sense of belonging that was recognisable to the community (Shuhana 2011; Idid 2004). The pressure for development and the inability to preserve these properties and attributes has taken its toll on the sustenance of public spaces of urban centres and cities in Malaysia. Many of these places have increasingly been demolished, for example the famous *Benteng* (outdoor eating area facing a river) that had for so long been synonymous with night life in Kuala Lumpur, which is now just another commercial building's back yard (Ismawi 1992). Bukit Nanas, known formerly as Weld Hill, is left as the only piece of virgin tropical rainforest in the Kuala Lumpur city centre.

The *Padang* and Square

The *padang* during this period fulfilled a multitude of public purposes (Home 1997), including as a site for parades to impress the local population with the coercive power of the colonial rulers. Apart from the open spaces mentioned above, there is another type known as a *medan* or square. It is usually formed by the shophouses located in the city centre surrounded by wholesale trading, retail and services. These vary in size from small to large, accommodating small groups to large crowds. In Kuala Lumpur, for instance, one of the famous squares originated from a settlement of Chinese miners and was among the earliest residences in the area of the confluence of the Gombak and Klang rivers. For example, in the case of the Gombak riverbank, the higher ground parallel to the river was the main thoroughfare, known for many years as the High Street, now known as Jalan Tun HS Lee. The square was surrounded by a trade settlement that served the outlying mines. The square started as a forum before it evolved into a marketplace.

The problem was made worse by the failure to appreciate and maintain the esplanade or *padang*, the open space, which is of historical and cultural significance for public usage. Padang Maziah in Kuala Terengganu, Padang Merdeka in Alor Setar and Padang Kalumpang in Kota Bharu are examples of *padang* located in front of the Malay sultanate palaces which have been converted into vehicle parking spaces. In the Malaysian scenario, the famous *padang* is currently seen and interpreted as a series of rooftop gardens that become a stage for singing contests and concerts, a far cry from its role in the past (Nor Zalina and Ismail 2008).

The Vernacular Spatial Pattern

Essentially, more organically developed urban patterns and identities stand in contrast to the more consumerist and rationalist layout of the network and context of cities which is an outcome of the previous model of a capitalist economy. Yet as cities undergo new development and new areas arise, there is a need to recall regional vernacular patterns and identities. The challenges in overcoming heightening carbon emissions in cities are also linked to a return to more traditional models. The rise of 'New Urbanism' and the key role of urbanism have highlighted the role of tradition (Calthorpe 2011), and these have given rise to urban principles of planning and architecture that focus on human-scale, walkable communities. Among others, Steuteville (2004) has highlighted the key role of urbanist principles on a number of scales, from buildings, lots and blocks to neighbourhoods, districts and corridors, and ultimately to entire cities and regions (Katz 1994). This is aligned with principles of neotraditional planning and green urbanism and their crucial role in shaping future urban patterns that will have an impact on sustainability. Low-carbon urban forms are increasingly linked with models derived from patterns and lessons from the past, locally derived histories and townships. More and more sustainability-related urban forms are linked to, and founded upon, local, traditional and regional forms, and without a return to more traditional lessons, sustainable development goals including the health and well-being of populations are also at risk; for example, imported models have been linked to a rise in obesity levels. There is a dichotomy between planned and traditionally grown pathways to future sustainable cities, as sustainable principles typically require an approach that is more organic, with regionally based principles founded upon naturally occurring forms and modes. A study of the histories of past historical urban centres in Malaysia, which lie beneath layers of history and past development, is essential to further identify the key sustainable principles and patterns of these past tropical cities.

Past Theories of Urbanism in the South East Asian Tropical City

The idea of a regional identity for a tropical city was suggested among others, in Yeang's book, *The Tropical Verandah City* (1985), in which he attempts to fuse the idea of the 'critical' with a vision of a 'tropical urban regionalism' for the city of Kuala Lumpur. To achieve a distinctive identity for the city, he envisioned: '*There must be a clear perceptual identity for Kuala Lumpur. The identity must be recognisable, memorable, vivid, engaging of attention, and differentiated from other locations in the Asian region.*' Yeang had fundamentally envisioned Kuala Lumpur as a 'tropical urban garden'. He called for the conservation and enhancement of 'natural features of Kuala Lumpur as part of its urban image and plan' and 'an optimum pattern of locations and linkages … which must include a movement network (pedestrian, open spaces and verandah-way network) that becomes the framework for an urban image of the city'.

An important feature of his 'image' of Kuala Lumpur is a city connected by a system of landscaping and 'verandah-ways'. The use of 'multiple variations' of this verandah-way system – including partially covered, multiple-level and landscaped walkways – was advocated. The 'verandah-way' was seen as a form capable of variations and permutations that would not only serve to connect spaces between buildings but be integrated as recessed elements into buildings.

> *'The verandah-way as an architectural device could be extended in its function as a linked walkway to a new role as an organising principle for urban design. ... This will reinstate the verandah-way as a viable contributing feature to strengthen the imagery of Kuala Lumpur as a unique tropical city.* (Yeang 1985)

Yeang outlines the parameters of his position: *'[T]he emergent regionalist architecture seeks its architectural significance through relating its built configuration, aesthetics, organization and technical assembly and materials to a certain place and time* (Yeang 1987).

Yeang presents the principles of tropical urban regionalism – developed from his theories of the critical vernacular – as consisting of five central tenets:

1) a direct connection which involves the creative adaptation for contemporary uses of an existing range of built forms
2) an indirect connection through the interpretation of forms which are designed based on an analysis of architectural heritage and cultural traditions
3) an inclusive contemporary connection in design through the selective use of current technology
4) a landscape connection that integrates the building with the physical context and natural history
5) a forward connection which includes the likely consequences of the building.

The Role of the Five-Foot Way

Contemporary architects and urban designers have highlighted that the ubiquitous five-foot way, a feature that evolved during the colonial area, is now one of the distinctive expressions of national identity for Malaysian cities, including Kuala Lumpur. Ahmad Bashri and Shuhana (2001) hail the five-foot way as the most recognisable identity element of Malaysian towns, and the urban elements have taken on a positive role in urban space as a result of mixed functions – commercial, social and retail. Lupaski and Jubilado (2014) summarise:

> *Our point is that the five foot way is a syncretic form of architecture where meaning is in flux, but which authoritative discourse attempts to purify and fix as traditional and authentically Malaysian.*
>
> *This architectural form draws together the geohistories of the Nusantara, with its own multiplicities and alterities being reordered as colonies and metropoles, … Only recently through discursive work, have they come to be understood as a matter of some traditional, authentic national culture (Kuala Lumpur City Hall 2003).*
>
> *[Its] contemporary designation as marker of Malaysian identity [is] an invented one.*

Identity and Greenery

A key consideration is that the tropical monsoon conditions must be re-engaged, and the issue of landscape, with cultural and geographic resonance, must be reinserted into any emerging theory of regional urbanism. That tropical jungle-like greenery constitutes an inevitable part of any identity for a place in Malaysia is expressed by the novelist Noel Barber in his historical work, *The War of the Running Dogs: Malaya 1948–1960* (2004):

> *It is the jungle, the jungle which none can escape. The jungle [which] reaches back to very compound, harsh and elementa, implacable to all who dare trifle with the suffocating heat, the jungle alone remained … unnamed.*

Due to the tropical context of Malaysia, the notion of regionalised identity cannot be separated from the role of greenery. In the post-colonial era, and in the context of modernity, Ismail Hafiz Salleh (2016) recalls how external concepts of the garden permeated ideas of the garden as regional identity. Antrop (2000) emphasises the inherited characteristics of both natural and cultural aspects to express a unique sense of the spirit of place, a *genius loci*, that helps to define its identity, which is conceptually referred to as the cultural landscape. Aziz and Osman (2007) have discussed how Malaysian landscapes have been shaped by foreign imported ideas and the lack of focus on the locally derived principles of a garden identity. An interview with SekSan, the renowned landscape architect from Malaysia, reveals that in contrast with other Eastern societies, such as Japan and Korea, Malaysia's own traditions and identity in garden design are still in the process of growth, consolidation and evolution:

> *In Japan or Bali, one can see a strong aesthetic sensibility rooted in their cultural worldview that is translated into their garden or landscape design, Malaysia was too young to have such a tradition and hence our main thrust was towards experimentation … in the hope that … the process would hopefully initiate something that can be distilled and developed over the next 50 or 100 years.*

The Vernacular Past

Warren (1991) stresses that the earliest gardens of the tropics were those planted in the compounds of religious complexes and around the palaces of local royalty. However, the perishable nature of all timber constructions and the absence of written reports prior to the fifteenth century limit our knowledge of Malay traditional architecture and landscape only to the last 500 years. The *Malay Annals* highlighted the imagery of *Melaka* palaces during the era of Sultan Mansur Shah, who ruled from 1458 to 1477. The Sultan built the palace on a hill known as Bukit Cina (Chinese Hill) in honour of his new consort, Hang Li Po, a daughter of China's emperor, as a symbol of friendly ties between *Melaka* and China.

Apart from the Malay timber palaces, the city of *Melaka* had many impressive buildings that were surrounded by high walls, and the gardens around the city were mostly maintained in their primeval landscape character. The royal palace of *Melaka* Sultanate covered some half an acre. The palace would normally have two large gardens located at the sides of the building (Nasir 1990). Abdul Rahman al-Ahmadi (2003) suggests the existence of a beautiful palace garden flourishing with a variety of trees, described as types of open spaces. The front of the palace was open space, with a line of palm trees planted along the fence. A group of bamboo, with slits cut in it, was planted at the main entrance gate of the palace.

Various plant species were recorded as having specific functions among the Malay community at that time. These include *pohon ru* (*Casuarina* spp.), *jambu laut* (*Eugenia grandis*), *bakau* (*Rhizophora* spp.), *api-api* (*Avecennia* spp.), *kayu mahang* (*Macaranga* spp.), *beringin* (*Ficus benjamina*), *kuras* (*Aquilaria malaccensis lamk*), *kempas* (*Koompassia malaccensis*), *tui* (*Dolichandrone spathacea*), *kulim* (*Scorodocarpus Borneensis*), *tulangdaing* (*Millettia atropurpurea*), *ibul* (*Orania macrocladus*), *gandasuli* (*Hedychium coronarium*), *pinang gading* (*Areca catechu*) and *seri gading* (*Nyctanthes arbor tristis*).

Reid (2005) explains that the healing properties of the water resulted from the medicinal plants that grew along the riverbanks, such as camphor (*Cinnamomum camphora*) and benzoin (*Styrax benzoin*). The water appears to have been central to Acehnese ideas of spiritual and physical health. In addition, both sides of the river were accommodated with a royal hall and a pool known as *Kolam Jentera Hati* where the water flowed with beautiful flower blooms.

The record reveals the significance of the garden through its many features that were intended to evoke the feeling of a heavenly garden, conventional in the Islamic vision of paradise. As highlighted by Feener et al. (2011), the Arabic terminology employed to designate the garden features pointed to its important role in expressions of the religious and political culture of the Sultanate. In fact, Sultan Iskandar Muda and his successor Sultan Iskandar Thani devoted considerable patronage to Islamic influences that were transmitted and transformed within the Sultanate's Islamicised idioms of symbolic power and social order through Islamic art and culture.

Colonial Legacy of Green Spaces

Most of the development of parks and gardens in Malaysia started in the late nineteenth century. Colonialism saw gardens as celebrating the growing wealth and leisure of the British residents and the upper-class populace. The gardens of the British residents with their manicured lawns provided a surreal image amidst the surrounding dense tropical jungle. With a modest allocation approved by the governor from public funds, certain areas which were originally jungles were rehabilitated and planted with ornamental palms and shrubs. Some examples of the earliest botanical gardens created by British are the Lake Garden located in the middle of Kuala Lumpur and Penang Botanical Garden on Penang Island. The garden was often initiated by the Chairman of the Sanitary Board of the city or the Resident ruling at a particular time. The garden development aimed to create a place for healthy activity, recreation and relaxation for British officers and their families. It was reported that in the garden suburbs, visitors were permitted to build stables for the ponies that pulled their carriages. With the rise of organised sports in the nineteenth century, they started to accommodate equestrian activities and lawn-based games such as cricket. *Padang* in Ipoh, Kuala Lumpur and Taiping were among the first *padang* developed by the British in the late 1880s. Morphological studies of the development of Kuala Lumpur also indicate that the early districts adjacent to the *padang* were Chinese and Malay settlements as well as the marketplace.

Historical disputes about the existence of a Malay garden have caused a loss of character and value in landscape designs. It has been argued by Jamil Abu Bakar (2002) that the development of gardens in the form of public parks was not recognisable in Malaysia until the development of Western-style parks by the colonialists. Aziz and Osman (2007) and Bunnell (2004) agree that the development of landscapes could be interpreted by considering the background history of the country. In her PhD thesis entitled 'Preferred Iconography for the Development of a New Garden Identity', Kaboudarahangi (2014) concludes that the development of a garden identity must be reflective of Malaysia's unique natural heritage.

Returning to the Roots of the Garden

In the Malay world, regional identity is somehow rooted in the vernacular *kampung* imagery which includes building and roof forms rather than garden forms. Gardens are inherently interactions between natural and cultural values, and traditional gardens developed gradually and were considered part of the Malay cultural landscape, translated into compound garden design. To examine the potential ways in which the elements, principles and histories of the Malay garden can play a crucial role in forming the identity of the Malay traditional settlement, one must begin by examining not only species and elements, but how the structural relationships among its components were formed within the Malay village and settlement, even such humble elements as greenery in the front yard, the rear and kitchen garden and, finally, the larger landscape.

The Malay *Kampung* Garden Tradition

The types of plants and their expression in landscaping are categorised as ornamental plants, herbs and spices, fruits and vegetables and native plants, and are often not linked with the form and presence of traditional Malay or vernacular identity. However, the garden throughout the Malay Archipelago has been documented as early as the second century in the form of the palace gardens intended for royal use and pleasure.

Past histories of the various royal Malay gardens, such as the royal garden of the Langkasuka Kingdom, the Śrīksetra park of Srivijaya Kingdom, the city garden of the Majapahit Kingdom, the palace garden of *Melaka* Sultanate and the pleasure garden of the Acehnese Sultanate, are depicted in classical Malay manuscripts. These writings, therefore, make possible a critical assessment of the existence of traditional Malay gardens recorded from the second century to the eighteenth century, focusing on their garden identity through examining nine selected well-known classical Malay manuscripts that were written during the blossoming of literature from the thirteenth century until the seventeenth century, such as *Sulalatus al-Salatin* (Malay Annals), *Bustan al-Salatin* (The Garden of Kings), *Hikayat Merong Mahawangsa*, *Hikayat Abdullah*, *Hikayat Hang Tuah*, *Hikayat Inderaputera*, *Hikayat Acheh*, *Hikayat Raja-raja Pasai* and *Hikayat Patani*.

The findings demonstrate that the identity of a traditional Malay garden can be determined from five aspects: spatial layout, softscape elements, hardscape elements, culture and beliefs. They also show that Malay gardens, with their distinct identity and dynamic evolution, existed throughout the various eras from the beginning of gardens to represent the majestic Malay Kingdom with its influence of Hinduism and eventually progressed to evoke the feelings of paradise gardens with Islamic influence during the Muslim Empire. Establishing a distinct Malay garden identity hence is an indispensable part of shaping the development of national landscape identity in Malaysia.

Open Spaces: Linking the Past and Present

The open space is basically a space allowing for regular local use that is accessible to the public, which can also provide an identity and a sense of place. From a vernacular viewpoint, the idea or the provision of open spaces in the city can be expanded from the Malay vernacular feature of a typical gazebo or resting area. The layout of the garden is determined by the social relationships, culture and lifestyle of the rulers and the community at large. In the Malaysian context, the vernacular open space includes an urban plaza, market square and religious square.

Historically, Malay royal courts were in fact the hubs of Malay society, which in the past were organised into city-states and functioned as the seat for the administrator and for royal residence purposes. At the royal court, the scribe who was in the service of the king would write little about actual events, but more of his interpretations of the events and happenings, particularly concerning those closely connected with the court. The court was an important element in the physical design of an urban setting in Malay society, and was one of the components in the construction of the fort associated with the royal institution of the Malay kings. The work of Siti Norlizaiha (2012) notes that the functions of the fort were not limited to defence, but also including serving as the administrative centre and royal residence.

The *Malay Annals* recorded legendary kingdoms, including that of Langkasuka, as among the earliest Malay kingdoms of the Isthmus (Malay Peninsula) which are believed to have existed in the second century, long before the *Melaka* Sultanate. The kingdom flourished for over 1000 years as the centre of an elaborate and splendid Malay civilisation. Referred to as Lang-ya-Hsiu, the Buddhist pilgrims calling at Langkasuka and its capital described it as being surrounded by walls on which towers and pavilions had been built to form a city that was approached through double gates. They also mentioned the plentiful aloe wood or gaharu (*Aquilaria malaccensis*) and camphor trees (*Cinnamomum camphora*) that were abundant in the kingdom.

Records of the Majapahit Kingdom of the twelfth to fifteenth centuries were linked to a book of poetry, *Nagarakartagama*, an Old Javanese work that contains detailed descriptions of the Majapahit capital city and its garden in the fourteenth century. An analysis conducted by Ahmad Zamil Zakaria et al. (2013) identified the existence of the exquisitely beautiful palace garden. The royal compound was described as surrounded by a thick and high red stone wall and an ornate iron gate. Features included in descriptions of this royal compound include:

1) The main gate into the palace was found to be located on the north side of the wall, accessed through a beautiful ornate iron door. Outside of the north gate was a long building functioning as a meeting place, a market and sacred crossroad. A courtyard containing religious buildings was located inside the north gate.
2) The west gate overlooked pavilions surrounded by canals where people bathed and in the middle there was a square. Lining the square were row upon row of Brahmana trees (*Ficus religiosa*), Bodhi trees (*Ficus rumphii*), Nagasari (*Mesua ferrea*) or Topen plant (*Mallotus floribunda*), Cempaka (*Michelia champaca*) as well as flowering plants shaped neatly and magnificently planted.
3) At the south end a gate led to rows of houses set on terraces in which the palace servants lived. Another gate led to a third courtyard crowded with houses and a great hall for those waiting to be admitted into the ruler's presence. The king's own quarters, which lay to the east of this courtyard, had pavilions on decorated red brick bases, ornately carved wooden pillars and a roof decorated with clay ornaments. Outside the palace were quarters for Shiva priests, Buddhists and other members of the nobility.

Conclusion

Shaded pathways, including the five-foot ways and greenery, the particular tropes or strategies of identity in the Malaysian city which were actively disseminated in the 1970s, can be linked to history and are presently experiencing a resurgence. Greenery is thus a symbol of national identity as it is a part of tropicality and engages the sense of imagination (Helmreich 2002; Ross 1998). Regional identity using landscape and garden elements can be elevated to national identity by reworking their contribution to the cultural-ethnic landscape with which each ethnic group can associate and in which they can find meaning and value. In the context of Malaysia as a unique multiracial country, garden and landscape development is thus one of the tools to symbolise the belief and cultural values inculcated in the living community, as each culture has its own origins in gardens and landscape, thus illustrating an intrinsic understanding of and relationship with their cultures and the living environment (Ismail Said 2001). Hence, there is an inherent potential for forging a national identity in urban spaces while conveying the cultural values of the nation through the development of gardens, shaded walkways and landscape as cultural tropes and settings that can form a vital part of the overall urban development and, simultaneously, achieve sustainability.

References

Al-Ahmadi, A. R. (2003). *Tamadun rumpun budaya Melayu*. Kuala Lumpur: Percetakan Watan.

Alexander, C. (1964). *Notes on the synthesis of form*. Cambridge, MA: Harvard University Press.

Antrop, M. (2000). Where are the Geneii Loci? Landscape our home. In B. Pedroli (Ed.), *Essay on the culture of the European landscape as a task* (p. 29). Stuttgart/Zeist: Freies Geistesleben/Indigo.

Aziz, M. A., & Osman, M. T. (2007). *Landscape architecture in Malaysia in search of identity*. Kuala Lumpur: IFLA.

Bakar, J. A. (2002). *A design guide of public parks in Malaysia*. Skudai: Universiti Teknologi Malaysia.

Barber, N. (1971). *The war of the running dogs: Malaya 1948–1960*. London: Phoenix.
Buder, S. (1990). *Visionaries and planners: The garden city movement and the modern community*. New York/Oxford: Oxford University Press.
Bunnell, T. (2004). *Malaysia, modernity and the multimedia super corridor: A critical geography of intelligent landscapes*. London: RoutledgeCurzon.
Calthorpe, P. (2011). *Urbanism in the age of climate change*. Washington, DC: Island Press, Centre for Resource Economics.
Feener, R. M., Daly, P., & Reid, A. (2011). *Mapping the acehnese past*. Leiden: KITLV Press, Royal Netherlands Institute of Southeast Asian and Caribbean Studies.
Fei, C. V. (1998). *Encyclopedia of Malaysian architecture*. Kuala Lumpur: Archipelago Press.
Forty, A. (2000). *Words and buildings, a vocabulary of modern architecture* (pp. 142–288). New York: Thames and Hudson.
Hall, P., & Ward, C. (1998). *Sociable cities: The legacy of Ebenezer Howard* (pp. 200–217). Chichester: University of Michigan, Wiley.
Hans-Dieter, E., & Korff, R. (2000). *Southeast Asian urbanism: The meaning and power of social space*. Hamburg: LIT Verlag Munster.
Helmreich, A. (2002). *English garden and national identity: The competing styles of garden design*. Cambridge: Cambridge University Press.
Home, R. K. (1990). Town planning and garden cities in the British colonial empire 1910–1940. *Planning Perspectives, 5*, 23–37.
Ismawi, Z. (1992). The evolution and morphology of Kuala Lumpur: A case for the conservation of a colonial urban form. *Edinburgh Architecture Research, 19*, 99–122.
Ismawi, Z. (1997, June). *Hubungan Manusia dengan Alam Sekitar.* Planning Malaysia, Issue No. 4. Kuala Lumpur: Department of Town and Country Planning Peninsular Malaysia.
Katz, P. (1994). *The new urbanism: Toward architecture of community*. New York: McGraw-Hill.
Meacham, B. J. (1998). *Regaining paradise, englishness and the early city movement* (pp. 88–111). New Haven/London: Yale University Press.
Miksic, J. N., & Goh, G. Y. (2016). *Ancient Southeast Asia*. London: Routledge World Archeology.
Miller, M. (2016). Garden cities and suburbs: At home and abroad. *Journal of Planning History, 1*(1), 6–28.
Nasir, A. H. (1990). *Kota-kota Melayu*. Kuala Lumpur: Dewan Bahasa dan Pustaka.

Nor Zalina, H., & Ismail, S. (2008, December 5–7). *Role and fate of Padang in Malaysian historical cities*. Proceedings of the 5th Great Asian Street Symposium. National University of Singapore, Singapore.

Ooi, G. L. (1990). *Town councils in Singapore: Self-determination for public housing estates* (Occasional Paper No. 4). Singapore: Institute of Policy Studies.

Reid, A. (2005). *An Indonesian frontier: Acehnese and other histories of Sumatra*. Singapore: Asia Research Institute/National University of Singapore/ Singapore University Press.

Ross, S. (1998). *What gardens mean*. Chicago: University of Chicago Press.

Said, I. (2001). Cultural-ethnic landscape of terrace housing community in Peninsular Malaysia. *Journal Teknologi B, 35*(2001), 41–53.

Salleh, I. H., Rashid, M. S. A., & Sakip, S. R. M. (2016). Malay garden concept from the traditional Malay landscape. *Procedia – Social and Behavioral Sciences, 222*(2016), 548–556.

Shuhana, S., & Ahmad Bashri, S. (2002). *The role of streets in influencing the sense of place of Malaysian towns and cities*. Paper presented at Great Asian Street Symposium: Public space. National University of Singapore, Singapore.

Steutevill, R. (2004). *The new urbanism: An alternative to modern, automobile-oriented planning and development*. New Urban News. Retrieved from http:// www.newurbannews.com/

Tahir, O., & Kaboudarahangi, M. (2014). The challenges, potentials, and experts' opinions on developing a Malaysian garden identity. *Journal of Pertanika, 22*, 19–33. Universiti Putra Malaysia.

Wang, Y. W., & Heath, T. (2008). Constructions of national identity: A tale of twin capital building in early post war Taiwan. *Taiwan in Comparative Perspective, 2*, 21–46.

Yeang, K. (1985). *The tropical Verandah city*. Petaling Jaya: Longman Publishers.

Yeang, K. (1987). *Tropical urban regionalism: Building in a South East Asian city*. Singapore: Mimar Publications.

Zakaria, A. Z., Salleh, I. H., & Rashid, M. S. A. (2013). Landscape furniture present in the ancient Malay garden according to old manuscripts and their effects on the formation of Malay garden design concept model in Malaysia. *Procedia – Social and Behavioral Sciences, 91*(2013), 28–35.

7

Between Criticality and Pastiche: The Putrajaya Boulevard

Mansor Ibrahim and Shireen Jahn Kassim

Putrajaya Boulevard is a planned city centre, and urban trends brewing in the late 1980s until the 1990s which represented the confluence of post-Modernism, eclecticism, critical regionalism and industrialisation, were all brought to bear onto a single axially planned urban centre that became the new administrative center of the nation. The range of stylistic forms found in the Putrajaya city centre reflect a central condition of post-modernity which saw interest and identity as a mix of historicism and modernity. The chapter attempts to discuss such underlying formative ideas, within the planning, intentions and forms of the Putrajaya Boulevard and their impact on public perception including some criticism and concern which revolved around the urban-architectural language of the boulevard some termed it a return to Islamic conservation, but other read its as a reflection of the difficulty of reconciling tradition of modernity in an urbanised style that expressed the local vernacular with a global identity. The search for a locally rooted urban vocabulary for the Malaysian context, is fraught with challenges and conundrums.

M. Ibrahim (✉) • S. Jahn Kassim
International Islamic University Malaysia, Kuala Lumpur, Malaysia

© The Author(s) 2018

S. Jahn Kassim et al. (eds.), *Modernity, Nation and Urban-Architectural Form*,
https://doi.org/10.1007/978-3-319-66131-5_7

Introduction

Putrajaya Boulevard represents the city centre of Malaysia's recently developed capital Putrajaya, and some have argued that it is the epitome of the outcome of a post-colonial world. While Kuala Lumpur City Centre in Kuala Lumpur (the former administrative centre of Malaysia) was modelled as a centre that would place Malaysia on the global map and help increase the global competitiveness of Kuala Lumpur (Jenkins 2000), it can be argued that Putrajaya Boulevard is the outcome and enmeshment of political and ideological forces that prevail in a post-independent nation-state, recalling the observations of Kahn (2006):

> *Apparently traditional forms of social, economic and political organization in Malaysia, along with the language that we have conventionally used to represent Asian societies, are modern and/or colonial constructions. These consequences, of modern empire are still with us, to the extent that anti-colonial nationalisms, along with the post-colonial nation-buildingprojets that they spawned were themselves thoroughly influenced by a European discourse on nation, race and culture.*

The beginnings and conceptualisation of Putrajaya a city must be seen against the Putrajaya development and masterplan which began with the need to reduce the overcrowding and density of Kuala Lumpur, coupled with the ambitions of a strong authoritarian leader who in the 1980s drove the Fourth Malaysia plan (1981–1985) which targeted the development of identified key 'corridors' of urban development. The new capital was intended to symbolise independence, both psychologically and physically. In 1993, the federal government invited a number of consulting firms to present masterplan proposals for a new capital city, which was to be strategically positioned along the 'economic corridor' linking Kuala Lumpur on one end and the airport city Aeropolis in Sepang on the other, with both Cyberjaya and Putrajaya straddling both economic centres. Putrajaya's conception came out of the Malaysian government's vision for the twenty-first century (known as Wawasan 2020) under the then Prime Minister, Dr Mahathir Mohammad. Vision 2020 was conceived by Dr Mahathir – known for his decisive and domineering style of leadership and strong vision – in order to chart a road map towards an industrialised future for Malaysia. Vision 2020 declared that Malaysia should strive to be a 'fully developed nation' by the year 2020, and this became the driving force of the economy and its policies from then onwards. Originally, all government administrative buildings were to be relocated there. Kuala Lumpur was seen as having transportation and infrastructure problems as well as population density and overcrowding issues, and many of its centrally located iconic buildings were architectural vestiges and reminders of a colonial past.

The Rationale of Putrajaya

The capital city, was conceived and envisioned based on ideas and a rational premise, similar to the vision of many other capital cities which in the 1960s had found themselves at the threshold of independence. Many developing nations had achieved independence around the 1950s and had idealised the beginning of a new leadership who will lead them forward into new economic era. Malaysia's trajectory into industrialisation from the 1980s and 1990s was also affected by a confluence of a new industrialised base and the rise of Islamic consciousness. To mark such a vision, a spate of iconic buildings and masterplans were undertaken. These projects of self-determination was also formulated towards erasing traces of a British-colonised past. Malaysia needed a new anchoring vocabulary to express its new capital; and to rid of traces of colonialism. A monumental vocabulary similar to a Classical framework must realign the urban language with an eclectic mix of Arab-Islamic vocabulary for large public and administrative buildings. Andaya and Andaya (2001) describes the 1990s:

> *The focus on Islam became more apparent. From 1983 Mahathir declared that the non aligned nations and the Commonwealth would no longer be as important to Malaysia as the Islamic bloc, but Islam formed only one facet of the new 'Malay' who would lead the country into first world status by 2020.*

It is recalled how Dr Mahathir, the then Prime Minister had insisted the government district be at the centre of Putrajaya, with the rest of the city radiating outward, symbolising Putrajaya's political position as the new centre of the country. Nichols (2013) how the philosophy of Putrajaya 'at its inception: the ideals and visions during this time would have a lasting impact on Malaysian approaches and developments in urbanism. They would set the conditions for various forms of new ideas in terms of physical structures, urban design and architecture.'

The Putrajaya Boulevard was constructed as the core administrative precinct. Located on Persiaran Perdana, it is the longest boulevard in Putrajaya, connecting Dataran Putra in the north to the Dataran Gemilang in the south. Oriented around a central 4-kilometre north–south axis, the axis is the Persiaran Putrajaya, which begins at the Putrajaya International Convention Center (PICC), passes through an as area around Gemilang Square, and running through a district of monumental government buildings, including the Perbadanan Putrajaya (City Hall), Palace of Justice, National Treasury, Ministry of Finance and the offices of Putrajaya Holdings Sdn. Bhd. It continues across the Putra Bridge to Putra Square. Then, at the other end, is the prime minister's office, Perdana Putra, which overlooks the entire boulevard and is the crown of the axis. The boulevard is impeccably manicured. There are pedestrian promenades and two lanes of vehicular traffic in each direction, interspersed by bike paths, planters and generous sidewalks (Fig. 7.1).

Monumentality and the City

Curtis (1996) has discussed how monumentality was part and parcel of urbanising cities in the 1980s. As part of the growth of urban centres and the consolidation of identities of nations in an increasingly competitive era. Putrajaya was part of this trend, eariler proponents had studied several planned city centres throughout the world, which consequently became basis of the urban form and iconography of Putrajaya.

Throughout history, urban and architectural forms have been harnessed as instruments of authority and political power. Monuments have evolved

Fig. 7.1 Putrajaya Boulevard from PICC to Prime Minister Complex

from archetypical ideas and local patterns of the past and then been transformed iconographically into new forms in the search for symbols of a nation. Vale (1992) aptly observes the relationship between the political regime of a time or a place and that such a regime can be understood by what it builds, particularly:

> *Buildings that house national government institutions are products of the political and cultural balance of power within pluralist societies 'and 'the manipulation of urban meaning is an important force in urban development.' The search for the basis of symbols was not only derived from an architectural search but from an urban planning perspective as well. Key buildings and monuments of a capital city were part of an abstraction and fusion of past and present and were orchestrated into specific formal layout and monumental outcomes to reflect such meaning or symbolism. The search was always for a dramatic symbol that could assert such an identity and embody the spirit of a nation in the midst of a key phase in its history. Architecture and urban design are almost as if carved into instruments of collective meaning, and control. Some are evolved into idealized forms and their spatial articulations that are more meaningful and layered and other sought an assertion of the presence and perceptions of a government of being in control and of 'ruling' over a group of people or populations or a nation.*

Past Models

Though many have associated Putrajaya with the vision of an individual leader, it must also be recalled that Putrajaya was modelled on, and perhaps took lessons from, several planned city centres throughout the world, each of which bears some resemblance to the eventual identity and form of Putrajaya. Each was an interpretation of the topography, culture and reflection of the population, distilled and modelled to represent their nations.

To understand Putrajaya, one must know the examples upon which it was modelled, including Canberra, Australia. Canberra was designed by Walter Burley Griffin, a twentieth-century American architect who sited the central area of the city near Lake Burley Griffin, a man-made lake similar to the man-made lakes of Putrajaya. Both Canberra & Putrajaya employed a concept in which major roads follow a wheel-and-spoke pattern rather than a grid. Griffin's proposal had an abundance of geometric patterns, including concentric hexagonal and octagonal streets emanating from several radii. In the planning of Canberra, the orientation of the components was related to the topographical landmarks, with lakes stretching from east to west and dividing the city in two. The axial principle from the central basin, which stretches from Capitol Hill to the eventual Parliament House on a mound on the southern side, north-north-east across the central basin to the northern banks along Anzac Parade to the Australian War Memorial, is evoked in the principles of mounds and hills interspersed among key structures in Putrajaya. In Canberra, Capitol Hill overlooks the Parliament, and the War Memorial stands directly at the foot of Mount Ainslie.

The straight edge of the circular segment that represents Lake Burley Griffin is perpendicular to the land axis and designates the water axis. It extends north-west towards Black Mountain and this recalls the high-rises of Dataran Gemilang. One of the strongest features of the Putrajaya masterplan is the central axis, which was the 4.2-km-long main ceremonial axis. A man-made lake was formed between the two natural waterways meandering across the site, adjacent to the prime minister's office. Like Canberra, Putrajaya is organised into a hierarchy of districts, town centres, group centres and local suburbs as well as other industrial areas and business hubs. These are surrounded by residential districts, each of which is divided into smaller suburbs, and most of which have a town centre as the focus of commercial and social activities.

Both Canberra's and Putrajaya's planning were to varied extents, influenced philosophically by the Western-based garden city movement. Hence both incorporate significant areas of natural vegetation that have earned Canberra the title 'Bush Capitol'.

Recalling Brasília, Brazil

Brasília, as planned and developed by Lúcio Costa and Oscar Niemeyer in 1956, was intended as a new, more centrally located capital city. The planning and design divide 'it into sectors for specified activities, such as the hotel sector, the banking sector and the embassy sector'. Named a UNESCO World Heritage Site due to its Modernist architecture and urban planning, it had caused some discomfort due to its embrace of what is termed plastic approach to Modernist architecture. Some have said it as a endlessly monotonous, and a few observers have referred to the city's large open lawns, plazas and fields as wastelands. One recalls how the Capitol in Chandigarh also resonated with the same formative ideas and gestures, yet it was modelled towards a vision of progressiveness and modernisation.

Chandigarh, India was similarly conceived against the dramatic backdrop of the Himalayan mountains and hills. Just as with Putrajaya, the basic masterplan of the entire city consisted of separate sectors of a functional city, at the core of which was the administrative precinct. In Chandigarh, the masterplan was often described as being 'capped' by its 'head', the Capitol, which is a planned conglomeration of monumental government buildings. The Capitol contains all the key administrative buildings such as the high court, the legislative assembly, the secretariat and the governor's palace, now known as the Museum of Knowledge, arranged in a park-like plaza. It was the then prime minister's vision that a new city for India would be not only a symbol of independence, but a visible and persuasive instrument of national economic and social development. Le Corbusier was then commissioned to design both the masterplan and the Capitol Complex, and he envisioned a new form of urban development which would arise from a liberated and democratic society.

Both Brasília and Chandigarh were at one time condemned as wastelands, yet as these two cities matured, their general ambience and environment have been improved by increased greenery and landscaping, giving an air of new urbanism and a sense of 'humanised' spaciousness, exuding an egalitarian and democratic persona. Although not fully accomplished, the utopian visions of Le Corbusier and Costa produced two cities now known for their relatively high quality of life, in which the citizens live in forested areas with sporting and leisure structures (the superquadras) flanked by small commercial areas, bookstores and cafes and benefit from efficient transit systems.

The Dialectics of Putrajaya

Developments in Malaysia from the 1990s onwards can be linked to global movements which coincided with the rise of a global post-modern era which saw trends of urban-architectural language moving towards historical interest and stylistic references. As described by Ghirardo (1996), the post-Modernity of the 1908s was an era of 'mass consumption' in which not only were products and services packaged and used at a rapid rate, but styles were also 'consumed'. By the 1980s and 1990s, many cities, in both the West and Asia, exhibited trends that were typified by those of 'late capitalism' – which tended towards consumption of multiple cut-and-paste pastiche approaches to urban expression. As cities grow, their densities increase, and taller buildings merely need façade dressings and aesthetic envelopes as their stylisation and physical individual expression. Motifs and ornamentation were applied as dressings to modern buildings without any deeper thought or layering. Ghirardo (1996) observes how, from the late 1960s, divergent paths of urban expression had followed a similar divergence in social and political ideologies and issues, and particularly the phenomena of 'megaprojects' were dressed in a range of stylistic tendencies that were no longer homogeneous and dogmatic and that reflected divergent post-Modernist ideas, trends and tendencies from the 1980s onwards. Thus, as summarised by Nichols:

> *Putrajaya represents a city derived from modern mapping and urban design process. Imaginative 'meaning' for this new greenfield city, was driven purely from borrowed aesthetics and form with a predetermined and ore-imagined sense of nationhood.*

Hence the post-Modernist ethos of historicism and diverging ideas that characterised the post-modern era were perhaps reflected in the breadth of styles and language in the institutional heart of Putrajaya. Putrajaya Boulevard became a form of concentration of architectural acrobatics in which styles were explored and enmeshed in one site. Visually, the boulevard became a parade of stylistic expressions with their different modalities and interpretations in a range of urban typologies. Some deemed it as reflecting a 'high fantasy' kind of architecture with its emphasis on a variety of Arab-Islamic elements, which some researchers have argued is a sign of rising 'Islamic conservatism' in Malaysia.

Moser (2010) observes:

> *Putrajaya's masterplan has the geometric formality of many planned capitals that make use of formal axis of other planned cities such as Paris, New Delhi and Washington DC.*

As discussed earlier, the masterplan divides the city into two main areas, the core and the periphery, and the aim was to showcase the nation's talents and reinforce Malaysia's identity through various civic buildings. The purpose was also to intersperse these with hotels, shopping centres, commercial offices, convention centres, tourism centres, leisure facilities and recreation clubs. Nichols (2013) describes Putrajaya as the nation's second major undertaking of national identity construction, after Malaysia's first wholesale nation-building exercise as a celebration of Independence in 1957.

King (2012) summarises: '*Characterising the scheme was an almost relentless formality of major, minor and radiating axes, symmetrical building complexes and setpieces.*'

The urban design guidelines also emphasised the general rules of architectural character and urban forms for central Putrajaya: the administrative government buildings were to reflect the syntax and language of high eclectic Islam, and the rest of the more commercial-type buildings were to be of in a modern Malaysian style, that is, expressing the International style yet with allusions to the Malay Islamic culture. Along the boulevard Islamic dome elements and Islamic-themed columns adorn mosques and administrative buildings. The Palace of Justice is striking with its Andalusian gestures of horseshoe arches and Islamic domes, whereas the Putra or 'Pink' mosque was derived from the synthesis of Persian architecture to that of the Moorish style and the Safavid period.

As also observed by Nichols (2013):

> *In order to stimulate national consciousness, a frenzied preoccupation with identity construction ensued in both of these cases, with new spatial and formal realizations promoted by the designers and politicians, Putrajaya assumed an identity of a pan-Islamic city with shared Islamic ideologies of global Middle*

Eastern centres. Imaginative 'meaning' for this new green field city was driven purely from borrowed aesthetics and form with a predetermined and pre imagined sense of nationhood.

Moser (2010) summarises:

Many of Putrajaya's architectural focal points and key government structures are based on various well-known classics of Middle Eastern architecture from a variety of origins including Iran, Iraq, Egypt, North India, Moorish Spain, central Asia and the Ottoman Empire.

Similar criticisms have since been levelled at Putrajaya due to the dominance of Arab-Islamic idioms in the midst of a multicultural Asian society. Some have labelled it a sign of the rise of Islamic conservatism, while others categorise it a kind of mindless post-Modernism. Moser (2010) summarises the general concern and sense of a lost cause: how 'rather the drawing from local idioms, vocabulary, expressive elements and grammar, the city from the traditions and imagery of the Middle Eastern'. King (2008) links the Arab-Islamic vocabulary with the underlying agenda of Putrajaya as the 'advancement of Malaysia as a Malay Muslim polity, a new kind of high modernist Muslim nation'. Goh and Liaw (2009) read Putrajaya Boulevard as 'the enmeshment of Malaysian nationalism within global Islam' which led to 'the pre-eminence of the Islamic over the Malay identifications in cultural forms; especially the key government structures reflect classical Middle Eastern language with origins from Iran, Iraq, North India and Moorish and Spain and The Ottoman Empire.' They further mention that:

It is the fantastical domes and arches that dominate Putrajaya's skyline and geometric Islamic landscape features that dominates streets and parks. Through its fantasy Islamic and hi-tech architecture, Putrajaya announces the state's ambitions to be known as a progressive Muslim country.

Moser (2000) summarises:

Putrajaya indicates a trend in Malaysian urban design and architecture to borrow from generalized traditional Middle Eastern motifs, rather than drawing on their own vernacular design traditions. In Putrajaya, any Greco-Roman

> *Classical leanings were to be avoided yet at the same time; urban design character cannot embrace the soul-less modernist language of the international style. Hence the Islamic dressing and language had become, by default, the medium of expressing nationalistic ideals in a modern city.*

Putrajaya Boulevard can thus be interpreted as part of a post-Modernist phenomenon carried forward by the 'swing of the stylistic pendulum' towards a more historical content in the language of modern urban design. Ghirardo (1996) observes a more rational basis for such historicism, linking the outcome of post-Modernism and its dynamics with reactions to deep laissez-faire capitalism. Certain traits of urbanism, planning and architecture in Kuala Lumpur from the 1980s are similarly reflective of such trends. They carried the same post-Modernist leanings and ethos. What Frampton (1999) describes as the kitsch tendency or predisposition in post-Modernism and its outcomes is perhaps played out in Putrajaya Boulevard. During the 1970s, kitsch architecture could be related to a certain level of immaturity in coping with the rapid rate of socioeconomic change within a specific country; however, by the 1990s, a degree of kitsch was an extension of the post-Modernist trend which sought to depart from homogeneity but embraced differences in an exuberant style.

Morrison (1998), in his biography of Louis Sullivan, summarises the two dynamic forces behind Chicago's rapid rate of development in the early 1900s: the influx of stylistic dressing from European cities, and those who wanted to pursue a more regional expression amidst the kitsch tendencies of his time, which Morrison describes as how 'various parties had resorted to the art of covering one thing with another thing to imitate a third thing'. Kitsch is an outcome of insufficient time to evolve a language due to the lack of depth in articulating the past in the forms and layerings of the present. It is an outcome of insufficient depth in resolving the paradoxical synthesis of modernisation and tradition and a certain level of impatience towards the demands of thorough understanding.

Though Moser (2012) claims this to be 'a manifestation of a growing conservatism amongst Muslims in Malaysia', it is argued that the embrace of Arab-Islamic language was brought about by a kind of 'anxiety' of a post-colonial nation. King (2010) observes, how Malaysia was anxious to assert & prove its status as an independent nation and urban design must consolidate an identity and represent a departure from the colonial past.

The Challenges of Urbanising the Vernacular

Historically, local architectural traditions and forms are rooted in essentially timber-based construction. Its formal language and its range of vocabulary reflect an evolution that stemmed from the core basis of the constructional outcomes of the post and beam in the Malay vernacular language of architecture. Such an essentially timber-based language has been lamented as 'ephemeral' and not able to be transcribed easily into modern masonry construction and technology. To evoke tradition, such timber-based elements and assemblies are abstracted, transcribed and transmuted into modern building construction. If tradition is to be carried forward into the future, there must be a sustained effort to transform such traditions into modern forms. The limitations of the Malay–Nusantara vernacular in, systems are evident not only in Malaysia, but elsewhere in regions and nations with such traditions. It can also be argued that both Britain and Asian nation such as Japan had a romanticist legacy, yet it was the classical and modern styles that managed to dominate their urban centres rather than the vernacular-based forms. These factors are among those which brought on what can be perceived as a quick-fix solution of implementing and transposing Arab-Islamic expression in public buildings, and these can be linked to conditions in Malaysia which can be summarised as follows:

- The development of an urban form derived from the traditional 'Malay' architectural language for multistorey public buildings would have required far more time and resources. Architecture and the city are means of asserting one's identity and displaying one's achievement – the position of 'arriving' at the 'developed' status. Typically, the local Malay vernacular constructional repertoire of timber frame and cladding elements are not readily transmuted into the construction of large structures and forms which are much more technologically sophisticated. Masonry and steel have more expressive and sculptural potentials than do timber tectonics.

- During any phase of the search for identity and enhancing one's symbolic place in the global world, both developed and developing nations need a certain level of monumentality in their public architecture and urban structures. This necessitates physical symbols and an identity of a country or civilisation. The aim is to evoke monumentality and a symbol of strength and permanence.

Vernacular traditions of South East Asia are steeped in timber frame construction and details. These are essentially ephemeral and are not easily transposed into the 'monumental'. Middle Eastern architecture and its vocabulary are originally masonry-based or earth-based. They developed building traditions with smaller windows and thicker walls. When coupled with the demand for air-conditioning and rising expectations of comfort in hot, humid cities, the masonry vocabulary lends itself more readily to the modern cubic forms and a sealed building is required to control infiltration, heat gain and operational costs of air-conditioned buildings. The essentially cubic or orthogonal earth forms of Middle Eastern languages lend themselves more readily to cast in situ concrete methods of construction and its viability.

The level of experimentation needed to transmute traditional timber-based forms into their counterpart or 'modernised' concrete, masonry and steel technology would have necessitated a longer process of thought and development. Mega-plans in Asia always sought a shorter process with the predominant use of concrete buildings with its grammar syntax to express the effect of monumentality. A syntax and vocabulary were needed to exude a sense of stability, solidity and strength, typical of masonry construction and forms.

Critical Regionalist 'Episodes'

Yet within the boulevard there are 'episodes' of the 'critical', which recall the notions and values of the critical in their attempt to combine the formal and the spatial in new ways, as expounded by Frampton and Tzonis-Lefaire (see Chap. 1). At the heart of their expression is a central argument, that modern expression should not be merely cut-and-paste and must recall Modernist expression and leanings, yet evoke local traditions and hence must contain certain elements of criticality. Criticality, as highlighted in earlier chapters, is a combination of spatial expression, in which internal space is reflected in outer forms, the principles of diffuse light, a more tectonic approach to form, a fusion of greenery and topographical elements, a fusion of inside with outside and an emphasis on the tactile rather than the visual or the scenographic (Frampton 1981). Tzonis' 'grid and the pathway', on the other hand, also represents such a position and recalls a juxtaposition of linearity and organicity, or an inflection of modularity and rationality, with emotive and curved forms of nature.

Putrajaya City Hall, by the architects Zaini and Riches, recalls the symmetry and rationality of the Classical, yet the classicality of Schinkel is regionally appropriated to fit the climate by extensions and layered and louvred treatments of façades and glazed openings. The Islamic arch which also acts as a framing device is entirely encased in an intricate weaving of stainless steel fins inspired by the traditional art of *songket* weaving; the feature archway or *Gerbang* is a major focal point of the square plaza that marks the intersection of the main and the *Qiblat* axes of the Core Island. Behind the *Gerbang*, the *Qiblat* axis is framed by the glass-enclosed atriums of the twin office blocks. These atriums serve as the public transitional spaces for the council, within which meeting rooms are incorporated, designed to float seemingly suspended in the light-filled space. Internal courtyards for both office blocks complete the design of the complex, emphasising the original design intention of lightness and transparency.

The 2C5 commercial complex by Malaysian architect Ken Yeang was purposely formed to break up the rectilinearity of orthogonal form into a more angular structure and faceted expression (Fig. 7.2). At the same time, tropical heat gain was reduced through the detail of a double wall façade. Within the building, multivolume daylit atriums pierced through a series of angled atriums and the façade was fritted glass. In terms of light there were diagonal multivolume injections to bring in daylight while providing shade from the intense tropical sunpath, yet there were also insertions of greenery that were perhaps fused with the body of the building. One recalls how, in composing the new capital city of Chandigarh, Le Corbusier had not only regionalised modern forms but modernised

Fig. 7.2 The Lot 2C5 commercial complex, Putrajaya Boulevard

past traditional forms in order to create a completely new language for the capital of a new masterplan (Jahn Kassim and Nawawi 2016). These were essentially cultural and climatic appropriations of approaches already formed and not challenged, representing the outcome of the dynamics of the old and the birth of the new.

Conclusions

Putrajaya Boulevard is perhaps emblematic of the dilemmas of identity-making in a post-modern era. Caught within a dichotomy or paradox between expressing identity through a series of positions, at times the critical outcomes get lost in the sea of kitsch. There is a collision of styles and 'positions' as each language competes with another. There is no competing and enveloping homogeneity to truly appreciate the critical. Although it allowed identity and critical positions to be expressed in a parade of forms, there was a danger of 'history' and its elements merely becoming façade dressing, or in the words of Frampton, 'scenographic'. Colquhoun (1981) warns of the dangers of post-Modernism, in which external expression is cut off or has no association whatsoever with internal space. Historically, post-Modernism represented the swing of the pendulum of theory and design towards the 'emotive' content of architecture and urban design. Yet it also ushered in an era of excess in which the need for decoration and 'features of interest' in façades degenerated into a kind of surface decoration in façade design in particular. Putrajaya Boulevard is perhaps a sample of such swings of styles which seem to be ensconced in one long axial exhibition in space. The combination of styles was perhaps the outcome of the opening of a Pandora's box and letting personal interpretation, intentions and ideas gravitate into one core centre. The design and dialectics of Putrajaya as embodied in the boulevard are representative of struggles to find universal grounds of expression in a growing and developing country with a multiracial mix.

References

Andaya, B. W., & Andaya, L. Y. (2001). *A history of Malaysia*. London, UK: Palgrave.

Azizi, N., & Mohd, A. (2007, March 6). *Putrajaya and the French connection*. Post-graduate seminar semester 2 session 2006/2007. Rumah Alumni, Universiti Teknologi Malaysia.

Colquhoun, A. (1981). Sign and substance: Reflections on complexity – Las Vegas, and Oberlin. In A. Colquhoun (Ed.), *Essays in architectural criticism: Modern architecture and historical change*. Cambridge, MA: MIT Press.

Curtis, W. J. R. (1996). Modernity, tradition and identity in the developing world. In W. J. R. Curtis (Ed.), *Modern architecture since 1900*. London: Phaidon Press.

Frampton, K. (1981). *Modern architecture. A critical history*. London: Thames and Hudson 1985. (First edition 1980).

Frampton, K. (1999, August). Seven points for the millenium: An untimly manifesto. *Architectural Record*, Vol 15.

Ghirardo, D. (1996). *Architecture after modernism (world of art)*. New York: Thames & Hudson.

Goh, B.-L., & Liaw, D. (2009). Post-colonial projects of a national culture. *City: Analysis of Urban Trends, Culture, Theory, Policy, Action, 13*(1), 71–79.

Jahn Kassim, P. S., & Nawawi, N. M. (2016). Allusions to Mughal urban forms, in the monumentality of Chandigarh's capitol complex. *Journal of Architecture and Urbanism, 40*, 177–190. Routledge, Taylor and Francis Group.

Jenkins, D. (2000). *Market whys and human wherefores: Thinking again about markets, politics and people paperback* (2nd Revised ed.). London, UK: Continuum, 4 January 2004.

Kahn, J. S. (2006). *Other Malays – Nationalism and cosmopolitanism in the modern Malay world* (p. 2). Singapore: NUS Press, National University Singapore.

King, R. (2008). *Kuala Lumpur and Putrajaya: Negotiating urban space in Malaysia*. Singapore: National University of Singapore Press.

King, R. (2010). Rewriting the city: Putrajaya as representation. *Journal of Urban Design, 12*(1), 117–138.

King, R. (2012). Rewriting the city: Putrajaya as representation. *Journal of Urban Design, 12*(1), 117–138.

Morrison, H. (1998). *Louis Sullivan prophet of the modern movement* (3rd ed.). New York: WW Norton and Company.

Moser, S. (2000). *Putrajaya: Malaysia's new federal administrative capital.* Hartford: Centre for Urban and Global Studies, Trinity College.

Moser, S. (2010). Putrajaya: Malaysia's new federal administrative capital. *Cities. The International Journal of Urban Policy and Planning, 27*(4), 285–297.

Moser, S. (2012). Circulating visions of 'High Islam': The adoption of fantasy middle eastern architecture in constructing Malaysian national identity. *Research Gate*, Retrived from https://www.researchgate.net/publication/255729902_Circulating_Visions_of_'High_Islam'_The_Adoption_of_Fantasy_Middle_Eastern_Architecture_in_Constructing_Malaysian_National_Identity on 1/10/2017.

Nichols, S. (2013). Mapping identity the rules & models of Putrajaya. In A. Brown & A. Leach (Eds.), *Proceedings of the society of architectural historians, Australia and New Zealand: 30, open* (Vol. 1, pp. 207–217). Gold Coast: SAHANZ.

SpringerLink. (2017, October 05). *Rock garden in Chandigarh*, from https://link.springer.com/chapter/10.1007/3-7643-7662-7_29

Vale, L. J. (1992). *Architecture, power, and national identity*. New York: Routledge.

8

Criticality, Symbolic Capital and the High-Rise Form

Shireen Jahn Kassim, Norzalifa Zainal Abidin, and Norwina Mohd Nawawi

Criticality and High-Rise Form

Colquhoun (1971) highlights that both ancient and modern cities have fundamentally two types of structures, 'representational buildings' and 'ordinary habitations'. 'Representional' buildings refer to those large buildings which are essentially formed and then elevated into the realm of the symbolic, while 'ordinary' habitations are those which are built as mainly utilitarian in nature. The high-rise is a kind of representational building of modern times; it is not only symbol that is a representation of a place, an identity of a nation and a community, but often formed as a representation of meaning:

> *'From an undifferentiated mass of houses and habitations, there have always emerged buildings which represent the mythos of collective life – social, political and intellectual'. Abidin Kusno, asserts on the significance of the highrise, in the context of newly independent nations of South East Asia: As cultural landmarks, high-rise buildings are thus attributed with a significant degree of importance in representing the achievement of the new nations.* (Kusno 2000, p. 198)

S. Jahn Kassim (✉) • N. Zainal Abidin • N. Mohd Nawawi
International Islamic University Malaysia, Kuala Lumpur, Malaysia

© The Author(s) 2018

S. Jahn Kassim et al. (eds.), *Modernity, Nation and Urban-Architectural Form*,
https://doi.org/10.1007/978-3-319-66131-5_8

The creation of regional and national identity, in the context of nation-building in a post-colonial world, refers to what Eco (1972) has summated that architectural forms, in certain cases, embody an inherent split between 'function' and 'symbol'. High-rise architecture is an example of such dichotomies, in which form and language can consistently be interpreted as reflecting 'two layers': a spatial and structural formal and character which often intrinsically expresses its function, and an external form which expresses a symbolic capacity. In modern nations, Architecture and urban form are often seen as a tool, and a form of mass communication and bearer of meaning and messages to the general public. Large structures are built as signs and sculpted to embody a certain message, whether it is for the individual entity, or a corporation, or an institution, or a nation. Aspirations, identity and ideals become embedded in large forms. Eco famously applied semiotic theory and associated this with 'any "architectural style" and its associated symbolic dimension and a connotative ability to communicate'.

Particularly from the 1990s onwards, the city has become inflected by what Jenkins (2000) terms as the link between architectural form, urban design, language and aspects of capitalist economics. Jenkins (2000) observes how, cultural theorists have long posited a connection between architecture and the development of capitalistic economies, '... if the contemporary burst of building campaigns is any indication, this relationship is more compelling than ever. Indeed, architecture appears to have become the semiotic tool of choice for cities seeking to enhance their economic and cultural status'. Malaysia, at the dawn of its independence, was rapidly taking up the International style, a nation initially buoyed with optimism and the vision of a new future, hence the embracing such new vocabularies. Its history and legacy as a British colony had left it with an irreversible path, and a gradual immersion and ingratiation into the fabric of global capitalism. Hence, the trends of the 1980s can be read as a struggle to reassert a new sense of self, amidst socio economic and physical changes that were tumultuous to its towns and cities. The International style was merely a change in the dressing and imagery of such changes, yet underlying and embedded within it is the same colonial organisation, economic interests and the legacy of frameworks and structures of a global presence. Kahn (2006, p. 136) describes changes in the late 1800s in Malaysia as follows:

> *'In the case of Malaya, ... in the process, people entangled in loyalties to traditional rules and Islamic leaders, were separated from their local context. ... the*

early decades of the 20th century was a period when colonial and local elites, began to articulate a view that the delocalization of colonial peoples, – their separation from ties to existing social, economic and religious communities and to traditional religio-political elites – was producing a crisis'.

At the same time, such transformation would serve to re-embed the diverse inhabitants of the Malay Peninsula within a new socio-spatial order constructed by the legacies & remnants, morphing into a colonial capitalism a modern state. The foreign and the 'imitative' at first seem 'progressive' and advanced, yet later, they spawned a series of local and climatic problems. Hence, despite these climatic challenges, the high-rise form initially acclimatised, became reshaped into a symbol of the developing tropical city. The achievement of the symbolic aim of a tower essentially lies with its distinctive form and profile. As Dovey (1999) succinctly summates the significance of the high-rise commercial building, not only in the context of the socio cultural developments of nations, but also in the context of socio economic status:

Despite functional inefficiencies, the corporate tower proliferates ... primarily because of its role in the symbolic discourse. The building image takes on a renewed economic importance as a primary generator of symbolic capital ... Distinction is achieved through a quest for uniqueness of form whether viewed in the city skyline or in relation to neighbouring buildings.

Through the evolution of high-rise stylisations and form in Asia both convergence of national identity and regionalism have spurred 'styles' and expression in a range of positions. Such tendencies and approaches of localising a global object or type-form, as a condition of modernity, or a result of forces linked to the dichotomies of modernisation, high-rise regional expression is achieved through the poetics of form and spatial dynamics. Both these strategies were seen as a driving principle behind architectural form, in the context of tropical Asia. Kusno (2000) observes:

South east Asian identity is achieved by virtue of its continuous involvement with the modernist chain that preceded its appearance as a subject of histories. The construction of 'cultural' difference is thus enabled by the imagined structure of 'foreign materials'; a condition enabled to a fundamental degree by a re-articulation of modernist codes.

In South East Asian cities, the approach or stylisation that focuses on the articulation of architectural form through the use of modern materials – such as glass and steel – was a strategy to express a connection with the global network and context. Metaphors and icons from the past and its traditions on the other hand represent the 'regional' of local means by which regional architects attempt to express a localised collective identity and establish a link to existing cultural traditions in terms of architectural form. These provide a mechanism by which local culture can be harnessed as identity-making tools in such new building forms. Economic, social, cultural and technological forces converge in cities and consequently the simultaneous pressures give rise to forms that reflect escalating land prices, the rise of the multinational corporation, rural-to-urban migration, rapid urban growth, and advancements in building and engineering expertise. Whereas in ancient times, social-religious forces gave rise monuments in urban centres which functioned as religious symbols, in modern cities high-rises function as symbols of the intertwining of modern economics and the local societies.

The evolution of commercial high-rise forms in Malaysia can be traced to same set of forces, which came just after Independence in the 1960s. The end of colonisation in 1957 – coincided with the dissolution of various regions in the colonial empires. The rise of Modernism as a style – brought about significant changes and consequences for the cityscape of many developing countries. These were formerly colonialised cities, and new forms were brought about a liberation of the economy and the opening of doors to foreign capitalist enterprises. As in various tropical Asian countries, Malaysia had laid out post-independence economic plans to accelerate its rate of development. These sped up the process of change, bringing drastic transformations of the urban fabric and forms. When Malaysia, like other developing countries, began to open its doors to foreign capitalist enterprises, the urban infrastructure and its forms began to change rapidly. The widespread use of Western-based building prototypes for public facilities, in order to modernise and to become more economically competitive, had however signalled a lack of localisation in a changed urban landscape. To some extent, there was a gradual abandonment of local forms and techniques as the use of industrial building systems, including materials and mass-produced components, intensified.

Due to what was perceived as 'cultural' reversion, there was a certain contamination from the generic West. A wave of protest and reactions arose against these form which were seen as values unthinkingly imported from the West. There was subsequently a need for a re-evaluation of Western values and Western-oriented trends in high-rise design. These gradually came to be perceived as symbols of the continuing cultural colonisation by the West. Identity must be articulated through formal means including spatial articulation and architectural form. The use of modern materials such as glass and steel must express a connection with the local, and not only the global context. Metaphors and the imagery of tradition became particular means by which regional architects and urbanists attempt to express a collective link with existing traditions. These provide a mechanism by which local values, ideas and culture can be reflected in such new building forms.

Hence these 'early' high-rise forms in the 1960s and 1970s were based on standard designs: the buildings were basically orthogonal and did not depart from the Modernist archetype. Yet climatic design and principles were seen as regionalising efforts that attempted to infuse the forms with naturally ventilated corridors and working spaces arranged in a rectilinear configuration with narrow floor plates to facilitate cross-ventilation. In many ways, these early high-rises were exemplary forms in terms of climatic design, as the narrow floor plates, extensive louvres, externally placed corridors and controlled openings collectively lend themselves to tropicalising an imported form and technology. Many of the major high-rise buildings in Kuala Lumpur, including the Parliament building (1963) by W.R. Shipley of J.K.R. (Jabatan Kerja Raya or Public Works Department) and the Kuala Lumpur City Hall (1976), were based on the classic model of 'podium and rectilinear tower' wrapped with climatically responsive and attuned sun-shading devices. The Kuala Lumpur City Hall consists of a similar rectilinear frame with glazed walls and a raised podium with sun-shading panels that are a modern abstraction of arch-like Islamic forms (Fig. 8.1).

The articulation of façade geometry and sun-shading systems were seen, at the time, as a form of regionalisation, in which sun-shading forms were typically derived not only from the elements of local traditions, but in some cases their texture and form were a function of the relative movement of the tropical sun. Such early attempts to 'regionalise' the high-rise through shading devices recall the brise-soleil and the Modernist ideas of Le Corbusier, who was himself inspired by Moroccan *claustras* and Arab *mashrabiyyas* and

Fig. 8.1 The Kuala Lumpur City Hall

had translated these into a concrete frame vocabulary. Tzonis and Le Faivre (2001, p. 35) summarise the contribution of such an approach to modern regional expression in the tropics during the early post-colonial period:

> *It freed tropical architecture of the region from narrow constraints of the bungalow, suitable for small-scale buildings only, and allowed it to adapt to larger scale urban projects such as extensive housing projects, banks, schools and commercial buildings.*

In later years, the emphasis shifted to transposing vernacular-based archetypes onto existing Western high-rise forms. Yet although Malay roof forms would adorn low-rise entrance podiums, the main high-rise tower blocks would remain in the ubiquitous International style. The 36-storey Hilton Hotel, Kuala Lumpur (1972), for example, featured a modern functionalist tower block with an entrance porch crowned by a *Minangkabau* roof form. Similarly the Bank Bumiputra, Kuala Lumpur (1980) by Kumpulan Akitek, comprised a 34-storey Modernist tower fronted by a banking hall whose overall form and façade design were directly derived from traditional Malay architecture (Fig. 8.2).

Fig. 8.2 National headquarters for Bank Bumiputra, Malaysia (1984)

At the same time, there was a need for cultural symbols that would not only represent political legitimacy and cultural consciousness, but embody the goals of a nation-state. 'After their respective independence from colonisation, the institution of the state became the very center of the post-colonial industrialisation process in a developing society' (Chua 2000). The aim was to represent in these high-rise forms a sense of collective identity, while at the same time express a 'connection with the global world' through an image that emphasised technology and efficiency.

By the mid-1980s, there was an ideological turn to the past in search of symbols that could be reconfigured to express the new-found sense of Malaysian identity. Among others, high-rise regionalism took the approach of an abstraction and simplification of traditional artefacts into high-rise forms which were exaggerated into monumental designs. By the 1980s, Malaysia had experienced a resurgence of Islamic ideals, and urban forms such as the high-rise pursued a link with past patterns. The Plaza Dayabumi (1985), for example, was essentially a high-rise concrete block based on an eight-sided geometric layout plan, and its entire façade was encased in integrated Islamic motifs. Both its shading design and its overall form, derived from the 'Islamic star' pattern, are symbolic of this revitalisation. More significantly, the design of the LUTH building (1986) was based on an inflated *rebana* or traditional Malay drum.

Beginning in the 1990s, industrialisation became the focus of Malaysia's development plans: the language of a tropicalised version of concrete aesthetics was gradually superseded and replaced with a focus on the use of steel and glass. A more iconic approach was to challenge the 'established' high-rise to make a greater visual impact in the city in order to create a powerful cultural landmark through a visually strong form. It is sometimes described as 'trophy' architecture, in which the overall form is manipulated and sculpted as one uncompromisingly assertive, and even competitive, form. Hijjas Kasturi is the principal of Hijjas Kasturi Associates, Malaysia, whose works include the award-winning Menara Maybank and the Tabung Haji/Malaysian Pilgrimage Fund Tower, and is well known for his approach. Though some may categorise his approach as simplistic, Kasturi's work must be seen against the evolution of Malaysia during its rapidly developing era. His was an approach that was particularly concerned with the need for cultural symbols to assert the notion of nationhood in Malaysia, and with expressions of the nation's identity in the face of the pressure of globalisation. The emphasis on 'strong' expressive forms must be read as the overall basis for using the essential forms of traditional artefacts and artisanal forms of Malaysia. For some, in order to look uniquely Malaysian and create an identity for the specific city, iconic intensity based on traditional forms is necessary, to assert: 'Why shouldn't function follow form?' Katsuri described his approach to form and its ability to connect with the memory and emotions of the general public in an interview with PAM (2000):

> *There is an art form in buildings. If the association of ideas is strong, there is no need to use expensive material. The building must be simple enough so that people can identify with it. The simplicity of Eiffel Tower makes it easily remembered.*

Criticality, Theory and Design

In debating the theoretical & formative principles of the 'critical' position in both modernisation & architectural regionalism, Boys (1996), with reference to Frampton, gives more detailed insight into the theory and principle of what Frampton has defined as the 'critical'. In his earlier writings, Frampton had posited a theory of what he calls critical regionalism, and he opposed this to a position that merely constitutes the scenographic or pastiche approach. He defines criticality as a form of resistance to an 'architecture of consumption' physically, it was a more layered approach to the problem of expressing regional identity. He advocates the critical approach as a kind of 'tight-rope' strategy 'between' a position that advocates 'mere surface that disguises the harsh realities of universal capitalism' and the romanticist regression into nostalgia.

At the time, the notion of the critical in architecture was related to the idea of modern regionalism as armour: to protect Modernism from what they saw as the excesses of post-Modernism. Since then, the critical has been linked to ideas underpinning a range of works of design significance, from small-scale residences to the largest structures. Ford (1996) links the recurrence of the 'critical' to the need for 'stability' through a deeper approach than merely catering for 'the whims of styles that change with increasing rapidity' (p. 413). However, what is not disputed is that the critical represents a position and approach that embodies the outcome of a certain depth of thought and strikes a balance between mere 'façade patterns' and 'iconism' in expressing identity. It does not represent the rushed approach of the quick and image-conscious. It is neither the regurgitation of the Modernist box which resonates with the forms of economic determinism, nor the degeneration of the articulation of modern-day cultural emblems into kitsch or cut-and-paste eclecticism.

The 'Spectrum of Criticality'

The basic problem of the design of a skyscraper is not environmental but formal and is universal throughout the world: how to counter the homogeneity of a high-rise façade, the tripartite problem of articulating its base, its main body and its roof, and the repetitive nature of its windows. Whereas Yeang (see Chap. 1) posits the critical as something opposed to the cut-and-paste approach, Frampton extends the definition further in saying that the 'critical' must go beyond a mere position that advocates architecture in the city as a 'free standing monument'. In addition to saying that criticality is opposed to 'an architecture of consumption', Frampton (1992, p. 327) asserts a form of language in that 'Regionalism is an inflection of disjunctive episodes in the overall structure.' Although not prescribing a style, Frampton nevertheless outlined several elements in articulating the language of critical regionalism in the face of post-Modernist language with a particular emphasis on the notion of 'place-form'.

Criticality is summarised as a series of principles, and which criteria can be implemented, as argued by Frampton (1983), by adhering to certain strategies and thought processes. These include 'the contingencies of 'climate' i.e. temporally inflected qualities of local light', and which formulate into 'an articulate response to climatic conditions is a necessary [corollary] to this … It tends to treat all openings as delicate transitional zones.'

Frampton emphasises the 'tectonic', which is referred to as a poetic interpretation or articulation of construction techniques based on a position in which 'the primary principle resides in the tectonic rather than the scenographic'. Frampton further asserts: 'We may speak here of the presentation of a structural poetic rather than the representation of a façade.' Boys (1996) then depicts this position as that of a fusion between an abstract cultural expression and critical regionalism which was almost always expressed in forms that represented a juxtaposition of linear/ orthogonal and circular/organic form, vocabulary or elements.

In the high-rise, the position of criticality of the language resides within a kind of resistance to the dominance of the monolithic homogeneous form by challenging that form. An essentially compact cylindrical form can be regionalised and elevated into symbolic form by the incision of deep balconies or skycourts or extensive landscaped rather than merely pasting patterns onto the main monolith of the high-rise. Davidson and Seralgedin (1995) describe the language of the Mesiniaga, which won the Aga Khan Award in 1998, emphasising the role of the skycourts in characterising its form:

> *Most notable are the two spirals of green 'sky gardens' that twist up the building and provide shade and visual contrast with the steel and aluminium surfaces. The reinforced concrete frame is further punctuated by two types of sun-screens and a glass and steel curtain wall, which along the sloping base and metal crown, make the essentially hi-tech image much more organic; one of the jurors termed the building 'organitech'.*

Mesiniaga, a subsidiary of IBM, literally means 'business machine'. features a tubular 13-storey composition basically made from pre-fabricated aluminium and glass façade elements. It has a circular plan and is fully glazed from the south to the north façade. A landscaped ground floor constitutes a base from which deep incisions made by the series of deep balconies with landscaping – rotate and pierce the cylindrical mass. The language counters the otherwise repetitive and monotonous façade of the conventional high-rise structure (Fig. 8.3).

Service cores are located on the east. A distinctive feature of the tower is the spiralling skycourts inserted into the cylindrical tower which spiral

Fig. 8.3 Telekom Tower, Kuala Lumpur by Hijjas Kasturi Associates. Different views of the skycourts and skygardens incised into a tapering highrise form. Photos courtesy: Hijjas Kasturi Associates

from south to north. Hence in the Mesiniaga, almost every floor is uniquely configured and has its own skycourt. A series of differentiated external sun-shading devices wrap around the tower, complementing the shading strategies of the deep skycourts.

Jahn Kassim (2004) describes:

> *Yeang affirms that his overall intentions and philosophy was focused on overcoming the 'rigidity' and 'blandness' of the homogenous highrise – seen as a symbol of global capitalism in an Asian city. Throughout this period in the Asian region, various cities in developing countries saw the emergence of the property developer as a major force in re-shaping the urban fabric of Asian cities.*

The 'bioclimatic' skyscraper was a response, in terms theory and design to the boom of skyscraper construction in Malaysia and rest of Asia during the early 1980s to the mid-1990s. By the end of the 1990s, the theory and design of the 'bioclimatic' high-rise (which was consolidated during this time), with its alternating projections and recesses was forwarded as a ecological yet 'rational' alternative to the prevalent Western-related 'glass box' form symptomatic of many of the urban landscape of Asian cities.

The skycourt represents a critical strategy in this regard, as it enables form depart from one that merely 'attaches' a climatic or regional device to an essentially Modernist form. Intending to challenge the prevalent form, spaces and structure emerge from an extensively landscaped base. The 'regionalised' form consists of a series of spaces, linked to columns where office spaces seem to be a series of massing plugged into an exposed armature. Its envelope system of fully glazed walls is partially protected through variable forms of vertical shading. Two kinds of solar protection wrap around the cylindrical form: one is a screen made of closely placed aluminium strips and the other consists of aluminium strips set farther apart in order to express the varying light of the tropics and which allow more light to penetrate. The Mesiniaga's form consists of floors of dissimilar configurations. Rather than conceiving form as a single volume, the architect sought to achieve an articulated block of cantilevered massing and spaces. Multilevel skygardens cause an interplay of shadows on the exterior cast by the cantilevered shapes elements. Varied designs of its shading systems additionally give a dynamic character to the overall envelope.

In an excerpt from the discussion of the Masters Jury during its five-day meeting in June 1995, Peter Eisenman (1996) – a member of the jury – commented on the singular achievement of the Mesiniaga, not only in terms of its regionalist form, but as a 'critical' symbol of a nation expressing collective self-consciousness as it emerges out from vestiges of colonial administration. In Eisenman's own words:

> *The Menara Mesiniaga is one of the few projects that contribute new thinking to the general culture in architecture. That provocation is particularly contextual, because it could not have come out of Morocco, Australia or Canada. It came out of a particular set of cultural intersections in Malaysia which promotes this kind of activity …*
>
> *We are talking about architecture's symbolic value to contemporary discourse and not whether it functions as a hospital or school. … The tower says something about the possibility of a tall building in a tropical climate. … All corporate buildings in Malaysia are nightmares of colonial capital implanted in a society.*

The 'critical' is seen as a regionalising position in high-rise form. It created a new form of symbolic capital, through it distinctive architectural language. Abel (1997) describes how:

> *The simple form is drastically corrupted by the irregular stepped incisions made by the skycourts, their spiral arrangement perfectly matched to the geometry of the cylinder.*

One recalls the position of the 'critical' as expounded by Tzonis and Le Faivre and in Frampton's writings in which critical regionalist ideas were positions which basically advocate 'an architecture of resistance'.

> *This position distances itself from the 'sentimental vernacular' and aligns itself with the Modern movement – while it draws a sharp distinction with the 'tendencies of Populism.* (Colquhoun 1971)

Such 'resistance' can be described as a reaction. Colquhoun (1983) further differentiates this 'critical' position as a reaction to the populist position linked to the postmodernist architects Robert Venturi and Denise Scott Brown. He explains:

This is a different position to the one that ornament should be related, plastically and iconographically to the real building, whose structural form was thought of as an integral part of its meaning. Ducks are external forms conform[ing] to a unified architectural image whose connotations overlap those of their use and interior arrangement and reinforce the meanings which have been associated with them.

Frampton (1998), further differentiates this critical regionalist 'position' from that of symbolic expression that is derived from the 'free standing monument'. He argues:

Technological maximisation, irrespective of whether it is bureaucratically enforced or ideologically adopted, also has the tendency to reduce the creation of built-form to the production of free-standing objects; whether the object in question is merely a technological instrument or the occasion for a spectacular aesthetic display. Against this, we may posit the critical strategy of the place-form, the ecological obligation that each new structure be inscribed into its site in such a way as to permit the creation of an articulated earthwork.

By 'free standing monument' Frampton refers to the tendency for architectured expression to rely on 'abstract' form to attain a distinctive addition to the city skyline. The emphasis on the strong prismatic volume, with the texture or detailed elements of the façade is obscured. Position of reverting to recalls the minimalist thin-skin smooth planes enclosing a volume in space. The aim must be to represent 'the hybrid nature of modern regional culture' (Frampton 1985, p. 307).

Boys (1996) further describes Frampton's position as that of attempts to negotiate a 'tight-rope' strategy between a position that advocates 'mere surface that disguises the harsh realities of universal capitalism' and one that advocates the 'free standing monument'. Frampton (1992, p. 327) outlines his position of 'Regionalism is an "inflection" to disjunctive episodes in the overall structure.' Boys usefully elucidates:

This is a crucial tight-rope strategy in achieving a balance between 'false progress' and 'false nostalgia' ... (which) is obtained by evoking spatial and visual representational meanings which offer a critical perception of reality.

Frampton also outlines several principles and elements in articulating this critical language and mentions a particular emphasis on the notion of 'place-form'. The criteria as include:

- An emphasis on climatic elements:

  [T]he contingencies of climate and temporally inflected qualities of local light. (Frampton 1983)

  An articulate response to climatic conditions is a necessary corollary to this. ... It tends to treat all openings as delicate transitional zones. (Frampton 1985, p. 327)

- A response to the topography of site:

  This inscription, which arises out of "in-laying" the building into the site, has many levels of significance ... for its capacity to embody its archaeological past, its subsequent cultivation and transformation across time ... the terracing of the site to receive the stepped form of a building is an engagement in the act of "cultivating" the site. (Frampton 1985)

- An emphasis on the tectonic:

  A poetic interpretation or articulation of construction techniques: '[T]he primary principle resides in the tectonic rather than the scenographic. ... We may speak here of the presentation of a structural poetic rather than the re-presentation of a façade'. (Frampton 1985)

- The juxtaposition of linear/orthogonal and circular/organic elements.

As described in Chap. 1, the critical position attempts to negotiate between polarities. Veering neither towards the more expedient forms of consumption nor the scenographical approach of post-Modernism. It is a negotiation within the act of regionalising a global form. The Telekom Tower, Kuala Lumpur, the headquarters of Telekom Malaysia Sdn. Bhd, is a more iconic attempt at a critical position, one that represents perhaps a more confident phase of the nation. The form itself not only evokes a Malaysian metaphor, the characteristic deep shading of the archetypical forms of the Malay traditional verandah or *anjung* is evoked. A position that veers towards the 'cultural/iconic' approach is intended to create a landmark design, yet still articulated within the Modernist dictum. The tower's overall tapering form exudes a strong presence and has a distinctive visual impact, yet functionally it caters to the need for the open-style organisation of twenty-first-century corporations.

Kasturi's work is often linked with his passionate involvement in and support of the local arts, and his high-rise forms can be read as 'sculpted' profiles by a master artist. The Telekom tower was said to be inspired by the work of the Malaysian sculptor and painter Latif Mohidin, particularly his acclaimed painting 'Pago-pago' and his sketch for the *pucuk rebung* a traditional bamboo plant. The typical floor plan is basically comprised of two quadrants and arches that are linked by the central service core. A key concept in inflecting the high-rise with topicality was the incorporation of large open-air terraced gardens scaling the heights of the tower. Selected floors have large skycourts which link the two quadrants together. Lower floors have larger and longer floor plates, and these floor plates decrease in size and length as they ascend towards the top of the tower. Another key contribution of Hijjas Kasturi Associates is the 4G11 tower in Putrajaya. Its form is essentially derived from two strategies resonating with the 'cultural patterns' approach: firstly, a floor layout which departs from the rectilinear or cubic toward a tapering form, and secondly, a façade composition which is made up of ingeniously 'woven' patterns which derive a vibrancy from Malay artisanal motifs linked to the local bamboo shoot or *pucuk rebung*. *Pucuk rebung* – the young bamboo shoot – is a delicacy in Malay culture and appears in many of its artistic and crafts traditions. The architect-designer in charge of the project, Azaiddy Abdullah, had related how he attempted to negotiate between rationalistic styles and eclectic tendencies that were characteristic of the institutional buildings of Putrajaya. He aimed to evoke a sense of Malaysianness and what it means to be 'Malaysian' by façade patterning and detailing which grew from observations of the Malay arts, including textiles. The dynamically organised tapering patterns was linked to the *rebung* which is reflected in Malay traditional *songket* patterns. This had simultaneously ensured effective control of heat gain and reduced overall thermal transfer values (OTTV), elements required by green building standards in the tropics, without elevated costs. As with many of the firm's designs, the point of departure is always a response to tradition, yet from an 'avant-garde' perspective and embracing modern technology.

One recalls tower seem to reflect how Boys (1996) elucidates on the fundamental nuances of the critical regionalist vocabulary

> *'... achieved through the juxtaposition within the building of two chains of associative concepts which are conventionally oppositional: external rectilinear/modular/universal/functional/secular and internal/curved/specific/unique/spiritual/religious.'*

By these descriptions, she refers to a juxtaposition of 'orthogonal and hard-edged themes in form' (characteristic of the 'Corbusian' language) with the more soft-edged, free-flowing abstract forms of modern regionalist architecture. On looking back at regional forms and their range of emphasis and position, it becomes clear that the period from the 1970s onwards was a time when there were different emphases on such strategies, including a dialogue with the local landscape and setting. The aim is ultimately maintain a connection with a universal global world yet find towards the roots of symbolic capital, among others, by juxtaposing orthogonal tendencies in form and design with the more 'organic' curvilinear elements to achieve a more balanced synthesis.

Conclusions

In regionalising the high-rise, the aim was to depart from the ubiquitous 'commercial' block, a symbol of economic expediency, into symbols would differentiate the city from a growing homogeneity brought about by a liberalised and capitalist economy. These were explorations of what was termed by Curtis (1996) as alternative social and urbanistic structures – to counter both economic and technological forces that privilege the modularity of the steep structural frame and the need to maximise floor space. Later the aim was to modulate and provide a striking image in the city as the high-rise is sculpted as a profile against monolithic surroundings. Ford (1996, p. 413) denotes the key motivation of regionalism as follows: 'it offers an escape from the monolith of industrialised processes.' The skyscraper was a symbol that added to the place identity and the growing density of the tropical city.

In the context of the urbanising economy in developing countries, where pressures such as increased land values, urban accessibility, expanding urban populations and the globalisation of the national economy have brought about the proliferation of the high-rise, these modern typeforms which reflect economic, social and technological forces have also been the arena where both regional and national identity are expressed, carved and incised into the forms. Even with the pressure of central land prices, corporate demands, engineering and economic expediency, regional and national identities expressed in the high-rise continue to create and instil identities in growing cities. The culturally differentiated form is a testimony to the will of designers, policy makers and stakeholders to enhance 'the symbolic capital' (Dovey 2000) of tropical cities. The form of the regionalist skyscraper, in the tropical city, is an attempt to infuse identity into the stark monolithic volumes. Hence regional and national identity harnesses the forms of high-rises to define the individual identity of a city. In later years, such forms need veered towards more symbolic assertions through the more formal tendencies. The KLCC Petronas towers is one result of such a quest to project a strong image and identity through a highrise complex, as will be discussed in Chap. 11. The search for symbols of an emerging nation and city continue, and present trends in high-rises have seen the emergence of more and more streamlined forms, in which details are submerged in the purity of the overall form, in order to appear seamless. The high-rise is, and will be, a symbol of global modernity and technology, in Asia with the effect of its profile, and form will continue to evolve as a symbol and imagery of growing cities and cosmopolitan centers.

References

Abel, C. (1997). Living in hybrid world. In C. Abel (Ed.), *Architecture and identity*. Oxford, UK: Architectural Press/Butterworth and Heinemann.

Boys, J. (1996). Misrepresentations of society? In J. Palmer & J. Dodson (Eds.), *Design and aesthetics: A reader*. London: Routledge.

Chua, B. H. (2000, February 21–23). *Living with capitalism in Asia, uncomfortably in 'we Asians – Between past and future'*. Proceedings of a regional conference. Singapore: Japan Foundation Center, National Archives of Singapore and Singapore Heritage Society.
Colquhoun, A. (1971). The superblock. In A. Colquhoun (Ed., 1981), *Essays in architectural criticism: Modern architecture and historical change*. Cambridge, MA: MIT Press.
Colquhoun, A. (1983). *Sign and substance: Reflections on complexity – Las Vegas, and Oberlin*. In A. Colquhoun (Ed., 1981) *Essays in architectural criticism: Modern architecture and historical change*. Cambridge, MA: MIT Press.
Curtis, W. J. R. (1996). Modernity, tradition and identity in the developing world. In W. J. R. Curtis (Ed.), *Modern architecture since 1900*. London: Phaidon Press
Davidson, C., & Seralgedin, I. (1995). Menara Mesiniaga. In *Architecture beyond architecture – Creativity and social transformation in Islamic cultures: The 1995 Aga Khan award for architecture* (pp. 95–101). London: Academy Editions.
Dovey, K. (1999). Tall storeys. In *Framing places: Mediating power in built form*. London: Routledge.
Dovey, K. (2000). Myth and media: Constructing aboriginal architecture. *Journal of Architectural Education, 54*(1), 2–6.
Eco, U. (1972). Introduction to a semiotics of iconic signs. *Versus, 2*, 1–15.
Eisenman, P. (1996). Masters jury discussion. In C. Davidson (Ed.), *Architecture beyond architecture – The 1995 Aga Khan award for architecture*. London: Academy Editions.
Ford, E. R. (1996). *The details of modern architecture* (Vol. 2). Cambridge, MA: MIT press.
Frampton, K. (1983). Modern architecture and critical regionalism. *Transactions of Royal Institute of British Architects, 2*(3), 15–25.
Frampton, K. (1985). Critical regionalism – Modern architecture and cultural identity. In K. Frampton (Ed.), *Modern architecture – A critical history*. London: Thames and Hudson.
Frampton, K. (1992). Riverside tower. In K. Frampton & P. Drew (Eds.), *Harry Seidler, four decades of architecture*. London: Thames and Hudson.
Frampton, K. (1998). Introduction. In K. Frampton, A. Specter, & L. R. Rosman (Eds.), *Technology, place and architecture-the Jerusalem seminar in architecture*. New York: Rizzoli International Publications.
Jahn Kassim, P. S. (2004). *The bioclimatic skyscraper – A critical analysis of the theories and designs of Ken Yeang*. Unpublished phd thesis 2004, University of Brighton.

Jenkins, D. (2000). *Market whys and human wherefores: Thinking again about markets, politics and people paperback* (2nd Revised ed.). London: Continuum, 4 January 2004.

Kahn, J. S. (2006). *Other Malays – Nationalism and cosmopolitanism in the modern Malay world* (p. 2). Singapore: NUS Press, National University Singapore.

Kusno, A. (2000). Imagining regionalism, re-fashioning orientalism: Some current architectural discourses in South East Asia. *Journal of Southeast Asian Architecture, 4*, 45–61.

Tzonis, A., & Le Faivre, L. (2001). Tropical critical regionalism – Introductory comments. In A. Tzonis & L. Le Faivre (Eds.), *Tropical architecture –Critical regionalism in the age of globalisation*. London: Wiley Academy.

9

The Transport Terminal: Marking National Landmarks

Shireen Jahn Kassim, Norwina Mohd Nawawi, and Siti Norzaini Zainal Abidin

Introduction

In the words of the acclaimed naturalist and writer Robert MacFarlane (2016), landmarks are 'key references of a place' which are richly expressed in the local lexicon of the people. He describes, with reference to the British landscape, how landmarks are defined as natural elements which define a place, and which are instinctively rooted in its identity and hence shape its individuality against a rapidly changing world constantly in flux. Yet the word 'landmark' can also be linked to man-made structures, those which are ingrained in one's memory as designating a 'marking', the remembrance of a certain moment in time or a certain location in space.

In any city or location, transport hubs are particularly linked to notions of place identity because they are seen as, and act as, national gateways, signifying the arrival at a destination. The main function of a train terminus is thus basically boarding trains, but through the centuries, the central railway station has evolved to fulfil multiple functions and often plays a

S. Jahn Kassim (✉) • N. Mohd Nawawi • S. Norzaini Zainal Abidin
International Islamic University Malaysia, Kuala Lumpur, Malaysia

© The Author(s) 2018

S. Jahn Kassim et al. (eds.), *Modernity, Nation and Urban-Architectural Form*,
https://doi.org/10.1007/978-3-319-66131-5_9

nostalgic role as the central hub through which urbanites and visitors move and undertake public transport. An airport terminal, on the other hand, is an arrival and departure point, a large shed, to facilitate the movement of a large number of people. As a typology, the airport terminal essentially represents the essence of the twenty-first century in which the world is connected globally whether by a network or by the rise of air travel from region to region or nation to nation. The airport is now looked upon as a gateway, and nations aim to build cutting-edge airports where high technology is fused with cultural resonance.

Airport

The Asia-Pacific region has seen some of the world's fastest growing markets, hence the emergence of air travel has spawned the rise of regional and international airport terminals, and their forms and architecture have been seen as an opportunity to make a statement within an increasingly competitive and connected world. Both Subang Airport and the KLIA Sepang of Malaysia epitomise these two distinct developments, and the evolution of Malaysia's journey from a colonial federation to an industrialised economy is embodied in the evolution of form, language and vocabulary of these two iconic structures. The airport terminal is a gateway to a particular region or nation. As the essence of a place, city or region, its form must reflect a specific character or tradition of a nation. These structures become the bearers of identity of a place, and regional and national identity are articulated through a more cultural-iconic approach with a predominant emphasis on rationality fused with imagery from traditional emblems.

Cultural Regionalisation of the Victorian Style

In his chapter on 'Architecture and the Nation: Building an "Us"', Paul Jones (2011) highlights how the Victorian age in Britain was a time when there was a moral search for the 'correct' language for a rising imperial power (p. 53):

Many British public buildings of the period (1850–1901) give testimony to the self-confidence of the Victorian nation state as an imperial power, architecture – alongside other codifications such as art, flags, national anthems – was drawn closely into the state's cultural project and mobilized to give tangible form to abstract national values.

Crinson (1996) in Jones (2011) explains that the volume of documentation, measured drawings and writings on Islamic architecture in Britain during the period 1840–1870 was intended to 'to make cultural differentiation' meaningful; as Jones summarises, 'In other words, to embed ethnic and national cultural differences'. However, in Malaysia, due to the absence of urban models, the Islamic Indo-Saracenic language was both meaningful to the local, predominantly Muslim, population and at the same time represented the glory of the British Raj. Jones (2011) also describes the use of the Islamic Indo Saracenic style as a form of cultural capital (p. 56):

Furthermore, knowledge of such 'exotic' architectural styles – whether they and the values they represented were only to be employed merely in a rhetorical binary with the Western canon – represented a form of cultural capita in the professionalizing architectural field of the day.

Language of the 'Terminus'

It was the British colonialist who introduced and built the first nationalised network rail systems on the Malaysian Peninsula, which were crucial for the development of the economy through the movement of people and goods. Smaller local train stations, however, were part of a public service network. These humbler structures are often expressed in a hybrid vernacular–colonial language. This essentially fused language of masonry and timber evokes the timber simplicity of the Malay vernacular and expresses modernity through elements of masonry and the brick solidity of columns and beams. The Sultan Street Station, for example, located at the present Jalan Tun Cheng Lock, Kuala Lumpur, was a tropical hybrid form, with a language of brackets and columns and a pitched roof structure which referred to Malay forms and, in combination, epitomised the tropical colonial style. The station itself has now been demolished, along with many other colonial-based stations, which is a loss to the identity of the city, as these masonry sensibilities of old are crucial in evoking the cool, naturally ventilated, colonnaded verandahs of the past.

Hailed by *Architectural Digest* (2014) as one of the most beautiful train stations in the world, the old Kuala Lumpur Central train station is one of the few colonial structures still preserved at the heart of the urban core of Kuala Lumpur. Designed by Arthur Hubback and completed in 1910, it was modelled on the Indo-Saracenic style and exhibited clear references to the Mughal vocabulary of arches and *chattris*. It was C. E. Spooner, Hubback's boss, who gave preference to the Saracenic style over the Neoclassical or Renaissance language, and hence the language of horseshoe-shaped arches surmounted by pavilions like *chattris*, were regarded as playful Indo-Saracenic language, mixing Mughal elements with those of Victorian vocabulary.

It was a time when British architects were searching for a British imperial style, and their use of Islamic vocabulary was a synthesised hybrid grammar linked to their aversion to the Neoclassical style yet forging a new style – derived from their knowledge to Oriental stylings – to represent British authority and presence. These elements of language were not merely used for stylistic predisposition or preference, but were seen to represent British modernity, from which the notions of civilisation, progress and modernity emanated. The use of the Mughal *chattris* to mark their pinnacles was for iconic impact, to rise above the general massing of the city, rather than due to a particular predilection for Mughal design. The effect is both Gothic and Mughal-Islamic, and the aim was a national style, yet it was intended as a symbol and an imprint of British imperialism.

In 1914, the Old Kuala Lumpur Station initially consisted of a main terminal building with three platforms serving four railway lines at the back. In 1915, an extension of the station was constructed consisting of a 30-room hotel, and several other buildings were built. As the central station, it linked Singapore to Kuala Lumpur and to British field stations throughout Malaya and to Bangkok. The platforms are covered by large steel-framed shelters, which were initially shorter during the station's early operation. The roofs were originally glazed, and were partially opened to allow smoke from steam locomotives to escape; corrugated roof sheets served as replacements later in the station's life. In the year 1986, the station was renovated and updated with additional facilities such as air-conditioned waiting halls, stalls and information counters. The extended platform built in the 1986 refurbishment of the station reflected a more Modernist approach, consisting simply of large concrete pillars supporting a latticed roof and a ticket office on concrete slabs at the north end, suspended two stories above ground. The new extension is connected to the Dayabumi complex via an elevated walkway. White walls and arches that serve the extension reflect the expressions of the Dayabumi complex rather than the original station.

The Kuala Lumpur Train Station – synthesising Mughal and localised vocabulary in a landmark of the colonial era

The station's three platforms conveniently served the four north- and south-bound railway tracks. On the north wing, a three-storey addition in a tropicalised version of the language exhibits a varied vocabulary with arches of different sizes and surrounding verandahs. The platforms are linked with the main terminal building by two underground passageways. The 1986 refurbishment had the aim of aligning the look of the station with that of the nearby Dayabumi complex rather than its original Maharaja-styled theme. Although in post-Independence Malaysia these functions have moved elsewhere, these buildings remain as a potent visual symbol of the country and its multicultural heritage.

Departing from his own position of nineteenth-century eclectic historicism, Hubback took Mughal forms and melded them with Byzantine, Romanesque and Gothic elements in order to syncretise a 'new' kind of architecture. Thus the combination of Mughal and Saracenic horseshoe and ogee arches, and large *chattris* (six originally, with two added later) by Hubback, is perhaps what makes the station one of the most iconic and memorable in the world. It rises poetically and distinctively from the dense urban fabric of an older zone of the city, and its pinnacles create a distinctive silhouette against the rising modern monoliths surrounding it. Instead of the muteness of blocks and flat roofs, the surmounting corners of the station with accompanying smaller variations at the front of the building instil a memory of an almost magical past. The same language is reflected in the iconic Sultan Abdul Samad building, which is perceived now as a national symbol. It was also largely attributed to R. A. J. Bidwell following the design direction set by the State Engineer Charles Edwin Spooner, and Hubback made additions and alterations to the building under Spooner's instructions. This strand of English colonial architecture was based on Indian Islamic architecture rather than native Malaya elements.

Subang: Kuala Lumpur First International Airport

Having attained independence in 1957, Malaysia was in need of an international airport. The proposed terminal building was not only meant to service the economy and the people, but it should also serve as an icon of an independent nation. A site in Subang, Malaysia, was earmarked for construction. The nation's first international airport terminal was to be state of the art yet buildable within the budget allocated. At the time of its completion in 1965, it was declared a national symbol. Built during the heyday of concrete technology in building, the form itself arose from a process that maximised the use of the modular concrete constructional method and technology, based on earlier international precedents of tropical airport forms in the Middle Eastern region.

In 1963, the firm BEP Akitek, headed by Kington Loo, was appointed to design the airport in Subang. Inspired by the architect Felix Candela, the form was conceptualised based on an expressive 'mushroom' structure recalling a more expressive approach to the International style during the 1960s. The final design was a terrazzo-clad concrete columnar structure based on a language which was essentially Modernist. From afar, the form leaned towards a simple horizontal exposed columnar structure held by a series of graceful pointed arches. A covered but open-air pier extended into the apron and the terminal building was conceived as a large open volume rather than an enclosed form (Fig. 9.1).

The massive roof was supported by soaring free-standing columns opening out onto the ceiling plane, almost like a tree canopy. The centrepiece of the terminal was a graceful spiral ramp in the centre of the arrival/departure hall. The roof was essentially 60 interconnected shell roofs, which were

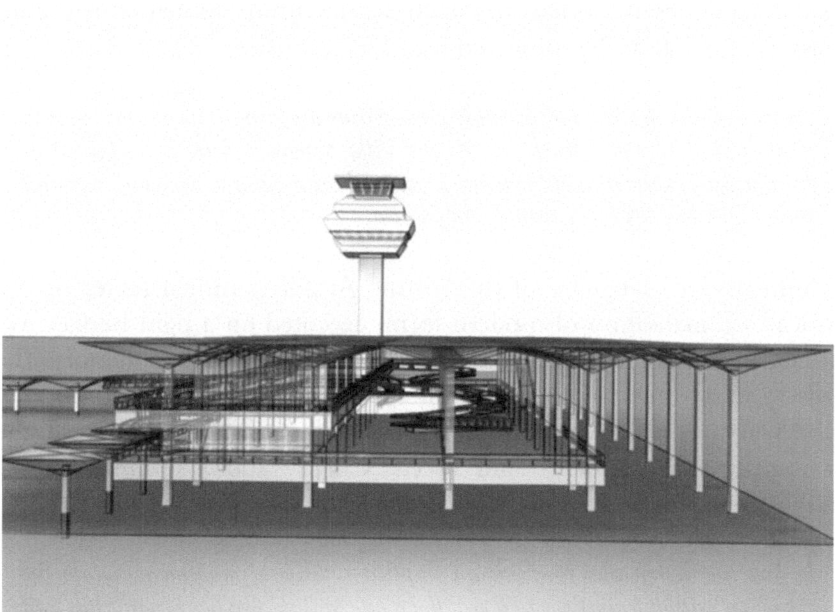

Fig. 9.1 Simplified three-dimensional illustration of the Subang Airport, Kuala Lumpur

constructed in early June 1964. The hyperbolic paraboloid shells were considered to be the natural modular yet methodological solution, to erecting the shells. The formwork around each of the shells had to be removed simultaneously and uniformly to avoid uneven stress, which might have cracked the large shells.

Architecturally, its form reflects a degree of rationality, yet the curvature of the ramp and the rhythm of the 'arches' create a counterforce to the 'functional' form and balance the austere and regimented expression of the columnar design. The circular ramp recalls the strategy and principle of the 'architectural promenade', a set of principles expounded by Le Corbusier. Le Corbusier's conceptualisation of his 'five principles' saw this element of the promenade (epitomised in his Villa Savoye, France) as an experiential tool that facilitates the experience of space and of walking through a cube-like space. The architecture is orthogonal, yet form and space are defined by a ramp. The curvature of the elements seems to pierce through a 'box', yet spatially the viewer experiences a pinwheel effect.

The juxtaposition of grid and curves recalls the same principles and spatial dynamics in Modern architecture but within a more tightly bound mass. Curtis (2006) has observed how Le Corbusier

> *clearly exploits the ideas of variable view-points and simultaneous perceptions of multiple layers and levels. … At the Villa Savoye, nature is celebrated as dramatically as the idea of the house as a 'machine a habiter,' views of trees and grasses are carefully orchestrated and framed.*

Similarly, the language of the Subang Airport terminal represented a critical regionalisation of modern form, executed on a tight budget, yet which embodies a resistance to the orthogonal language of modernity. The inflection or softening of form is symbolic of a regional characterisation of modernity, yet with evocations of the key changes in the modern era: the symbolism of technology and speed. Curtis (2006) summarises key insights in terms of the Villa Savoye which can be applied to this airport:

> *In fact the design also contains an implied rotational movement, while the actual transition from floor to floor allows one to link together inner vistas and events with outer ones. The Villa Savoye might be understood as an analogue to the flux and relativity of the modern experience.*

Colquhoun (2002) has also stated:

> *One could describe as the enclosure of function in a generalized cubic container not committed to any particular set of concrete functions – a tendency partly derived from his early allegiance to Neo-Classicism, The other was the articulation of the building in response to the fluidity of life.*
>
> *The inculturation of the tropical modernist design to the architecture of the terminal building to the Malaysian way of life was easily adopted and adapted. The nation's pride, the terminal was seemingly neutral to all cultures. The terminal's open architecture, humble in its treatment and friendly to all walks of life, made it a must-visit national building to any Malaysian visiting the city of Kuala Lumpur. The spacious departure concourse, mimicking the 'anjung' of a Malay house, augured well with the entourage of family members sending off their loved ones abroad. Spaces for the public extended well into the waving gallery at the upper level of the terminal building, providing the last chance to see each other before departure. Prior to the advent of the aerobridge and long before its becoming mandatory, the spiral and linear ramps provided access to the less abled, especially during the annual Hajj pilgrimage flights. The architecture was essentially utilitarian, with an easily cleanable terrazzo-clad triangle-shaped column canopy with a rainwater downpipe running through the column, a space planning utilising natural daylight and thorough ventilation, in line with the green architecture standards of today. The black rubberised flooring of the public concourse acted both as an acoustic and safety cushion for children and the elderly. The foresightedness of the architecture was also reflected in the use of the natural stone-grey colour of the terrazzo on the overall building in contrast to critical spaces and details. To Malaysians of the 1960s right to the 1980s, the terminal building, which was located just 30 minutes from Kuala Lumpur City Centre, was more than a city hub and international gateway to Malaysia; it was a significant contribution to the nation's emergence from the colonial past, a sign of global mobility and connectivity that underlines today's country's success. However, in a mean capitalistic world that Malaysia had inherited, to go global, the terminal building was silently demolished without a trace, and the new terminal in Sepang soars. The Subang Airport is survived by an upgraded city air terminal – former terminal 3 – into the current Subang SkyPark Terminal, Sultan Abdul Aziz Shah Airport, for selected local and regional destinations.*

The KLIA International Airport, Sepang, Malaysia

By the 1990s, the Subang International Airport was superseded by a new airport, the KLIA (Kuala Lumpur International Airport) in Sepang, expressed in the next evolution in long-span steel construction, and demonstrating its own modality of expression in regional and national identity infused and integrated formally and spatially. These terminals were built to represent the idea of a progressive nation and act as infrastructure that would support the growth of a range of economic sectors. The KLIA was designed to symbolise an industrialised era for the nation, just as the Subang airport signals its beginning. Both were expressed in terms of different technology and material which gave rise to a different vocabulary and expression in representing the nation. KLIA, as affirmed by Shireen et al. (2017), was conceptualised to bring out the essence of the place through a reflection of climate and key elements of local culture. Criticism of the recent destruction of the old international airport at Subang is highlighted and read against the lack of recognition given to the historical value of 1970s-style structures.

The KLIA main terminal building consists of six levels with a total floor area of 170,640 square metres. The main terminal spans 38.4 square metres along a grid pattern, allowing for easy expansion in the future. Kurokawa (1999) derived ideas from his personal philosophy of 'architectural symbiosis' and envisioned a 'total' work of architecture for the airport. Typically, the hyperbolic roof was curved to recall traditional roof forms, and abstractions were sought after a deep study of elements of its culture, landscape and artefacts. The roof's hyperparabolic (H-P) shells evoke the 'curvature' and pointed forms of the Minangkabau roof. The regional character of the architecture is complemented by extensive landscaping and courtyards interspersed throughout the terminal (Fig. 9.2).

The goal, as architect Kisho Kurokawa (1999) states, was to attain 'symbiosis'. The high-tech materials needed to articulate a distinctive imagery that evokes the memory of cultural forms and traditions. Some felt the overall flattened, dome-like structure externally reflected the curves of the dome. Such gentle curved inflections are repeated throughout both in

Fig. 9.2 The Kuala Lumpur International Airport's canopy and column module

section and plan, while the roof is supported by a dynamically raked structure. Additionally, as seen from outside, the overhanging eaves of the roof evoke traditional Malaysian architecture.

Rather than a direct expression of tradition and its iconography, KLIA's regional identity is essentially contained in 'resistance' or differentiation of an essentially Modernist position of structural rationalisation and volumetric forms in terms of its allusions to climate, landscape and culture, through tapering columns and the gentle sweep of its hyperbolic-shaped roofs and its use of timber-strip-look aluminium and interspersing of space with 'islands' of tropical greenery.

KLIA, as discussed by Jahn Kassim et al. (2017), is a cultural departure from or differentiation of an essentially Modernist form, the similar essential universal form: service-column structures with almost floating roof structures that can be found throughout the world, for example in London's Stansted Airport. The terminal is a combination of columns and overhead skylights derived purely for functionality, as the composition is distinct in exhibiting a rational and orthogonal approach to terminal design reminiscent of the geometric yet idealised pure forms of Modern architecture. The primary aim of the architect was to symbolise the drama of flight by focusing on efficiency and optimum passenger experience. The terminal is similarly a series of lightweight modular roofs of shallow geometric domes, supported by structural steel 'tree-like columns' intended to give clear circulation to its users. The Stansted roof structure is punctuated by pyramid-like skylights with underlying reflectors which diffuse the daylight. The columns 'cloak' views of typical mechanical and electrical nozzles, and unifying such services into one central trunk provides enhanced control for technical and maintenance strategies. The undercroft contains baggage handling and accommodates a mainline railway station, which was integrated late in the design process. Service distribution systems are contained within the 'trunks' of the structural 'trees' that rise from the undercroft through the concourse floor. The unification of structure and services made the huge expanse of roof seem to be floating without effort. Visitors to Stansted have likened the column supports to 'trees', with some relating the form to gigantic 'hands'. As an organic analogy, each 'hand' has four fingers splayed out to 'balance' and support the roof.

Yet KLIA constitutes an act of departure from normative rationalised form. Both conical columns represent the most critical cultural strategies in the terminal; these, with the inspection of the tropical island atriums, inflect the rational form to culture and geographical region. The H-P modular roofs are held aloft by cylindrical column forms tapering towards the top in a series of curved undulations of wooden-look anodised aluminium strip ceilings (Fig. 9.3). These are pierced with tiny spotlights and constructed with a single-layer pipe lattice structure and straight-line wood panels. The distinctive tapering column forms and undulating curved roofs set in a modular grid are inflected further with greenery that reflects the key design motto, 'forest in an airport, airport in a forest'. Kurokawa wanted to capture the uniqueness of Malaysian cultural identity through forms that expressed the local vernacular architecture and local landscape transformed through modern structural technology and materials. Malaysian cultural allusions

Fig. 9.3 The hyperbolic paraboloid roof form depicting the rain-forest canopy

are also evident in the abstract elements through the provision of public, semi-public and private spaces of the terminal building, cleverly articulated based on Malay architecture.

Further, allusions to the curved form of the Minangkabau roof can be discerned in the distinctive hyperbolic forms of the highly distinctive roof, similar to the roof form of Negeri Sembilan's state mosque of reinforced concrete structure and fat conical columns. Skylight roof features and extensive landscaping and courtyards are interspersed throughout the terminal to create a tropical aura that is Malaysian in its essence.

KLIA is perhaps the apotheosis of criticality in the range of regionalist works that have been discussed. KLIA, like Bangkok International Airport, was designed for a hot and humid climate (Kessling et al. 2004) in the context of the twenty-first-century situation of an international airport that is expected to meet 24-hour working days, high internal heat loads from people, electric equipment and lighting, as well as desired indoor climate conditions of 24°C room temperature and 50% to 60% relative humidity, among others, which calls for a completely new approach to design. By the 1990s, Heynen (1999) had expressed that there was a degree of maturity to the region and nation, and Kurokawa managed to synthesise key tropes of topicality and cultural forms into a single architectural masterpiece. Criticality, according to Frampton (1983, 1992), is a departure from iconography and the scenographic; it is a critical inhalation which reflects a certain ethos of Modernism in which external form reflects internal space and vice versa. It also involves all the key elements of topicality and place-making such as light, greenery, Malay roof form and nuances to timber and reference to the forms of greenery in both language and actual irrigation. In all, a newly independent sovereign nation, as the country progresses and utilitarian needs already fulfilled, elements of identity with a sense of place and design details gradually crept into transport gateway designs. The move from KLIA in Subang to KLIA at Sepang, is the desire in the search for one's root or identity. The year 1998, as the country opened to the Commonwealth Games, KLIA, as nation's terminal supported by the Light Rail Transit (LRT) system catapulted the Malaysia industry to myriads of soul-searching approaches. Terminal buildings act as transit spaces and shelter. Malaysia had delivered the KLIA2 terminal, the first terminal for low-cost carriers that had won the LEED Green Building Certification. The terminal is equipped with state-of-the-art surveillance system and boasts of a robust architectural design. This is a remarkable contribution by the government, because it provides every individual with air travel that is stylish and comfortable, albeit affordable.

References

Colquhoun, A. (2002). *Modern architecture*. Oxford/New York: Oxford University Press.

Crinson, M. (1996). *Empire building: Orientalism and Victorian architecture*. London: Routledge.

Curtis, W. J. R. (2006). *Le Corbusier -ideas and forms*. London/New York: Phaidon Press.

Frampton, K. (1983). Modern architecture and critical regionalism. *Transactions of Royal Institute of British Architects, 2*(3), 15–25.

Frampton, K. (1992). Critical regionalism – Modern architecture and cultural identity. In K. Frampton (Ed.), *Modern architecture – A critical history*. London: Thames and Hudson.

Heynen, H. (1999). *Architecture and modernity: A critique*. Cambridge, MA: MIT Press.

Jones, P. (2011). Architecture and the nation: Building an 'Us'. In *The sociology of architecture: Constructing identities* (pp. 49–66). Liverpool: Liverpool University Press.

Kessling, W., Holst, S., & Schuler, M. (2004). *Innovative design concept for the New Bangkok International Airport, NBIA*. Symposium on improving building systems in Hot and Humid Climates, Dallas.

Kurokawa, K. (1999). Futuristic flight plan, lighting design and application, IESNA, 1999 International Illumination Design Awards.

MacFarlane, R. (2016). Landmarks 'dazzling spectator'. London, UK: Penguin Books.

Shireen, J. K., Noor Hanita, A. M., & Nawawi, N. M. (2017). *The resilience of tradition: Malay allusions in contemporary architecture*. Penang: Areca Books.

10

The Tropical Metropolis: A Review of History, Identity and Climatic Idealisations in City Form

Nurul Syala Abdul Latip, Norwina Mohd Nawawi, Shaiful Nadzri Shamsudin, and Elias Salleh

Introduction

As a city, Kuala Lumpur evolved from the confluence of two rivers in the Klang Valley (hence its name, which literally means 'muddy confluence') where traders, immigrants and workers settled it had evolved and grew from a conglomeration of two- to three-storey shophouses into its present form as a dense metropolis. By the 1990s, major cities in tropical Asia were centres of business, tourism and urban life, including Kuala Lumpur, from which post-Independence commercial areas had further extended

N. S. Abdul Latip (✉)
Department of Architecture, University Sains Islam Malaysia, Nilai, Negeri Sembilan, Malaysia

N. Mohd Nawawi
International Islamic University Malaysia, Kuala Lumpur, Malaysia

S. N. Shamsudin • E. Salleh
Department of Architecture, Kulliyyah of Architecture and Environmental Design, International Islamic University Malaysia, Kuala Lumpur, Malaysia

© The Author(s) 2018

S. Jahn Kassim et al. (eds.), *Modernity, Nation and Urban-Architectural Form*,
https://doi.org/10.1007/978-3-319-66131-5_10

and evolved. In some cases, several urban centres gradually grew into a range of disparate small towns and villages, which had been consolidated into new centres of urban life and development.

More recently, the rising densities of these urban centres has spurred the rise of satellite cities. Both Putrajaya and Cyberjaya in Malaysia are planned cities, satellite developments which arose from the need to reduce the pressure on the central core by relocating administrative functions to surrounding areas and linking them through an interconnecting network of highways and public transportation systems.

Urban Histories

Rather than having a single unifying identity or national image, Kuala Lumpur was a city which grew out of 'compounds' and cultural 'enclaves' of some of which have competing identities and evolve from different communities and traditions. Other than Kuala Lumpur, Singapore also evolved from a colonial past and catapulted into a bustling metropolis of the twenty-first century, and its recent spate of urban reconstruction was part of its agenda of developing a competitive edge to the city, and its development of key icons and the bay area were part of its long-term strategic initiatives to spur and sustain continuing economic growth. Tourist attractions were developed vis-à-vis a series of highly modern mixed development and iconic structures. A key example is the urban core development of the Marina Bay, with its range of entertainment and shopping complexes, and public transport which is an evolvement from many recreational spots such as the zoo, Jurong Bird Parks, Science Centres and centres of refurbished eating places along the Singapore River to name a few. These developments had attracted investors and became the catalyst of the city and its urban development. Indonesia, is also rebuilding its cities with new zones and business parks with the idea of new urban living centres termed *superkampung* or vertical *kampungs* (Frausto 2011).

In a similar vein, Kuala Lumpur had mapped out a masterplan which began in the 1990s with the KL City Centre, yet Malaysian urban centres had subtle divisions based on ethnicity and the consequent impact on historical patterns with which it had to grapple. Both malaysia and Indonesia, face the issue of ethnicity with the existence of many ethnic groups with a similarly created series of social 'islands' in the city itself. Each ethnic group developed its own inner social zone within the city. To tackle this issue, an increased number of iconic structures were built to create unification symbols and an identity for the city and a point of focus for the multiethnic population. This reflects a central role of urban-architectural form as a means of unification of the people. The capital city of Indonesia, Jakarta, is the home of a much denser population whose urban form was termed an 'involution' by Evers et al. (2000). Described as 'urbanization without urbanism' (Evers et al. 2000), it was a condition in which monuments and grand plazas were built as symbols and to provide a sense of urban life, but the whose symbols were in fact, sculptures and physical monuments. It created a form of identity which evoked a sense of nationalism among those ethnic groups. Such monuments depicting the history of Indonesia became instant urban symbols. After the 1980s, similarly to Malaysia, a rapid pace of industrialisation was seen. New government offices were then built to create a sense of the centre of an urban city. Shopping malls and other public places were also constructed to meet the social and economic needs of the people.

Urbanism: Relooking at Kuala Lumpur as a City Centre

Kuala Lumpur, in slight contrast to Singapore and Jakarta, began with the emergence of settlements and businesses along its main rivers. After Independence, its continuous urban growth revolved round these new centres of urban life. Its growth reflected on how Malay settlements in the region were conventionally formed: through the adjacency or confluence of rivers. The city itself was originally opened in the 1800s by immigrants, including merchants and tin miners who settled at the meeting point of the Sungai Gombak and Sungai Klang rivers. The location became a seed, and its consequent impact had signified an urban catalyst of a major economic centre; its governance and surrounding natural resources had attracted many business-related activities to Kuala Lumpur. In contrast to the general understanding of Yap Ah Loi representing the founder of Kuala Lumpur, it is now known as Sutan Puasa, the founder of Kuala Lumpur, was a trader and central business figure originating from

Mandailing. Just before and after colonisation, there was a rapid influx of cultures, skills and communities into Kuala Lumpur, which rapidly evolved from a settlement into a centre of work and business, and the city grew with the help of national policies that spurred rapid economic development.

Malaysia was on a path that required new national symbols, including strategically located administrative buildings and monuments. Yet the colonial imprint remains distinct and urban spaces which were the centre of colonial administration later became a form of public space that accommodated public activities, and became symbols of democracy. In Kuala Lumpur, what were previously centres of trade and administrative spaces have evolved into such public spaces. The Padang Merdeka, at the centre of the old administrative centre and town, is as much a space for leisure as it is a place for public gatherings, and occasional demonstrations. Yet such observations have shown that there are two forms of public spaces, spaces for consumption and spaces for public participation (Fig. 10.1).

Fig. 10.1 Kampung Baru, Kuala Lumpur – a Malay 'cultural' enclave amidst the urban core

A typology that has recently grown rapidly is the shopping mall. These have proliferated in Kuala Lumpur and other cities in which a range of functions, such as hospitality, convention centres, event venues and retail spaces, all converge into an interconnecting and fluid space, designed for the air-conditioned comfort of the shopper, visitor or tourist. The immense popularity of the Kuala Lumpur City Centre spurred the linking of mixed high-density developments such as other high-rise developments, now known as Lot 91 and Lot 185, linked to the KLCC. In addition to seeing the growth of business-related buildings, the Chinese and Indian communities have maintained certain traditional districts in the city centre. Petaling Street still mainly consists of two-storey shophouses where the Chinese community does their daily business and resides. Similarly the Indian community has consolidated their own commercial space in the zone of Brickfields which becomes a centre of festivities and lights during key celebrations and events. The growth of residential housing in the city centre of Kuala Lumpur is also escalating and more and more high-end accommodations consist of complexes in which urbanites work, eat and play in the same place. The programme of 'Malaysia as your second home' has attracted foreign buyers of city centre residences and such forms of high-end living have made Kuala Lumpur a magnet for expatriates and overseas visitors.

Urban Traditions and Histories

The present urban forms of Kuala Lumpur are also a consequence of past racial division which were born of an economic urban–rural segregation. The Second and Third Malaysia plans in the 1970s included an expedited programme of education by which Malays became more involved in government and businesses, including as administrators. This was the turning point when Malays were seen to enter the city centre and play the role of land administrators. These changing patterns can be seen particularly in the greater KL city centre development. Colonisation had imprinted a form of centralised administration in the city centre. Hospitals and schools were constructed to support local population growth. Social activities between different races were seen to be rather a part of a healthier daily life.

Dynamic public spaces were constructed to be part of the urban form. Greater appreciation of the public place was expanded, whereby the physical and social functions are elements that provide pleasure, safety and care to urban users (Lynch 1960; Abdul Latip et al. 2010).

Kuala Lumpur has been a colonial administrative centre in the 1880s and such historical layerings and legacies can be observed on closer inspection of the city fabric and forms. These include swampy and uneven grounds which were turned into settled lands, including one plot immediately to the west of the Klang River which was then levelled and drained to be used as a training ground for the police. This patch of land, originally named the Parade Ground, would become the *Padang*. Ten years later, in 1892, the Acting British Resident Ernest Birch who was a keen cricketer started to smooth over the ground so that it might be used as a cricket ground and for other sports. The urban tradition of city management set by the British had provided basic administrative foundations and turned the city into a financial and commercial catalyst.

The post-Independence years saw a rapid rate of development as people from rural areas flocked to the city centre to occupy the areas left by the British. This was also contributed to by the government policy to urbanise the city centre and become more modern. The influence of the ruling political government took the form of overseeing the growth of the city centre. More modernised buildings were constructed to boost economic growth and attract investors. Lines of transportation were then improved to link the city centre to more outskirt areas. Housing developments were constructed comprising landed properties and low-cost high-rise residential developments to serve all states of socioeconomic status. High-rises were located within the city centre, and adjacent to most administrative offices. Farther away, landed residential developments were constructed. Only recently, after 2000, was there a return of the urban pattern of erecting high-rise residential buildings and filling in the missing urban pockets in the city centre.

Presently, Kuala Lumpur is a city with a combination of all kinds of social activities, from residential to economic activities, all in one place. In recent years, a few important structures, notably the Petronas Twin Towers and KL Tower, have been added which have significantly altered the character of Kuala Lumpur's skyline. However, the organic growth of Kuala Lumpur and particularly the recent rapid growth and scattering of new urban development within the city centre has resulted in a city with no planned formal large-scale visual structures. The linear nature of the old city and its small-scale grid patterns has created some smaller view corridors and axes. Generally, for the city centre, the broader visual linkages are not well developed.

Apart from the larger-scale metropolitan parks and forest reserves, there are some plazas and smaller parks such as Merdeka Square and the KLCC parklands that are major contributors to the amenities of the city. However, there are many areas in the city where there is a lack of spaces such as urban parks and open spaces, especially within the city centre, district and neighbourhood centres. Places for informal civic uses and cultural performances can help to bring life back onto the streets and provide opportunities for street artists to display their skills. A part from the open spaces and pocket parts, notably at Taman Titiwangsa and Jalan Masjid India, there is a need to look into the adequacy of such amenities in a growing tropical metropolis, which must reflect a 'sense and image' of the tropical city.

Present Deficiencies

Another deficiency, especially in the city centre, is the lack of pedestrian linkages. In some instances, the activities of unlicensed hawkers and vendors encroach onto pedestrian walkways and some buildings do not permit public access across their property boundaries, thus leaving little or no space for pedestrian movement. In recent years, there has been a gradual improvement in the provision of pedestrian linkages in newer buildings, but the shortcomings of earlier development remain. Similarly, not many buildings provide pedestrians with proper protection from the sun and rain. In recent cities such as Putrajaya it too suffered from what was essentially an imported model of 'the garden in the city' template inspired by the early ideas of Ebenezer Howard. Yet such ideas was not tropicalised for the region. Hence the present effects of this urbanism model are felt not only in terms of carbon emissions in the city due to long travel distances, but the increasing levels of urban heat island due to lack of shade and wider, larger exposure to the sun. The increase in open paved spaces and increased skyview factors have brought some unintended effects in the long term. In tropical cities such as Kuala Lumpur, the optimal width-to-height ratio of street canyons to take advantage of self-shading physical structures is 1:3 (Salleh 2006). Additionally, there is better shading of the street spaces if they are oriented in a north–south orientation pattern (Salleh 2006). This must bring forward a reassessment and rethinking of imported models of urbanism and urban planning, which must 'be tropicalised' with heightened interest and integration of local patterns and models.

Various microclimatic researchers have also reported on the urban heat island effects of Putrajaya, whether through a general survey of comfort of occupants and workers or through a measured study of the surrounding daily morning and night temperatures (Shahidan et al. 2012), and a few studies on the boulevard have recorded urban comfort conditions over the adaptive thermal comfort range for tropical residents. A recent article, 'Putrajaya is 5 degree[s] hotter than other local cities' in the *Star*, Malaysia, from 19 June 2007 reported that:

> *It was revealed that Putrajaya is 5 degree[s] hotter than other cities in Malaysia, … while we cannot stop concrete jungles from being built, a simple strategy to avoid the UHI phenomenon is to plant large shady trees.*

The Modernist City Versus the Tropical City

Schumacher (1971) interestingly argues that the twentieth-century city can perhaps be described as a spectrum that ranges or diverges into two extremes in concept: on the one hand is the idea of the traditional city, one that emphasises walkable elements such as corridor streets, grids, plazas and squares, and on the other extreme is the idea of the modern 'city in the park', which is essentially the idea of a city filled with high-rise blocks set apart from each other. Essentially this phenomenon can be seen in Kuala Lumpur and its satellite cities, in which sealed air-conditioned buildings sit amidst hot, humid developments and urban space. The notion of public space here is dissimilar to that in more temperature countries; activities increasingly occur indoors, sealed off from the intensity of the climate outside. Under these circumstances, public spaces in such tropical areas have evolved into what has been described by Ghirardo (1996) as how

> *public space constitutes the spatialised realization of the public sphere. The public sphere … refers to the setting in which citizens engage specifically in political participation, and indeed … this is essential for democratic political practices. … What we often see as publicly accessible spaces – theme parks, shopping malls, festival market places – are more appropriately described as social space.*

In the tropics, the conditions above are multiplied many times over, as the hot, humid outdoors is increasingly shunned by an urbanised public. Translated as everyday experience, it means there is a distinct disjuncture between the hot, humid outside and cool, serviced environments inside. When translated into the Asian context of tropical cities, city folks and urbanites encounter, with increasing frequency, the rupture between the dry, cool, internal environments of such modern blocks and the hot, humid outdoors, and as the heat island effect takes place, the contrast is significantly felt as more acute. As cool indoor environments become more highly serviced and free from pollution, the hotter and more polluted outdoors is an environment from which the pedestrians or city dwellers seem to do their best to escape.

Hence as Asian cities develop and nations urbanise, urban patterns which seem to mimic the Modernist ideas from more temperate climates result in increasing carbon-lock-in effects of rising energy and carbon emissions. What is emphasised is the individual 'super-block' rising amidst an efficient network of roads and superhighways. The trajectory of the urban populace is always from outdoors into indoor serviced environments as they jump from air-conditioned cars and air-conditioned public transportation systems into highly serviced indoor environments. Those of the professional classes occupy gleaming, highly serviced high-rises that proliferate in the city centre, while the average urban dweller thus becomes more and more divorced from the outdoor urban spaces.

A Climatic Idealisation of the Tropical Metropolis

The tropical urbanism of the past is infused with corridor streets, permeated with five-foot walkways. Yet new cities can be described as transplanted idealisations in which the traditional parts of the city are rapidly decreasing and even rarely discussed as part of the city's history. Similarly there are several disparate *Kampung* islands in Kuala Lumpur, yet these have increasingly become islands of marginal traditions within an increasingly dense and massive construction of concrete and glass within the urban fabric.

Yeang (1984) had once envisioned the tropical city as urban blocks and densities connected by verandah ways and covered boulevards. He perhaps aptly prophesied a city, based on his ecological dictums, which must consider the issue of comfort in order to increase its permeability, walkability and liveability. To support a 'walkable' city under tropical conditions, climate and comfort remain the main issues. Although a compact city may have a denser urban fabric and narrower canyons, the reduced airflow between buildings will be acute. Traditional ideas related to 'urban shade' must be explored, and standards related to the level of adaptive outdoor comfort conditions can be implemented. The traditional principles of increased eave projection and projections of verandah-like spaces with shading must be reworked into the higher densities, finer urban grain and narrower streets of sustainable tropical cities and implemented within morphological characteristics of traditional patterns and urban forms of the past. The more organic character of old townships must be explored as the overall impact of the self-shading of buildings will be higher. Narrower distance between buildings not only create a self-shading mechanism to the city.

Psychologically, it exude a feeling and perception of safety at the human pedestrian level when buildings has entrances open up to these walkways. The height of the buildings will need control to respect the human scale in giving the feeling of enclosure to the pedestrian. The human scale and human level of visual perception, the incentive to walk involves a psychological factor as one perceives less of a possibility of encountering speeding vehicles as pathways or urban canyons are narrower.

A Reconceptualisation of the Sustainable Metropolis in the Tropics

A city built on a more sustainable model can perhaps be conceptualised as the complete reverse of the 'city in the park'; which is generally composed of isolated buildings and will present a city experience to the pedestrian that emphasises 'building volumes' rather than the spaces between buildings. Such experiences are characteristic of more historic towns and such cultural spaces have physical, cultural and perceptual attributes (Yoke Lai et al. 2013) that generate sociocultural and economic vitality. In realising the goals of low-carbon frameworks in cities, the overall approach cannot ignore the contribution of local cultural modes and morphologies of more traditional urban spaces in history which did not grow from the freedom of private vehicle use and hence can affect the carbon equation. To achieve such low-carbon targets, individual buildings and spaces between buildings, and as well as the urban city model, must be considered. The Malay vernacular urban form and architecture play a role as these traditional type-forms have grown from the locality. Although the Malay vernacular is often related to a simple house elevated off the ground, its morphology and spaces can be extended into urban forms, with semi-outdoor spaces that better respond to the diurnal variation of climate throughout the day. Such climatic characteristics have given rise to urban forms which are improved and naturally attuned, organic extensions or growths of the character and intensities of the climate.

The very notion of the local vernacular essence suggests elevated structures and architecture which, in turn, suggests a city form that departs from sealed building blocks as concrete masses stamped onto plots of lands. Rather, the city must recall the fragmentation of organic morphologies infused with the climatic ethos of the Malay traditions in which pathways and semi-open areas are elements that punctuate city form, with pathways and roads around the ground level of cities. These can be perceived as an open continuous space connecting both the horizontal and vertical movement of people where there are insertions and walkways with covered pathways through buildings and blocks. This can also be punctuated by the vertical, such as nodes of pocket parks and urban courtyards integrated naturally into the fabric of the city. Under equatorial conditions, such pockets or punctuations of air can be ventilated by diverting the downward flow of air from the higher levels of a multistorey building to the more stagnant strata of air-conditioning at ground level. Past studies of trends in urban airflow and bioclimatic data have shown that air stagnates within the lower levels of urban pathways including any enclosed plazas or courtyards.

Hence high-rise structures can be viewed and treated three-dimensional urban forms with a climatic function and purpose. They can be strategically placed to ventilate the tropical urban 'corridors' and pathways, rather than merely consertions. Interspersed with plazas they can be seen as outdoor rooms, srategies that allow the city to breathe. Hence urban form is valued and optimised for its urban microclimatic impact, city form is optimised to extract from the ambient climate the necessary energies, such as diversion of higher-level winds for thermal comfort on the pedestrian level and the shadowing of pedestrian walkways and thoroughfares at critical times of the day.

The key criterion is comfort to the pedestrian. This includes a metropolis in which large structures optimised for shaded outdoor space and optimum windflow are planned for comfort. Bioclimatic devices can harvest and divert cleaner and faster air at higher levels down to the humid ground space which may be blocked by continuous low-rise building blocks. Semi-public areas in the tropical region are typically open on all sides and these extend the spaces underneath buildings into a conducive permeable area that is thermally comfortable in the city. The dominance of cultural intentions within the making of architectural form must be seen in the context of the necessity of Asian cities to create a recognisable identity for its urban spaces and cityscape while complying with rising standards of sustainability. The semi-open spaces, the open plan layout, multifunctionality of spaces, family intimacy and spatial intimacy should be identified as the key influential sociocultural factors to be embodied in the city as a result of the study of vernacular architecture, which is a generational result of the confluences of the climatic, cultural and religious life of the people. The fusion of the decorative, ornamented with recessed projections and openings, and shading are strategies that not only achieve their respective thermal, daylight and energy-saving reductions in terms of building operational performance and lifecycle annual carbon emission, but a distinctive language and identity of the city.

'Low-Carbon' City Form the Future

The future target of a low-carbon city in the dense urban tropics must combine identity goals with sustainable targets. Hence it must constitute a move towards deriving a basis of form derived from local climatic principles the challange is using place-identity as an associative strategy towards a climatic & low-carbon agenda. This not only includes city that targets the reduction of energy consumed by individual buildings, but the aim must be to increase the walkability of cities in order to reduce carbon emissions by the 'business-as-usual' activities of private vehicle usage and travel. Culturally, this coincides with strategies that can support economic growth in diverse sectors including tourism. Traditional principles, founded upon the abstraction of history and local tradition, will contribute to economic growth as the city, at ground level, becomes a source of historical and cultural reference for past vocabularies and values.

In contrast, in the cities of the Western world, the green movement has evolved an increasingly 'anti-city' stance, meaning the conventional concept of cities is replaced by walkable neighborhoods and green urbanism.

For example, in recent studies conducted comparing four factors – drivable versus walkable location, traditional construction versus green building, single-family versus multifamily housing, and conventional versus hybrid vehicles – it was found that while the above factors have had a measurable impact on sustainability, there was no strategy that produced nearly as much impact as 'walkability' in reducing the carbon consumption or output of a city. In car-dependent areas of a city, transportation energy use had consistently overwhelmed total building energy use, including residential household energy use. In a typical city, as much as 70 percent of carbon emissions is derived from the effects of non-renewable energy transportation. Hence, a number of cities with a comparatively lower per capita carbon footprint in the Western world have moved rapidly to reduce their dependence on private vehicles. Cities with old heritage urban fabric such as Paris have been particularly effective as they have resident populations and enjoy support from a large percentage of the inhabitants. In other major cities in the Western world, there is actually a reversal of trends in automobile dependence, as younger populations in the range of 25–34 years of age are increasingly choosing those cities with vibrant urban cores defined by mixed use, greater density, opportunities for connectivity, and a balance among transportation modes (walking, biking, buses, and cars). Such trends are similarly reflected in the outer suburbs of Kuala Lumpur, in which new suburbs with excellent connectivity and walkability such as Mont Kiara and Desa Sri Hartamas have seen their land and property values accelerate, due to the marker forces and preferences of the younger professionals for the everyday connectivity they offer.

Increasingly, quality of life is also related to another factor: health. In new emerging cities in Asia, the driving force for the growing population of young professionals is the critical link between health and the city form. Past research that links health and cities has suggested that characteristics and features of the built environment such as low density, poor connectivity, and the lack of linkages have been associated with decreased physical activity and an increased likelihood of health risks, including the risk of being overweight. As the World Health Organisation (WHO) has claimed, obesity is 'the epidemic of the 21st century', and with the prevalence of obesity increasing since the 1980s, (according to 2005 WHO statistics, at least 400 million adults were obese worldwide; this figure will increase by 300 million to 700 million in 2015), researchers have essentially found links with aspects of the local external environment and the growing interest in how physical inactivity, obesity, and chronic health problems are affected by external environmental factors. Future ecologic and environmental models will recognize the importance of both physical and social environments as determinants of long-term health and urban form factors such as (1) a population widely dispersed in low-density residential development; (2) rigid separation of homes, shops, and workplaces; (3) a lack of distinct, thriving activity centers, such as active commercial cores or centers; and (4) a network of roads marked by large block size and poor access from one place to another. These have become crucially important as a determinant of the health of urban populations.

References

Abdul Latip, N. S., Shamsudin, S., & Liew M. S. (2010, January). Evaluation on the functional dimensions of the contextual integration at Kuala Lumpur Waterfront. *Asian Journal of Environment-Behaviour Studies, 1*(Maiden issue), 9–23. ISSN 1394-0384.

Cerin, E., Saelens, B. E., Sallis, J. F., & Frank, L. D. (2006). Neighborhood environment walkability scale: Validity and development of a short form. *Medicine and Science in Sports and Exercise*, 1682–1691. https://doi.org/10.1249/01.mss.0000227639.83607.4d.

Evers, H.-D., et al. (2000). *Southeast Asian urbanism: The meaning and power of social space*. Münster: LIT Verlag.

Evers, H.-D. (2011). Urban symbolism and the new urbanism of Indonesia. In P. J. M. Nas (Ed.), *Cities full of symbols. A theory of urban space and culture* (pp. 287–296). Leiden: Leiden University Press.

Frausto. (2011). *Superkampung: The densest, liveliest and most diverse*. http://www.theberlage.nl/galleries/projects/details/superkampung

Ghirardo. (1996). *Architecture after modernism*. London: Thames and Hudson.

Gullick, J. M. (1990). The growth of Kuala Lumpur and of the Malay community in Selangor before 1880. *Journal of the Malaysian Branch of the Royal Asiatic Society, 63*(1 (258)), 15–38.

Jacobs, J. (2016). *The death and life of Great American cities*. New York: Vitage Books ed.
Karuppannan, S., Zainul, M. B, Sivam, A., & Daniels, C. B. (2014). Urban green space and urban biodiversity: Kuala Lumpur, Malaysia. *Journal of Sustainable Development, 7*(1), issn 1913-9063 E-ISSN 1913-9071. Published by Canadian Center of Science and Education. https://doi.org/10.5539/jsd.v7n1p1.
Lai, Y., et al. (2013). The role of cultural spaces in Malaysia's historic towns: The case of Kuala Dungun and Taiping. *Elsevier Procedia-Social and Behavioral Sciences, 85*, 602–625.
Lynch. (1960). *The image of the city*. Cambridge/London, UK: MIT Press.
Salleh, E. (2006). 'Tropical urban street canyons', Chapter 11. In J. H. Bay & B. L. Ong (Eds.), *Tropical sustainable architecture: Social and environmental dimensions*. London: Architectural Press. ELSEVIER (ISBN 0-7506-6797-4).
Schumacher, T. (1971). Contextualism, urban ideals and deformations. *Casabella,* (359–360), 79–86.
Shahidan, M. F., Jones, P. J., Gwilliam, J., & Salleh, E. (2012). An evaluation of outdoor and building environment cooling achieved through combination modification of trees with ground materials. *Building and Environment, 58*, 245–257.
Yeang. (1984). Notes for a critical vernacular in contemporary Malaysian architecture. UIA International Architect, No. 6. London, pp. 16–17.

11

Urban Syncretism: Conscious and Unconscious Architectural Formation of National Identity

Shireen Jahn Kassim and Zumahiran Kamaruddin

Introduction

Syncretism has always been a phenomenon across civilisations, and its recurring nature attests to the fact that the multicultural and multireligious nature of civilisations have always cross-bred and congeal into physical expression and nuances in traditions artefacts and the built environment, including urban-architectural form. It is either consciously invoked the fusion of elements, on unconsciously fused in patterns and devices of art & architectural language in order to forge two or more identities. Elements from two or more distinctly different cultures with different meanings, semantics and vocabularies are fused to forge a new language. In some cases, these evolve into a new-found common identity between cultures. Hence syncretism, which some may define as how 'two opposed forces unify when facing a third …' (Leopold 2001), can broadly be understood as how two or more seemingly widely divergent or different traditions, cultures, beliefs and civilisations with widely divergent

S. Jahn Kassim (✉) • Z. Kamaruddin
International Islamic University Malaysia, Kuala Lumpur, Malaysia

© The Author(s) 2018

S. Jahn Kassim et al. (eds.), *Modernity, Nation and Urban-Architectural Form*,
https://doi.org/10.1007/978-3-319-66131-5_11

expressions can unite to produce a third form of expression. In the more traditional polities and cultural forms of the past, a ruler or a monarch may envision a fusion of cultures as in way to breed a common bond between different tribes and races in an empire. He would see the potential of urban-architectural form as a tool of unification. The capacity of such syncretic language lies in its ability to physically express the idealism of sociopolitical, and at times religious, goals. Form symbolises an underlying perennial search for unity and 'national identity', which has taken on many forms and expressions throughout the ages, and the idealism of co-existence between different socio-religious communities.

An example is the Mughal Empire, within which Indian and Arab-Persian elements were used as formal devices to fuse the meanings of the differing forms and traditions. Formal devices were used as a syncretic means, including brackets and capitals fusing expression from different traditions, with corbels and archways from the Indian traditions. Shaukatt, Denan and Jahn Kassim (2014, p. 75) observed the syncretism of the enigmatic buildings in Fatehpur Sikri, the metropolis & complex built by Akbar: 'The Diwani Khas's architectural form was influenced by ... Gujerat, Persia and resonated with ... India. Example of features (with multiple influences) are the ... plan, lantern ceiling, corbelled pendentices, pillars, three-tiered brackets, *chajjas*, ... and lotus shaped finials,' and '... a prominent example of (Indian) indigenous influences is the serpentine bracket and the *chajja*.' One recalls also the fusion of multiple devices and forms with references to both Islamic and Western elements as found in the renowned and central Ducal Palace, now a key landmark of Venice, which was described by Crinson (1996, pp. 51–53): 'The greatest example of what Ruskin saw, as the coming together of northern and southern cultures was the Ducal Palace, Venice. In Ruskin's words ... the building was a glorious ethnic hybrid... Ruskin's geological metaphor ... smuggles in the idea of racial mixture or hybridity, as the very sources of architectural achievement ... For Ruskin, the city of Venice ... was the progeny of a coital struggle between races, and its most representative building, the Ducal Palace, was a mogrel refinement and fusion of all that was best in its threefold parentage ...' In China, the nation's imperial past also gave rise to a range of syncretic forms and traditions. On closer inpsection, its key monuments, display evidence of fusion and representations of its position, in past eras, as a multicultural empire. Yi (1989, 2000) relates this to the traditional and monumental architecture of imperial China, and Ding highlights the point as part of a legacy of critical architecture of China, stating that it is a project that created a new cultural type beyond tradition and modernism:

> *The Garden Square Pagoda is a new public cultural type, neither private nor imperial.*

In the famed Fatehpur Sikri, of Agra, India, the syncretic strategy of Akbar was a path towards 'national identity' due to its culturally and spiritually diverse population. Akbar aimed at uniting this diversity by syncretical form-reflecting, fusing & combining Hindu and Arab-Persian architectural elements into a single continuum. Urban and architectural form became a tool for eliciting a synchronous ideal of unity. It was a monumental instrument of the state. Form was used to disseminate and embody such aspirations. Akbar, in the fifteenth and sixteenth centuries, orchestrated a new architectural language to embody an ideal. Jahn Kassim and Nawawi (2016) discuss how Le Corbusier used the varied-forms of the pavilions and courtyards of Sikri as a seed for the language of the Chandigarh, inflecting it with a new formal dynamism in a fusion of layout and climatic elements of both urban space & key buildings. Shaukat et al. (2014) discuss such fusion in terms of a vocabulary of two different cultures – the Indian-Janain and the Arab-Islamic – employed as new forms of language it was a form of 'national identity' and form was a means to unite two major cultures, races and religions in an empire. Shaukat et al. (2014) also highlight how the elements of Sikri were part of a process of 'modernisation' and 'syncretisation' at the same time. During its era, it represented a powerful visual communication tool, in which different physical expression of different cultures were brought together into an orchestration of form. Such syncretism is used towards embodying the ideal of co-existence by not veering overtly or dominantly towards either culture.

> *The buildings of Fatehpur Sikri show a synthesis of various regional schools of architectural craftsmanship such as Gujarati and Bengali. … the indigenous craftsman from various parts of the empire were used for the construction of the*

buildings. Influences from Hindu and Jaina architecture are seen hand in hand with Islamic elements. Akbar's great interest in craft and technology became a source of encouragement … the artisans, architects and builders from all parts of the country were allowed to express their designs freely under the Emperor['s] supervision. The bracket and chhajja were, by far, the most important constituent[s] of such syncretic facade composition in Fatehpur Sikri architecture. Chhajja was essentially required to protect from the scorching tropical climate, that is the sun and rain, and to provide the necessary shadings, and bracket was used to support it.

Syncretism in Vernacular Architecture

Key aristocratic structures of the Malay world during the 1800s and 1900s also reflected syncretic, yet it was an 'unconscious' outcome. This syncretism was the result of extensive and age-old trade networks and diplomatic gestures – reflected different variations of hybridity along the peninsular and its water ways. At the same time, the absorption of new technology in the form of hybridisation of new Neoclassical and Georgian stylisation began in the colonial era and reflected the pervasive influence of colonial presense on the local context. The late 1800s and early 1900s were seen as a 'watershed' era in which the local social structure came under pressure from modernisation due to the extension of colonial control and influence. Malay palaces were the barometers of such change – form essentially rescaled and refined versions from the vernacular. In the 1800s and 1900s, under growing colonial presence, elements of external cultures because fused with the dominant vocabulary of the local Malay style. One key example is the *Balai Besar* or Audience Hall, in Alor Setar, Kedah, built by Sultan Muhammad Jiwa Zainal Adilin Shah (1710–1760), the first Sultan of Kedah, at times also known as the *Balai Penghadapan* or Grand Audience Hall. It is essentially a structure built in front of the main Kedah Royal palace, called the *Istana Pelamin,* where ministers reported to the Sultan on government matters and where official meetings were held. The original timber-based building took several years to complete and was finished in 1735. It then evolved into a form of unconscious syncretised architecture, as different elements and influences were gradually fused with external influences in the form of vocabulary and elements, and later a British vocabulary, designed to elevate the language of the palace from a simple building with a projection into a transnational 'dignitaries' palace.

The front portion of *Balai Besar*, Kedah – the tropicality and syncretic aspects of a northern Malay palatial form and language of the late 1800s

The original structure of the hall was built in 1735 was essentially a timber palace, reflecting the classical Malay form of the *bumbong panjang* or long pitched roof, with post-and-beam language and vocabulary. Kedah had then faced several attacks from foreign forces. The attacks by the Thais and the neighbouring Bugis forces were mainly for political reasons and caused the original building to be severely damaged. The first attack came from the Siamese because Kedah delayed delivery of the *Bunga Emas* to Bangkok in 1767. After these challenging times, the gradual syncretisation processes saw the absorption of neighbouring elements into the decorative language of the palace without losing its Malay archetypical form. A key element is how the roof still resonates in the form of the Riau-based 'double' pitched roof. The frontage of regularly spaced double-height columns resembling a large-scale veranda protrusion recalls the archetypal Malay vernacular house set on stilts, and its quintis-sential wide open-air projection. The strong influence of Thai traditions is notable in its roof finials in which the cross finials of Riau origin were merged with the 'ogee'-like curve of a perpendicular finial enclosing a *selembayung* ornamental motif. Though the motif is Malay, the form of the dominant finial recalls the *makara* forms of Thai roof embellishments. Neoclassical designs and Palladian motifs were later integrated into the structure, as a reflection of the growing British control as Kedah formally came under British 'non-Federated Malay states' administration in the late 1800s. The structure was still surmounted by a *Bumbung Panjang* roof, and in later years, the *Balai Besar* was further improved and reno-vated, with craftsmen utilising an eclectic mix of Malay, Javanese, Thai and colonial influences. In the late colonial period, the 'unconscious' syn-cretic form was a vibrant amalgamation of both local and external mod-erning forces demonstrated by the surreptitious influence of the Georgian and Victorian styles, Renaissance arches, sweeping Viennese staircases and a Malay/Thai roof.

The architecture of the *Balai Besar* was a reflection of the forces of power in the region. Later Siam had forged closer relations with Kedah and in later periods, both nations had welcomed an era of close political and cultural ties. The ornamentations decorating the roof, combining the sharper Riau-based roof finial with the curved finial, reflect the symbolic the link between the Malay center of power and with the center of Siamese civilisation. In addition, the motifs that span the columns sup-porting the roof over the foyers and verandahs are reflected of Siamese traditions in their temples. Colour schemes of yellow and green recall the varnished roofing tiles of palaces and temples of Siam, with slender col-umns reaching a height of over nine metres, with openwork at the joint between the roof and column. Influences from the Regency era and early nineteenth century are found in the metalwork of the staircase. The cast iron staircase recalls similar decorative forms from Glasgow with geo-metrical forms and floral details derived from the classical repertoire known as the *Rinceau* design. Column capitals on the upper floor recalled Victorian-style cast iron columns – possibly modelled by styles in neigh-

Fig. 11.1 Roof forms and finials that recall influence of Thai architecture

bouring Penang – but regionalised with the Malay *sulor paku* motif – eight pieces of local fern patterns carved from wood were secured to the plain column capital with two nails each around the octagonal cross-section of the column. The *kerawang* and the 'star motif' as shown in Fig. 11.1 were symbols of the dynamic interaction of Thai and Malay culture. The roof finials not only depict the 'scissor-form' of Malay Riau palaces but also the *kranok* forms of Thai palaces and temples. The *kranok* represents a recognisable pattern hinting local cultures to Thai symbolism; it recalls the form of a mythical creature – the *makara* – with its head turned up and facing away from the roof, fused with the form of a 'flame' or 'fire shooting from a dragon's mouth'. In this palace, features the Thai *kranok* form was evoked and syncretically combined with the *selembayung* motif of Malay culture. The sun motif or 'La Dawandi' refers to a medal conferred by King Chulalongkorn on the late Sultan Abdul Hamid of Kedah in 1895, and the motif on the roof gable in the form of the sun's rays was a singular commemoration of this event. The two brackets ornamenting each column around the Viennese staircase and in the *Balai Lepau* reflected a triangular form, of local floral pattern (Fig. 11.2).

In short, localised elements of the Malay syncretic language evolved into the palatial scale reflecting traditional archetypes in a type of wood carving in what is known as the traditional *sesiku* (ornamental bracket), also known as *sesiku keluang*.

Fig. 11.2 The columns of the portico showing syncretism between Malay vegetal motifs, Victorian-style columns and Siamese traditions

The Syncretic *Melaka* Style

From the fifteenth century, as a result of the growth of *Melaka* as an entrepôt in South East Asia, trade and diplomatic relations resulted in Chinese delegates, had expanded and strengthened culture of syncretism between two nations evolved into a new style, known as the *Melaka* 'Peranakan' style. Its syncretic architecture is also a result of a fusion of two different vocabulary in a consistent style, and later became generally known also as the *Melaka* style. Variants of the vernacular long-roof house with heightened columnar expressions and tall windows facing the front, and balanced with an open verandah (*anjung*) at the entrance of the house are fused with the dominant and curved masonry staircases adorned with multicoloured tiles, typically on the stairs and open long windows. The patterns of the coloured decorative tiles recall Chinese and European influences fused through past trade activities. Hence even today, the *Melaka* houses often feature multicoloured tilings including staircases that are adorned with bright tiles. Chinese motifs such as peony flowers and flora and fauna are clearly featured in the interior design of houses and mosques. A prominent example is such syncretism is the *Rumah*

Penghulu Abdul Ghani (or Abdul Ghani House) in Merlimau, *Melaka* built by Penghulu (Demang) Abdul Ghani bin Penghulu Abdul Majid, who was a trader from Palembang, Indonesia who came to Malaya in 1894. The house, believed to have been constructed in 1894 and is estimated to be around 122 years old, distinctively combines Malay heritage elements, Chinese oriental style and reminiscences of the European vocabulary. The flora and fauna decoration that can be seen applied to the pillars relates to the influence of Chinese ornamental motifs.

The Syncretic Palace of Selangor: An Expression of Modernity of the Early 1900s

Syncretism in form sometimes risks 'synthesising' too many cultural references and elements into one hybrid complex. Yet in some cases, the syncretisation of two vocabularies from two different cultures seems to result in a coherent whole, a new language and consequently, a new identity, in others, there may be elements that are juxtaposed yet not fully syncretised. The *Istana Bandar*, or 'Bandar Palace', in the town of Jugra, Selangor, is an example of a 'conscious' syncretism conceptualised by a Malay leader increasingly aware of the cosmopolitan and multicultural society of new Selangor, which had rapidly boomed due to the economic opportunities afforded by the resources in the locality and the infrastructure provided by the colonialists. Designed and built by the Sultan Alauddin Sulaiman Shah, the reigning 5th Sultan of Selangor, from 1899 to 1905, the Sultan and his family then lived in the 40-room palace for the ensuing 30 years until his demise in 1938. The palace has two structure frontages, one which has an open-air verandah-like space extending from its main masonry structure, and the other façade extending from an audience hall which dually function as a welcoming portico for official events. Overall, the language of the palace is a vibrant syncretis of three cultural references into a simultaneous whole. From the three cultures, there were gestures that recall even other cultures in the region. The main elements were resonating references to Malay, colonial British, Indian and Chinese traditions can be observed. Indian-Mughal elements such as the pinnacles bordering the roof parapets, whose ornamental form echoes the roof finials and turret forms of the Sultan Abdul Samad building – formerly known as the British Colonial administration in Kuala Lumpur – evoke both Indian cultural and British imperial references. While attempting to reference the Chinese elements in its jade-green ventilative blocks, there were distinct references in the roof form to the pitch and form of Malay-Acehnese origins, as the *bumbong panjang* roof is derived from the local Malay archetypical roof. The distinctive pinnacles are influenced by Indian architecture; recall how the 'British imperial' style had affected many of the buildings in its colonised protectorates. In Indian tradition, pinnacles symbolised a reflection & demonstration of 'strength' and protection. Chinese references can be seen in the glazed green tiles of the ventilation blocks interspersed throughout the palace, walls, while the stuccoed patterns of ceilings walls refer to the Greek and classical vocabulary (Fig. 11.3).

Istana Bandar and its syncretic vocabulary

While some may view the overall composition as highly hybrid and eclectic, and the reference to Mughal Indo-Saracenic elements as a copying of British 'Raj' style, it must be highlighted how the British were representative of what was 'dynamic and modern' during the era. The aesthetic intention of the reigning monarchs was not only to represent the 'modern and progressive' but to highlight the possibilities of unification – in the syncretic form – which embodies a multicultural vision and hope – in which formal devices were inset to afford and ensure an almost equal reference to each ethnicity: Malay, Indian and Chinese. The Sultan was known for his cosmopolitanism and as one who would engage with people of many races, and he was active in receiving guests from many countries, including regular visits from British colonial representatives. The style is representative of a vision of unification – in eclecticism was harnessed into a form of national identity. While at first glance the *Istana Bandar* appears more 'imperialised' rather than 'localised', yet it must be seen as an attempt to be 'representative' of rapidly changing times. In this case, the monarch himself was attempting to forge a stylistic form – one that would refer to each culture and which spoke to a range of ethnic 'audiences' within a population. The aim of synthesising multicultural and inclusive vision of architecture – is an alternative to the more imported or externally influenced Neoclassical style – and a brave attempt to express a vision in urban-architectural form. The syncretic approach was made possible in an era of profound change within his state, yet within which a challenge for a more cosmopolitan approach to palatial expression. It was a new language that could provide meaning in a rapidly changing socioeconomic context. It represented the possibility of a multicultural identity for a growing multiracial and multiethnic community. Yet *Istana Bandar* can also be read as an outcome of modernity that assailed Selangor as the centre of colonial government who presided over dominant cultural forces. One can argue that *Istana Bandar* had prophesied the future of Malaysia, which would become a nation formed by a tripartite 'ethnic hybrid'. The palace was reflective of the perennial attempt to balance and unite the three main ethnicities. The *Istana Bandar*, rather than an eclectic Oriental product, struck a tenuous balance between the iconographic elements in almost equal proportions.

It is almost the eclectic version of national identity, the outcome of a threefold parentage – in which the upper roof forms and pilastered ornaments were local Malay forms fused with the distinctive pinnacles of Indian-Mughal origins, while the ventilation block motifs and interior elements are Chinese in an eclectic model. Sultan Alauddin was attempting to offer a new syncretic model and preempted a multicultural Malaysia. As Crinson (1996, p. 277) observes a condition of colonial form in Islamic nations: 'Architecture had to address a number of specific audiences, such as the groups, that provided its funding or intended users of the building ... in its attempt to address myriad audiences and to represent different aspirations of clients ...'

The language and form still resonate a vernacular essence. Elements recalled Malay roots particularly in terms of its roof treatments and forms – modelled after the *bumbung limas*. Its roof form strengthens and locks the whole structure – yet helps to maintain its link to the root culture. While finials and decorative eaves recall Malay references, certain formed gestures subtly recalled the stupa forms of Buddhist traditions. Such treatments symbolise such multicultural references, with must be references seen as a unique trait of South East Asian form, even occasionally recalling motif of a mythical dragon originating from China and Hindu Buddhist elements in their syncretic form and style.

The 'Vernacular' Archetype

Throughout such changes and syncretic forces of the era, some of the characteristics of classical traditions still persist. The Malay aristocratic form – like the vernacular house form – appears as a 'natural growth' amidst its topography, climate, ecology and geography. This archetypical form of the palatial vernacular is a reflection of the essentially timber-based language of the vernacular with its elevated, columnar character, with decorative variants represented by elements such as decorative eaves, roof finials and filigrees. The roof gable ends, for example, in both house and palace, are decorated by panels in the shape of the blazing sun or ornamented with a carved pattern (*tebuk timbul*) and end in finials in the form of *silang gunting* or crossed scissors. Malay vernacular architecture is defined by key characteristics, yet most prominently figuring archetypically in Malay architecture is the element of the Malay verandah or *serambi*. Ethnic Malays are historically found not only throughout the peninsula of West Malaysia, but also in coastal East Malaysia, Brunei, southern Thailand, parts of Sumatra, Java, the Riau Islands and Kalimantan in Indonesia, southern Philippines, and even as far as Colombo, Sri Lanka, and Cape Town, South Africa, the Chams in Cambodia and Vietnam; a recurring element found in all these communities is the verandah or *serambi* representative of the culture of hospitability and the tropical need to cool down and experience the evening and night air. The *Sejarah Melayu* (also known as the *Malay Annals*), a seventeenth-century text on the history of Malays, says that for almost 2000 years, the non-stop traffic between India and the archipelago, as well as with China, Champa and Cambodia, provided a multitude of cultural influences through trade, culture and intermarriage. Traditionally Malay society was made up of rulers, warriors, artisans, farmers and seafarers with a close-knit feudal organisation that reflected sharp divisions between nobility and commoners. The archetypical 'verandah' and its derivations of *anjung* and *serambi* can be found from the smallest-scale house to the larger-scale palace.

The adaptations of traditional Malay settlements to the native environment and climate have been quintessentially related to the Malay vernacular house-form which appears as a 'natural growth' amidst its topography, climate, ecology and geography. The prevalent hot, humid climate alongside a jungle-infested inhospitable ecology has shaped a form attuned to its environment from its elevating form, wide openings, layered yet wide protective roofs and linear-like arrangement of spaces. Over time, these developed and were refined as timber-based construction, and artisanal skills were put to the test by the reigning power and the wealthiest patronage of the land presiding over the largest construction undertaking: the Sultanate and the palace. Variants of the vernacular palace abound, yet its cultural form is a generic outcome of evolving technology, forms, techniques and innovations that grew from the land, but later included foreign technology. Whether house or palace, variants abound in its form and expression including elevational characteristics – full-height windows, decorative walls, wallboards, decorative eaves and finials and ventilative panels – which were all expressed in a variation of decorative motifs reflective of the climate. Interpretations vary from state to state and from region to region yet there are several key defining attributes and a common denominator.

A persistent element of the vernacular reflective of the culture and lifestyle of the Malays is the *serambi* or *anjung* (the Malay verandah). This refers to the characteristic outdoor room or large protruding verandah that extends significantly from the main body of the house or main spaces. The Malay word *serambi* means a space that is extended. Although its variants differ across different states, essentially the *serambi* is a covered but open outdoor portico in which the host or owner of the house can sit and entertain guests and/or relax and enjoy the evening and night air. After eating, the people would sit on the porch to chat, relax, lie down and have supper. At times, the *serambi* extends to the left and right parts of the house and the space is extended adjacent to the main room. It is typically lower than the main room, distinguished by finishing with the surrounding wall or pole position for each corner. It is a symbol that evolved from a culture of hospitality and decorum towards receiving guests. Forms reflect a culture through centuries of attunement with the prevailing climate and the culture and lifestyle of the traditional population.

Beside the Straits of *Melaka*, the colonial-Malay aristocratic regions were also subject to subtle influences of Chinese and Arabian traders throughout time. Their cultural nuances and elements appear in built structures, yet their overall external built and formal expression remained in the Malay vernacular essence. As the decades progressed, forms of structures including palaces and their architectural expression changed and modernised and began embodying a kind of hybridity. The shifts of power within Malay society occurred and their sociopolitical systems were gradually subsumed under full control of the colonialists. Such dynamics constitute a quagmire of forces that exerted themselves in the social, political and physical fabric of society and gradually became inscribed as part of the palatial elements of language and aesthetic expression which can be argued as the monumental vernacular of the times.

In the *Rumah Panglima Ghani*, the layout plan is typical of a generic Malay house which is divided into three main areas, clearly demarcated with supporting spaces for public area, semi-private and private space. The public area was designed through an open verandah or *serambi* and it was known as the place to hold meetings to discuss community affairs raised among the villagers. In the present final form of the house, the syncretisation is also found in the built-in Victorian style bench between two pillars for the guest to rest while waiting to meet the Penghulu. The row of the bench created ample space in the middle and is comfortably fit for cross-legged sitting. The decorative timber balustrade along the perimeter allows natural cross-ventilation throughout the verandah.

The *Melakan* style is a variant, and a significant element of this style and vocabulary is the grand staircase. The multicoloured Chinese-made tiles create the sense of warm welcoming hospitality for the guests. Its main house or *Rumah Ibu* is separated by a unique pair of decorative doors with Chinese-influenced dragon wood carving as a motif. Floral motifs of birds in the head doors, windows and couches highlight the richness of craftsmanship of Chinese Peranakan.

A unique element of this house is the elemental woodcarving fitted as a panel and in a form of *pola pemidang* (frame pattern) with *awan larat* design. This decorative panel is placed directly below the roofline and seems to serve merely as a decorative screen at the open spaces or welcoming porches like *serambi* and *anjung*, which are typically found in traditional Malay houses in the northern region of Peninsula Malaysia. A type of embellishment is also found in the states of Perak and Kedah, the Malay royal palaces of the Northern Malay Peninsula. It reflects the degree of external influence on form and elemental composition, motif and colour scheme. The design and syncretic fusion also reflect the colonists' adoption (in the colonial era) of their architectural style in local buildings (on a micro or macro scale) modified to the climatic context by maintaining the vernacular style. There are nuances of Palladian and Neoclassical motifs and the Art Deco style which has resulted in a hybrid edition of architectural elements and motifs.

The 1980s

In the modern era of the 1970s and the 1980s, modern forms of syncretic architecture with vernacular nuances can be found in the early high-rises. The language of the Plaza IBM recalls the tropical regionalist forms of the 1970s and 1980s by tropical architects such as Maxwell Fry and Jane

Drew. It recalls Ken Yeang's theories on the environmental filter, which was used as a 'general armature for design ideas' and acted as a guiding framework to implement design elements and principles for the design of the high-rise based on climate in the tropical context. It was aimed at highlighting how architectural elements from local traditions can be selected, abstracted and incorporated into new building types.

According to this idea, various elements of the building envelope can be seen as 'modifiers' of the internal climatic environment. Says Yeang (1985):

> *The basic role of the filter analogy is in its basic role in describing the enclosural systems in terms of general systems and functions. The proposition simply provides an analogy that can be used for design synthesis and for use in the analysis and selection based on the local architectural heritage.* (Yeang 1985)

Traditional elements such as the verandah-ways, porches and terraces are 'intermediary enclosural layers' that play an environmental mediating role within the building enclosure:

> *This treatment of the building enclosure as an environmental filter – focuses the attention on the roles of envelope components as modifiers of the internal environment. The 'valve' is used as an analogy – that which regulates the filtering of the undesired climatic elements.* (Yeang 1984)

This 'filter' should function as a 'sieve' to control any interaction between the internal and external climate. 'The filter acts like a sieve that enables selective exchanges between the external climate and the internal climate that are designed to achieve the desired internal conditions' (Yeang 1984). The influence of Yeang's PhD thesis can be clearly seen: the building enclosure is treated as a 'system' which 'interacts' operatively with the external environment. 'The climatic elements are sieved so that certain unwanted influence[s] are excluded while those which are desirable are admitted' (Yeang 1985, p. 47).

In addition to a climatic role, the 'function' of the building enclosure includes how the various internal spaces are used by the building's occupants.

It might even be a systemically operative with the rest of the building or it might facilitate its performance, say in the way the building is utilised by its occupants, or in conjunction with the actual physical valve-functions of the built form in a spatial or even structural way. (Yeang 1984)

This set of ideas was eventually expressed in the Plaza IBM (1984), a high-rise that consists of a 24-storey office tower and a three-storey annex block housing a single-storey restaurant/food court in the lower block linked by a curvilinear bridge. The tower is located in the centre of one of the affluent suburbs of Kuala Lumpur. Adjacent buildings that surround the Plaza IBM include three-storey shophouses and shop offices, linked townhouses and low- and medium-rise condominiums.

Yeang explains the principles involved in the articulation of form:

The building does four things. It sets out to respond by plan and form to the climate. It responds to the requirement for landscaping by introducing planting upwards diagonally across the face of a high-rise built form. It seeks to break away from the conventions of a straight plan, curtain-walled modernist tower block. In terms of urban design, it provides linkages to the surrounding base.

Yeang's initial concept for the building was that of integrating 'open-air' sky gardens at ground level, mid-way and rooftop level of the tropical high-rise. The vegetation was designed as 'climbing the face of the tower'; it begins to ascend from the ground floor garden or landscaped base that surrounds the main tower block. This vertical landscape climbs diagonally up the building in a zig-zag manner across the north and south face of the tower through an escalating system of planter boxes. At mid-way, these planters continue on the opposite face of the building, culminating in a roof garden.

In the initial stages of design, the sun's path, the geometry on the building and the contextual geometry of the site did not coincide. The orientation of the main tower was then adjusted to meet the sun's geometry, leaving subsidiary elements (service cores housing toilets and lifts) oriented towards the geometry of the site. The service cores, fire-escape areas and toilets are located on the hot east and west sides of the tower.

With minimal windows on the façades in order to limit heat gain, the building form consist of the ground floor lobby, the mid-level mezzanine and the rooftop terrace.

The roof basically consists of a concrete structure overshading a rooftop garden. The design was based on a 'sloped' roof form and was intended to recall the traditional slope of the roof of the Malay house. This form is abstracted and synthesised with 'arches' reminiscent of the colonnades of the Chinese shophouse. The roof is basically an environmental filter-like structure which has been adapted to the Z-beam concrete section. The Z-beams are laid at an incline in order to create the 'pitch-roof' form at the top of the tower.

Although it is indicative of Yeang's early ideas on the bioclimatic high-rise and his early affinity for the Modernist Corbusian language, the Plaza IBM also juxtaposes distinctly multiracial elements from both Malay and Chinese traditions. Basically the expression of a reinforced concrete interpretation of pitch forms of a Malay protective overhanging roof demonstrates Yeang's ability to observe key schemata in local tradition and tropical climate and ultimately synthesise the syncretic forms with abstractions from a range of sources and origins. In Yeang's conceptual diagram for the IBM tower, Modernist principles are evoked in the overall organisation: references to the *pilotis* or vertical columns which lift the box up in space while freeing the ground underneath, the use of strip windows, and the roof garden can be found in the ground floor and subsequent upper floors. These are fused with elements taken from the vernacular traditions such as the arched verandah from the traditional Chinese shophouses and the shape of the traditional Malay sloping roof (Figs. 11.3, 11.4, 11.5, 11.6).

Its 'wedge-shaped' floors were intended to create a departure from the typical vertical tower block. A curvilinear bridge connects the main tower block to the lower podium and weaves like a snake over the pedestrianised ground floor, based on an abstraction of the 'weaving' Chinese dragon. Generally these elements inflect and break the crispness and regularity of the main body of the tower.

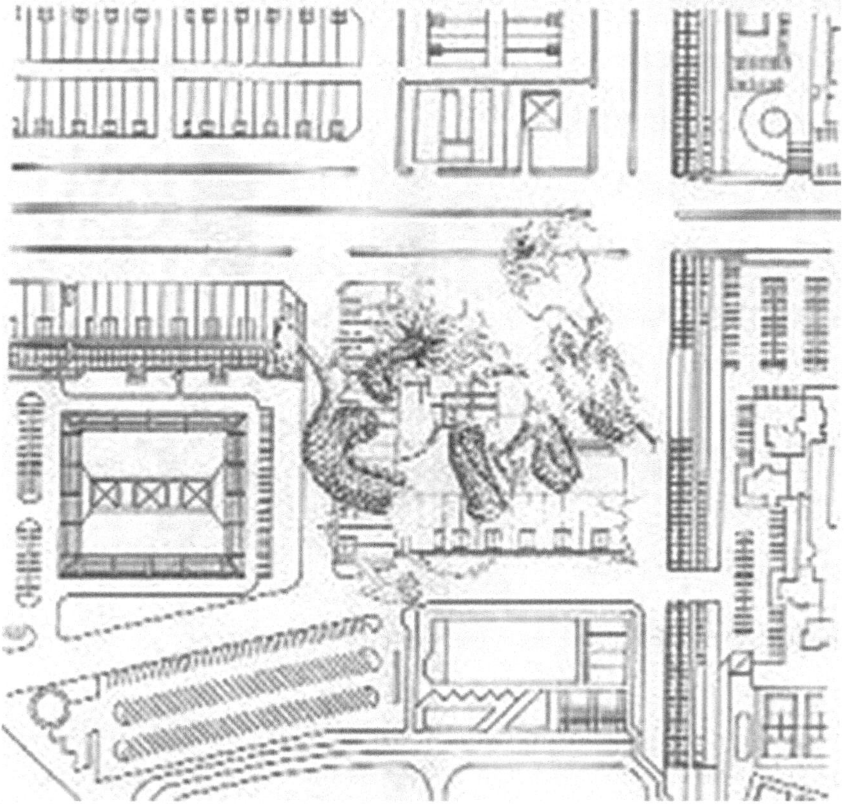

Fig. 11.3 Plaza IBM – the 'dragon' icon superimposed on site plan

The Year 2000 and Beyond

The Petronas Twin Towers is another example of the syncretic form of modern expression. This form now dominates the Kuala Lumpur skyline and is a monument the language of steel and glass, with references to different traditions. The Petronas Towers were built not only as the headquarters of this large national oil corporation, but as a modern icon and cultural landmark for Malaysia. As mentioned earlier, the then Malaysian Prime Minister, Dr Mahathir, saw the construction of the towers as part

Fig. 11.4 The 'iconic' elements in the roofscape of Plaza IBM

of his vision for Malaysia in terms of development and industrialisation, the vision he termed 'Wawasan 2020'. As the design of the towers was supposed to reflect the national aspirations of Malaysia as an industrialising nation, their façade reflected a combination and juxtaposition of elements derived from Malaysia's multicultural traditions. The structural system of the towers consists of a ring of 16 cylindrical columns (made of high-strength reinforced concrete) placed on the inner corners of the star-shaped plan. As the tower ascends, it is set back six times. An inverted three-pinned arch supports the bridge at the centre, designed to accommodate the differential movements of the two towers.

Bunnell (2004) points to the role of the Petronas Twin Towers as an icon of Malaysia's rapid development:

> *The conceptions of Malaysianness and progress are manifested in a single landscape artefact – the highrise. The building is at once a representation of individual taste … as well as broader social and cultural processes, prevailing*

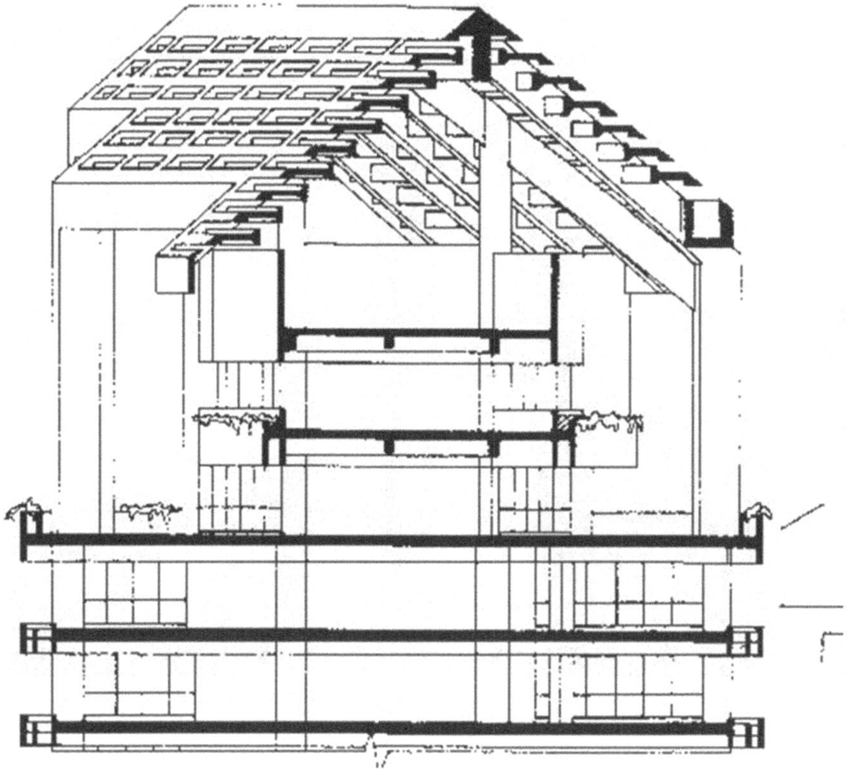

Fig. 11.5 Plaza IBM – roofscape

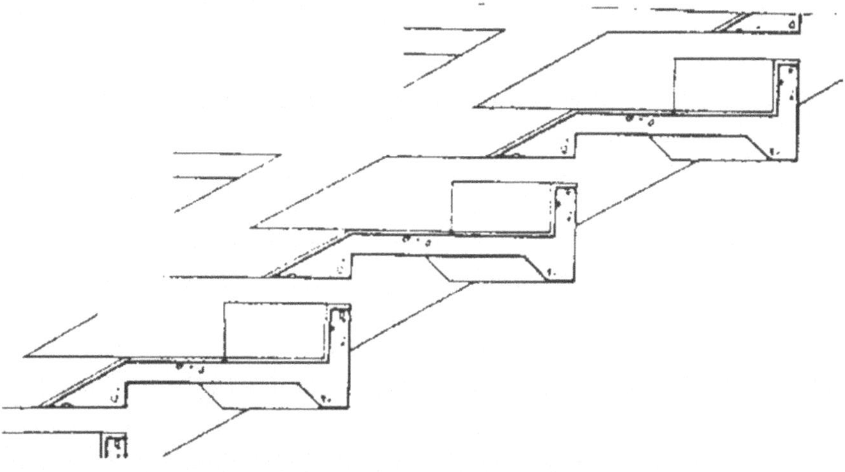

Fig. 11.6 Sectional detail of roof section showing 'filter' elements

Fig. 11.7 The Petronas Towers, Kuala Lumpur

practices and dominant ideas. Official representations of the building, political and commercial, do powerful work in defining an appropriate vision of the nation and a vision of national development.

The twin towers combine a recollection of cultures; recalling the multifarious ethnic traditions of Malaysia through cultural references, including Islamic references. Two intersecting squares based on an eight-point Islamic star motif, are linked to references to other imagery and key traditions that make up the vibrancy of Malaysia. In addition, the outward curve of the wall of each point is said to have an arabesque appearance (Asia Now 2006, p. 63). Cesar Pelli, describes his effort as responding 'to the climate, to the dominant Islamic culture, and to the sense of form and patterning that I could perceive in traditional Malaysian building' (Munro 2000) (Figs. 11.7 and 11.8).

Unintentionally, the final roof profile recalls the layered stupa of Indian-Buddhist traditions, yet the total number of floors, 88 in all,

Fig. 11.8 The Petronas Towers – entrance

recalls Chinese tradition. The layout design and composition of the plan was based on the eight-sided star in Islamic geometry.

Based on a winning entry by César Pelli Associates and selected from an international design it was the winner in a competition held in 1990 in which 20 firms took part. Its form basically comprises two towers, connected by a 'skybridge'. Pelli and Crosbie (2001) link the twin-form to the 'symbolic space' between the towers: an important decision was to make the towers figurative. This resulted in a design that is unabashedly symbolic, announcing its presence as a landmark and a gateway to an important new development.

Pelli explains, at length, the overall concept and underlying significance of the 'twin-form' of the towers:

> *The Petronas Towers are not only symmetric in themselves, but they also create a distinctive, symmetric space between them. Each tower has it[s] own vertical axis, but more importantly the space between them also has a recognisable form.*

> *The center of the composition – the axis mundi was transferred from the solid forms to the space they defined. This central space is free of functions and the onlooker can assign spiritual or civic roles to it. … The symbolic attribute resides in the space between the buildings. … The most artistic decision made was to design the towers skyscrapers with distinctive silhouettes and to make the pair a single form.* (Pelli and Crosbie 2001)

Yet one observes that the twin towers – reflect the message of 'co-existence' which is recalled every time one gazes at the two giant spires or towers standing side by side. Whatever the basis, the form of the twin towers – whether unconscious or consciously intended – seems to represent and encapsulate some enduring message of co-existence between cultures, which is the very basis of the constant negotiation and balance sought by the leaders of the nation. Malaysian architecture, which is often associated with the vernacular folk-built forms, here has found a mature expression. Its form embodies a kind of dichotomy between the search for national identity and a unity between 'equals'.

Conclusions

In his seminal book *Leaves of the Same Tree: Trade and Ethnicity in the Straits of Melaka* (NUS 2008), Professor Leonard Andaya recalls the memory of lands bordering the Straits of *Melaka* as a rich and 'rhizomic' dynamism of forces. The South East Asian region, for centuries, has been the crucible of multiple cultures, within which each ethnicity, race and group was able to sustain its identity. Yet they have co-existed, collided and criss-crossed with one another in such a way that they have fused and grafted onto each other, and bred new visions, patterns and forms, including the vocabulary of arts and architecture. Much like species of grafted flora, they appear to offshoot and grow from each other as different trees, yet they support and sustain one another as they grow from the same 'root'. Malaysia lies within such a region and in fact at its epicentre. Historically, its settlements and urban centres have been a cultural melting pot of influences, with its forms of tensions and hybridity. As Asia modernises, the speed of its urbanisation is outpacing its socio cultural movements. Syncretism is a phenomenon of the region, and its physical expression seems to transcend an architecture of hybridity from which new synthesised form and vocabulary seem to emerge from disparate traditions yet combine into a language that is innovative, new and urbanised. The case studies discussed represent different forms of syncretism, ranging from a Malay-eclectic style, into a colonial eclecticism to modern syncretism. The search for national identity began even before the Modernist era of the 1960s; multicultural forms are expressive of the constant state of evolution of Malaysia reflecting the relative 'porosity' of its ethnicities. Offshoots and derivations are a character of a genealogical development of Malaysian architecture from its beginnings. These cases are evocative of a time when people became more conscious of a 'modernity', becoming aware of palpable change or on the threshold of change. Each form of architecture becomes a means of expressing the 'spirit of the age', and the elites of a society attempt to embody and express the currents of change in their monuments and symbolic representation of society through forms that arise from new building materials such as cast iron and concrete. The infusion, then dominance, of different forms, construction methods and architectural styles have given rise to structures representative of the dynamic and cross-cultural forces and streams of a region.

One branch may die while another root is formed; thus the relationship between cultures, dynamics of powers and influence and impact of the colonial era are couched in urban-architectural forms which are a concrete manifestation of the utopian idealism in technological advancement. It is argued that the co-existence of a global force with local talents as the cultural standard-bearers often produces unique works of architecture. Form becomes a physical testament of co-existence and the ability to syncretise cultures yet respecting a way of life, celebrating differences yet diffusing the common grounds. These recall some of humanity's greatest achievements in terms of hybrid architecture, which may lurk not in twenty-first-century cities, but in the quiet regions and even backwaters of what were once colonial outposts. Lastly, it posits that when local and global interests collide, yet refrain from control, local ingenuity and centuries-long traditions are facilitated and new ideas emerge. Urban-architectural form is a result of a constant tension or 'play' between such dominating forces. Modernity and nationhood serve as both instigator and the backdrop as the dynamics of forces played out again and again in the larger context of region. The syncretisation of cultures, without compromising the local host culture, must be seen and valued as one of the highest attainments of urban-architectural form and expression in an increasingly globalised world.

References

Article. (2016). *Article of Konservasi Bangunnan-bangunan Tradisional: Rumah Penghulu Abdul Ghani at official website of Jabatan Warisan Negara*. Retrieved December 13, 2016, at http://www.heritage.gov.my/index.php/konservasi/konservasi-bangunan/bangunan-tradisional/rumah-penghulu-abdul-ghani

Bunnell, T. (2004). *Malaysia, modernity and the multimedia super corridor: A critical geography of intelligent landscapes*. London: RoutledgeCurzon.

Crinson, M. (1996). *Empire building – Orientalism and Victorian architecture*. London/New York: Routledge Publishers.

Newspaper. (2014). *Newspaper article, Kosmo online written on 3 June 2014, Keistimewaan Rumah Melayu Melaka*. Retrieved December 13, 2016, at http://www.kosmo.com.my/kosmo/content.asp?y=2014&dt=0306&pub=Kosmo&sec=Horizon&pg=ho_04.htm

Yeang, K. (1984). Notes for a critical vernacular in contemporary Malaysian architecture. *UIA International Architect*, (6), 16–17. London.

Yeang, K. (1985). *The Tropical Verandah city*. Malaysia: Longman Publishers.

12

Conclusions

Shireen Jahn Kassim, Norwina Mohd Nawawi, and Mansor Ibrahim

Regional identities principally refer to larger geographical boundaries comprising of possibly, different ethnicities but with shared identities and traditions. There is a commonality of cultural traditions that have evolved along a trajectory, hence embodying a cultural network that represents a single continuum. On the other hand, a 'nation' resonates a more recent phenomenon, an almost 'modern' construct that has, at times, been imposed by others, external to the region.

In discussing the context of post-colonial nations such as Malaysia, one must recall a similar nationalistic experience of India, which on achieving independence from Britain in 1947, had experienced a resounding rebirth and saw this independence as a new threshold from which to rebuild from the fetters of the past. The birth of a new nation was, as aptly described by Charles Correa (2011), symbolised by the construction of its new capital in Punjab, i.e. Chandigarh, a city being born out of the harsh plains of Punjab '*without an umbilical chord*'

S. Jahn Kassim (✉) • N. Mohd Nawawi • M. Ibrahim
International Islamic University Malaysia, Kuala Lumpur, Malaysia

© The Author(s) 2018

S. Jahn Kassim et al. (eds.), *Modernity, Nation and Urban-Architectural Form*,
https://doi.org/10.1007/978-3-319-66131-5_12

(Correa 2011). In the post-colonial context, new nations emerging from the colonial experience as anxious entities that sought to obliterate traces of its colonial past. Urban-architectural form became a means and a representation of such ends. It paved a path of evolution, from the 'birth' of a nation to its maturity, a phenomena that resembled the growth of a human being, from birth, going through infancy, childhood, youth with its identity crisis, adulthood and eventual maturity. The era of modernity in this region is thus characterised by the same evolving continuum – akin to birth and infancy. The birth of a new nation is akin to the birth of a human being who on achieving independence, is essentially anxious to be independent of control.

Thus the South East Asian region, similarly with India, was characterised by an initial period of **absorption**, in which external influences were absorbed without any critical resistance. The tropicalised expressions of the International style, seen in both India and Malaysia, became symbols of nations due to their very novelty. Watkin (2000, p. 564) describes a similar trend in the Western world: 'are memorably inventive attempt to create monumentality without recourse to traditional Classical vocabulary.' The diffusion of Modernism was a form of 'avant-gardist' movements in style; a sociocultural movement which congealed into physical expressions. Global capitalist entities including multinational corporations became the sponsors and drivers of large and complex structures. These structures are requisite to the functioning of modern societies, as they house modern functions to enable the complicated web of socioeconomic life. These can be read as an outcome of a certain level of 'anxiety' and a by-product of post-colonial societies and nations. In expressing the identity of a nation they attempt not only to regionalise their forms amidst modernisation, but also to symbolise an independence in an increasingly complex modern world. The evolution of the Asian nation, in the early years of Independence, was characterised by these ideas, some which were unquestionably absorbed at times, the expressions of urban-architectural form were thus a reflection of the pressure of global ideas and movements. Modernity is defined as an external set of forces – whether cultural or social or economic – that had been diffused, dispersed and disseminated due to the simultaneous occurrence of a range of factors, including the end of two destructive world wars. In Europe, nations felt the urgent need to quicken the pace of development, and the anxiety of reflecting the new, had spurred forms that would throw off the 'yoke of the past'. At the onset of Independence, Asian nations were faced with a sudden vacuum left by the colonialists, and professionals returning from studies abroad acted as carriers or 'vectors' of modernity. Their influence has been decisive and distinctive up to the present day. In contrast to Europe and North America's period of post-Industrial Revolution which had spanned 200 years, Asian nations had evolved within a much shorter period of time; a pressurised and condensed time span of 50 to 60 years. In the midst of nations including Malaysia, grappling an intense period of development, changes were a form of 'fast-forward' evolution, as if making a giant leap through the 'worm-hole' of progress. In a comparatively short pace of time, there arose projects constructed in few decades involving large, and complex building types characterised by complex functions. These spurred spatial patterns, architectural elements and special functions that were characteristic of a period of growth. Some reflected kitsch, while others became part and parcel of the emerging complexity of urban forms in new cities, thus contributing towards a vastly changing urbanising and industrialising landscape. Concepts and aesthetic intentions of regionalism and national identity became part of a synergistic reaction, at times conflated, and at other times constituting different forms of 'cultural' pressures. Yet both simmered and brewed out of the need to counter the widespread, ubiquitous and natural tendency towards expedient economically-efficient forms. Each typology, even in the eclectic examples by colonial agents, had epitomised a struggle against the tendency to create conventional forms and structures. These forms are characteristic of the more complex nature of the evolution of developing cities amidst the race to urbanise, grow and modernise. Cities in Asia became part of not only the local landscape, but was infused into a global network and rapidly flowing field of pressures. As Jenkins (2006) observes:

> *Those with pretensions to global-city status must present their urban environment as a cosmopolitan, culturally vibrant place to live. In other words, if you want to be globally competitive, you have got to be cultured but in an avant-*

> *garde, global sort of way. The stodgy old national model will no longer do. … They represent a laissez-faire competitive aesthetic—a culture so intertwined with international economic competition that it is impossible to separate the two …*

Jones (2011) further describes that the efforts to infuse indigenous or idiosyncratic elements of the 'local' are part of the need to assert national and regional identity through formal strategies. These were also inflections that would localise building forms from Modernism's universalising tendencies. In the 1800s, both the Gothic and Classical languages were nationalised in Europe into different stylistic tendencies and vocabularies that have been known as universalising tendencies. Jones (2011, pp. 53–54) highlights how the national agenda had, at one time, harnessed the regionalised forms of modern architecture to inflect the universality of the language of public design into an acceptable form across races. This phenomenon is not only representative of the post-colonial nations, but was found even in earlier eras, societies and cultures in modernising Europe. 'A desire for representation, with attempts to construct and express idiosyncratic national cultural codes against the more universalizing tendencies inherent in modernity, was key to this cultural project' (Jones 2011).

In the Asian context, both vectors – the modern and the local – were fused into hybridities and new forms of regional and national derivations arise from archetypes. Regional and national identity conflated into national and regional derivatives and were at times synonymous and at other times, dissimilar. The South East Asian region became a source of expression towards regionalising the International style, and the local traditions are extracted and appropriated into the new complexities of an emerging nation.

In earlier years of independence, both a regional and national identity search had conflated in, these forms and expressions. The International style constituted a new form of language that was considered not only progressive, but a departure from the memories of a Colonial past. It signified freedom and freeing oneself from dependence. Yet some saw the International style as merely a change in the dressing and imageries of an underlying capitalist system, a legacy of Colonial sub-structures already embedded in urban patterns. Kahn (2006, p. 136) describes changes in the late 1800s in Malaysia:

> *In the case of Malaya … in the process, people entangled in loyalties to traditional rules and Islamic leaders, were separated from their local context. … the early decades of the 20th century was a period when colonial and local elites, began to articulate a view that the delocalization of colonial peoples, – their separation from ties to existing social, economic and religious communities and to traditional religion-political elites – was producing a crisis. … At the same time, transformation … would serve to re-embed the diverse inhabitants of the Malay Peninsula within a new socio-spatial order constructed by colonial capitalism and a modern state.*

A series of projects conceived in the speed of rapid development is part of the reembedding of a population in a new spatial order. This initially is represented by the novel forms of the Modernist style but which later, had evolved into a 'post-modernist' tendency of sculpting symbols of a new civic order. The strategy of amplification of artefacts from local traditions had a populist appeal – with an emotive dimension to the population. In the 1960s and 1970s, the transient influence of colonial remnants of power had determined the direction of projects as the architects and urban designers were either British or British-trained. By the 1980s and 1990s, Malaysian-born and educated architects were making their mark. Clean lines and minimalist expressions of the 1960s arose yet later became associated with homogeneity and monotony. Modernism, seem to suited to a nation anxious to build economically yet over time, it became increasingly anachronistic. What followed were attempts to imbue identity through heightening hybridity between a predominantly orthogonal language and the more emotive-organic style of Asian forms. In mosques, cultural centres and airports, these tensions simmered, and were brought to surface in a series of regionalised expressions which became symbolic of the synthesising forces between modernity and tradition.

These phenomena can be read as urban-architectural outcomes representing a kind of youthfulness and enthusiasm of a new nation, yet as the nation matures, just as a single human being does, it will forge path to find its own identity and its own independent footing. The foreign and the 'imitative' which at first seem 'progressive' and advanced, had later, spawn a response to the homogeneity it had triggered. Watkin (2000, p. 572) summarised the western world's similar and eventual reaction to Modernism, particularly linking such reactions to its casting off of history and tradition: *'The mass of banal International Style buildings, lacking all poetry or historical resonance, … produced all over the world, contributing to a state of alienation on the part of the public which erupted in the 1970s in a hostility to modern architecture on both sides of the Atlantic.'*

When referring and drawing from the vernacular palette, there is a fine line between 'criticality' and 'kitsch'. Kitsch, as outlined in Chap. 1, is the outcome of a rush to 'cut-and-paste' elements onto essentially modernist structures, without delving deeper into the substructures of tradition. In the early 1980s, architects such as Ken Yeang (1984, 1987) coined the 'critical vernacular' and theorists such as Kenneth Frampton coined the seminal theories of critical regionalism. Both proponents were essentially Modernist, who wanted to 'protect' Modernism from the tendency of degenerating into 'Post-Modernist' kitsch or what Yeang (1984) terms as 'cosmetic' elements. Hence Yeang (1984, 1986, 1987) formed a series of positions initially termed as 'the tropical skyscraper' and the 'environmental' filter, in which 'climate' is brought forward as the dominant source of form and architectural trope. Climatic design became the 'armature' of the Modernist position. However there is an essential limitation of drawing solely from a climatic position in an essentially equatorial climate. The nature of the climate, which is characterised by a monotonous weather throughout the year, lacks variation. This makes it an extremely limited source of form. Hence when Yeang mentions how some of his design initiatives fall short of its intended performance throughout the year, he is essentially lamenting on the difficulties of working with such a climate. Yet as a true 'modernist', he continues to champion it as an essential principle. However in later stages of his theories and designs, the tropical and 'filter' trope evolved into the 'ecological' theory from which the mulivariate nature of tropical ecology makes it a richer, and more dynamic source of form (Jahn Kassim 2004).

One of the universally accepted basis of form is the climatic ethos. Though the principle itself is inherent in the vernacular architecture, its archetypes and forms have a contrasting basis of design – one that is derived from an analytical basis of climate. While this principle has been utilised worldwide, the use of the climatic parameters as the source of architectural regional expressions has its limitations within a monotonous equatorial climate context. Temperate climates generally have a higher degree of variations with extreme changes occurring throughout the different times of the day and seasons of the year. Hence the climatic position assumes that such dynamic variations exist and thus constitute a source of architectural expression or differentiation in form and make. The climatic position under certain conditions may even reinforce an aesthetic preference or pre-disposition towards certain Western-based forms. A climatic functionalism may exert an opposite pressure against the much-needed regional differentiation in cities. As implied by Hagan (1998), although in another context, '[W]hen tendencies swerve towards the purely functional, the outcome may "spill" into the symbolic.' Thus under such conditions (i.e. when the intention is purely functional) the effects of its mechanisms can penetrate domains beyond the functional into the symbolic.

The Cultural esplanade complex, a distinctive addition to the urban skyline of Singapore is a curved hemisphere, with a layer of 'scales' that are optimised in terms of angle of incidence, in response to the movement of the tropical sun throughout the day. While the varied expression of the angling series of scales on its envelope help create interest and differentiation on the building envelope and shading devices, the form itself is distinctly neutral, a hemipherical form that is mute and silent in terms of referencing or evoking any specific cultural tradition may not be acceptable in Asian cities which struggle to assert a more culturally differentiated identity. The overall neutral hemispherical shape was particularly efficient in accomodating ancillary spaces and functions which must support cultural and theatrical productions, yet it does not evoke the memory of Asian forms and traditions, although finalised with 'scales' that were computer-optimised to cut out direct sunlight at different orientations under the Singapore climate. The device shaded a neutral form to signify a universal position which can be defined as 'without any racial overtones' to create an icon through a cultural centre in the middle of the city. Powell (2000) observes how such an approach would not have been possible without the use of advanced computer simulation tools. He further described the predominantly climatic approach behind the design of the centre:

> *Climatically the architects argue that it is inappropriate to have a naturally ventilated structure since we have come to expect the comfort of air-conditioning. … They have attempted to reconcile the inherent conflicts that arise between the exploitation of views, the exclusion of direct sunlight and high insolation, and the need for efficient air-conditioning.*

Contrary to theory, a climatic approach to regionalism or regional differentation is not consistently 'expressive' with all types of climates. The tropical zone is particularly challenging as it is characterised by anually consistent high ambient temperatures (23–34°C), high humidity, high and fairly evenly distributed rainfall, throughout the year with only small diurnal and annual variations of temperature, little seasonal variation, light winds and periods of still air. The main causes of discomfort are high daytime temperatures and high level of humidity. In traditional buildings such as village houses, continuous ventilation is provided by its essentially elevated structure and fragmented form with generous openings, in order to ensure a sweat evaporation rate sufficient to maintain thermal equilibrium and minimum sweat accumulation of the skin.

Climatic and Cultural Basis of Form: An Epistemological Difference

Jencks (1993, p. 94) insightfully observes: 'The potentially depressing point is that good ecological building may mean bad expressive architecture; in the trade-off between these two competing concerns, it often makes more eco-sense to push the building down, pack it tight and minimise surface'. Hawkes (2000) similarly points to a central difficulty in the design process and its basis of form: architectural designs are cultural-aesthetic matters and it is difficult to ground such decisions in the technical dimensions. Maxwell (1999) highlights a similar paradox – and links it to the architect's search for architectural expression:

> *If you accept the principle that the programme is the source of unity, the crucible of the architect's creative endeavour, you cannot postulate another principle, another crucible at the end of the designer's process, to satisfy the architect's craving for conspicuous self-expression. You cannot have it both ways. You certainly cannot have two sources of unity! ...*

Gerlenter (1995) describes, at length the basis of architectural form and the underlying difficulty and the source of the architectural paradox:

> *Although one intuitively feels that designing involves both sides of the equation, the logic of duality makes it virtually impossible to link the two together. It makes the individual who knows who takes in information from the outside, an object in a larger system and a recipient of objective, transpersonal material, while it makes the individual who creates, the individual who generates ideas from within, an autonomous and subjective being who transcends the existing and even the shared.*

Regionalist theories or intentions in 'regional' identity in form are romanticist and refers to design as an individual task. It encompasses the architect's personal expression and makes reference to architectural design as a totality. Rooted in the specifics of the situation, it reinforces the role of the architect as an artist and is less concerned with abstract and rational issues – and more with adding character and depth to designs. Such romanticist theories or philosophies favour the notion of organic 'wholeness' – *'where a solution springs from the artist's unconscious mind'* (Gerlenter 1995). It regards the conception of design as a matter of organic creation – in which the entire composition grows spontaneously and as a whole. There is a strong emotional dimension to romanticism and cultural-iconic intentions in regionalism is a response to the onset and impact of globalisation and the subtle and gradual destruction of local interests and identities in the various localities and countries.

Bioclimatic theories, on the other hand, imply a diametrically opposed idea regarding the source of architectural form. It implies an attitude to form-making that reflects the theories and methods of the exact sciences – where the performance of certain functions and fulfillment of objective or physical criteria would then suggest architectural form and then result in the transposition of these functions and criteria into built form. The reliance on scientific methods is inherently positivistic – it maintains that the source of form lies outside the designer. It emphasises the role of external phenomena unmediated by the individual mind. Taken to its extreme, it means discovering an architectural form that is innately contained in the external constraints of the design program without imposing one's own preconceptions upon that form.

Colquhoun (1970) interestingly observes this central paradox between iconic/romanticist intentions and functionalist paradigms underlying theories of the Modern Movement. This is due to the fact that:

> *The more rigorously the general physical or mathematical laws are applied to the solution of design problems, the less it is necessary to have a mental picture of the final form. The essence of a doctrine of functionalism contradicts any theory which would give priority to an intentional iconic form.*
>
> *A shift from the processes of knowledge to the processes of creation necessary entails a change in the underlying conception of the individual and his/her relationship to the external world. The two processes cannot be related together within the logic of the system.*

The climatic basis in regionalist identity assumed that external factors impinge upon architectural form and give it shape while national identity arise from a mental schema in which the designer who envisions the design as an organic 'whole' and 'conceptually'. Rowe (1976, p. 131) highlights this dilemma and suggests a reconciliation between the ideas:

> *The attempt to relate the spirit of the age to the function-structure-materials triad was entirely understandable. But in reality, there are natural anti-theses*

and not harmonious partners. They are positive and negative charges which authenticate any genuine process of creation. But they can be brought together only in a relationship of tension.

Symbols are necessary in a nation. The struggle for selfhood and collective consciousness must depend on certain type-forms. These must be rooted in a nation's need for independence and assertion. National forms are symbolic gestures that evoke meaning in terms of collective significance. This is arguably crucial during certain thresholds of nationhood. It restores the role of architecture and urban form as semiotic tools capable of collectively representing values other than itself. In an often disparate and diverse population, Curtis (1981) observes that monumentalism or monumentality is essentially needed to a nation,

This is because to create symbols laden with meaning and memory, the creative agent must choose between competing cultures and interest. Political power structures often determine the selection of the means of forging a national identity.

Islamic Architecture and Asian Form

Islamic architecture has been harnessed to represent such agendas and power structures, and a link with a global past. As noted in Chap. 2, Crinson (1999) describes how the language of Islamic architecture constituted a formal grammar that not only represented itself, but was harnessed to assert the presence of British imperialism in the 19th century. In more recent times, Jahn Kassim, Anis and Latip (2017) describes how the Islamic dome – rather than the Malay roof – was essentially used a strategy to assert the iconic presence of a new administrative palace built in Kuala Lumpur in the early 2000s. The *Istana Negara*, or National Palace, was designed as a hierarchical mass elevating it with a certain monumenality. Compared to the more subdued form of Malay traditional roofs, the dome was a marker of symbolic form amidst multistorey buildings. In the 1980s and 1990s, the use of Islamic vocabulary was as its height in Kuala Lumpur, expressed in commercial developments including highrise form and expression in the city, including the Dayabumi complex. Islamic architecture has a syncretic range of vocabulary accepted in various cultures, and in certain cases, the use of such Arab-Islamic elements has engendered contrasting effects, including discomfort. Putrajaya's vibrant use of Islamic architecture in mosque had made it a tourist destination, yet it evoked 'pastiche-like' dressing of administrative centres. Some had even the questioned the vcabulary in terms of its multicultural relevance. In the 1990s, Yat (2013) commented on rise of the Islamic style through Islamisation of the urban landscape which had cause some discomfort in a multiracial society:

> *The Islamisation of the urban landscape, which he claims is at the core of Malaysia' decolonisaion projects has somewhat marginalized the Chinese and proposes recuperating an urban and architectural history.*

Jahn Kassim et al. (2016) observes how the eclectic language of mosque architecture had consistently converge stereotypically on domes, arches, 'muqarnas' and calligraphy. Such arabesque decorative elements (Othman and Zainal-Abidin 2011) are used in representing Islam. Malaysia has reflected similar conservative trends when it comes to mosque forms. Their overall massing, features, forms and vocabulary, are almost always configured to eclectic expressions derived from conceptualisations, processes and imageries related to the Arab-Islamic origins. In the modern Muslim-state, the mosque is conventionally seen as a representative of the official religion of the nation, Islam, along with a long association with vocabularies and grammars derived from its Arab Islamic origins (Saniei and Delavar 2012). As Kassim, Anis and Latip (2017), discussed, with reference to the National Palace of Malaysia, the dome, instead of the Malay roof, was used to assert the presence of a national symbol rather than the Malay *bumbong panjang* roof which is comparatively subdued. In terms of elevation, there is also a lack of elements in local grammar in order to create a iconographic expression of identity. Although Malay traditions are replete with motifs, the hibiscus (Tengku Anis et al. 2017) was focused upon as ornamentation that could impart a national identity meaning.

Such discussions of national identity arising from regionalist elements bring to the fore the recurring dynamics of 'national' vs 'regional' forms. It is represent in continuing discourses and design decisions and these interactions essentially, the dynamics that has been played out in every era and region. Colquhoun (1989) observes the continued dialectics of a regional and national agenda which have given rise to episodes of 'critical regionalism,':

> *There is another phenomenon which might equally be called 'regionalism' that has nothing to do with any vernacular utopia or any critique of industrialization. This regionalism exists as part of unconscious 'ideologies' underlying current practice and is actually connected with political economic survival. … It is the result of a complex interaction between modern international capitalism and various national traditions ingrained in institutions and attitudes.*

National identity as a driver of urban-architectural form pursues a more intense and emotive sentiments. This often spurs a drastic insertion of form in the urban lanscape. Metaphors are means by which regional architects elevate traditions into such form. Hans Dieter Evers (2000) writes about how certain cities in Asia represented a kind of 'urbanisation without urbanism', in which the pace of rapid growth and the need to reconfigure nationalistic fevor, had brought about the building of monuments and sculptures in cities, while there was a slow evolution towards urbanism, '*Lacking a strong tradition of urbanism and having to battle with urban involution, … urbanism was symbolically constructed through the architecture of significant buildings, monuments and the planning of city space.*'

A constant challenge is how to protect regionalism from a degeneration into kitsch. As highlighted in Chap. 1 kitsch or pastiche is when a decision is made without sufficient time and processes delving deep into the layers and substructures of tradition. Stern (2009) attempts to articulate principles of a post-modernst architecture highlights the difference between a genuine allusion to historical references, to 'simplistic eclectism' or what he terms as 'predisgested imagery'. Yo be allusionistic, demands that architecture communicate meaning through metaphor and by direct reference. Most of the language became a kind of surface-patterning rather than a critical layering of local memory and regionalisation. Urban expression of traditional forms must transcend such cut-and-paste solutions into the 'critical'. This position inhabits a negotiated or tight rope zone between mere surface cut-and-paste, or a 'puffed-up' version of cultural identity in which artefacts are merely amplified as building form. In order to create a sense of monumentality and civic style, there must be a degree of layering rather than merely surrounting Modernist blocks with a pitch roof or a bulbous dome. It is this form of resistance to kitsch and grounding in local idiosyncracies that constitutes a persistent challenge. Such intentions, and expresisons, must range from regionalist nuances or inflections with a degree of formal explorations and alternative modalities of identities.

To move closer to the values and representation of depth and criticality, localised strategies must penetrate into the substructures of traditions. This is to unearth layers of memory and into enriching the present stock of buildings through a critical interpretation of the past. A position must be formed, one that ranges from a minimum differentiation to highlight a position of resistence to an architecture of 'consumption' to one that can create a symbolic impact of new cities. Such issues, had also surface during the early years of Post-Modernism, from which designers such as Robert Sterm has outlined three principles of which to reinvigorate the city, contextualism, allusionism, and ornamentalism (Stern 2009), which recall the very themes of regionalism in modern South East Asia. A significant achievement must be linked towards achieving a minimum balance, a 'form' that achieves some collective significance and cultural-consciousness of a rapidly developing nation at the same time. This may then encourage alternative but culturally differentiated forms that contribute to the formation of cultural and locational identities in rapidly developing cities.

This is a process that must go beyond the type, as usefully described by Herkert (1999),

> *to generate solutions not only within the narrow bounds defined by the characteristics of the archetypical form but to introduce a new style which differs radically from the prevalent archetypical style.*

The Vernacular Identity

The tropical city is a conundrum, while on the one hand, historians and urbanists observe the absence of a distinctive urbanism in its historical urban cities and forms, yet on the other hand, tropical cities has inverted itself into a city of highrise airconditioning blocks separated by wide empty spaces with introverted shopping malls and complexes. While the idea of a tropical urban regionalism has been highlighted in the past, there is a lack of classical model derived from traditional origins. Yet as part of movement of new urbanism, traditional models must again be relooked and in tropical South East Asia, the vernacular Malay world, hold the promise of extended pavilions, outdoor pavilions, shaded walkways and treelined boulevards characteristic of an indigenous tropical urbanism. At the oneset of Colonisation, such tropicality was sustained in the siting and construction of administrative buildings yet as the same nations became free from their colonial past, and race to progress, such tropical urbanism – a means of acculturising and indegenising public space – has been lost. One must again define these spaces in terms of shaded 'pools' or zones, and they range from detached and attached spaces, and is a salient and crucial part of the tropical language of urban design, and which can then be used to generate new ideas in tropical urban design. The Malay vernacular architecture must be expanded by defining key characteristics – including its elevated form, wide openings, layered yet wide protective roofs and linear-like arrangement of spaces. Its elevational characteristics – full height windows, decorative wall, wallboards, decorative eaves, finials and ventilative panels – are at times, expressed in variations of decorative motifs and reflective of its climate and interpretations varies from state to state from region to region; yet there are several key defining attributes and common denominator. One of the most critical hallmarks of the lifestyle of the Malays is the *serambi* or *anjung* (the Malay verandah) – which in general, refers the characteristic outdoor room or large protruding verandah that protrudes or extends significantly from the main body of the house or main spaces. The Malay word *se•ram•bi* means a space that is extended. While its variants differ across different states, essentially the *serambi* is an covered but open outdoor portico in which the host or owner of the house can sit and entertain guests and/or relaxes and enjoys the evening and night air. After eating, they would sit on the porch for chatting, relax, lie down and have supper. At times, it extends to the left and right parts of the house and the space is extended adjacent to the main room or the main room. It is typically lower in the main room, distinguished by finishing with the surrounding wall or pole position for each corner. It is a symbol of the habit of a culture, which evolved from a culture of hospitality and decorum on receiving guest. Forms reflect a culture – through centuries of attunement with the prevailing climate and the culture and lifestyle of the traditional population. The Malay palace is the heightened, and at times, grandiose, form of the Malay vernacular – the result of artisanal expertise at its highest form. By the early 1900s the vocabulary itself began infusing the colonial (global) influences, while certain palaces were a result of a tension between local control and Colonial influence. Yet, amidst such influences, elements of the 'Classical Malay', a kind of controlled and proportioned aesthetic form and language can be discerned which is related to the roots of the archetype in the timber house. 'Classicality' can also refer to a kind of symmetry and concordance with the rules of local traditions, one which reflect the essential stability of the old system of life. Palatial Classicality can be defined as (Jahn Kassim et al. 2017): 'Salient features such as the "awan larat, tunjuk langit and tebar layar" (translated as the malay decorative ventilation panels, roof finials and decorative barge board) and a "symmetrical internal spatial order" which is essentially how "the traditional rules of the vernacular house" were essentially translated to a grander scale'; and

Classicality reflects a kind of: 'triadic principles of symmetry, axial planning and harmonic proportions'. Malay palaces can be viewed as the apotheosis or final branch of the Malay architectural genealogy, but which evovled in times of modernity, to include essentially the last 'remnant' of 'modernised' Malay-Asian vernacular which had infused the effect of a global Colonial trends before the style is compromised by an overwhelming dominance of Colonial influences.

One recalls ulimately what represents an architecture of identity is the expressive outcome of what is 'endemic' in the region. Yet a key challenge, as highlighted in Jahn Kassim et al. (2016), is how to avoid the pastiche or cosmetic approach and strategy of merely surmounting essentially Modernist structures with Malay roof form in order to evoke identity in the city. In discussions in Chaps. 3, 4 and 5, early attempts to evoke a monumental identity, saw the amplication of traditional forms such as the roof, which adorned modern 'boxes' into an exagerrated form of Malay houses.

While new materials such as steel and glass have been articulated to evoke history, and fuse a reference to both progress and tradition, the use and present of timber still carries a powerful identificaion with Asian tropical trraditions. Currently worlwide, timber as a building and interior material, is making a comeback due to the low embodied carbon content of the material, yet it advantages may prove to be more of its psychological impact, rather than physical. Recent research have attributed timber to soothing and warm effects to the building occupants, which are valuable in certain programmes. Yet even without resorting to timber, certain spatial and tectonic expressions recall traditional identities such as a columnar space, the use of elevated structures, wide windows and steeply pitch roofs, even when expressed in steel and concrete. A key example of one of fusion of local and global 'archetypes' is that of Masjid Negara which can be said to have successfully carried both cultural tropes –local and Western – and cultural iconography as a symbol of national identity.

In this case, form and language are harnessed not only to successfully evoke a regional identity, but also simultaneously a symbolic landmark of national proportions. Many have attributed to Masjid Negara's success to not only its modern & tropical attributes, but universal appeal to a population of multicultural backgrounds. These can be related also to (1) a propensity towards 'hybridity' or 'neutral' elements, and (2) form based on constructional forces or controlled ornamental expression and (3) the play and interspersing of vocabulary, that refer directly to the tropics, yet refer the current ideas of modern civilisation, including precision and science, industrialisation and modernisation.

In retrospect, Masjid Negara's success was part of its ability to 'tropicalise' and 'vernacularise' an international language which was then hybridised with Malay emblems and abstracted references to local symbols. Through this hybridisation, a basis of the 'rational' was still maintained, yet traditions of the local were fused with the global, resulting in a new form of architecture that is appreciated and acclaimed to present day. Architecture became a marker of time, a statement of hopes towards a progressive future yet keeping a hold of the comfortable familiarity with the past with its traditional emblems, and symbols.

The intersection of multiple cultural identities is a particular challenge of urban-architectural forms. What is particularly challenging are the persistent calls for the neutrality of the International style and the appropriation to climate, but the reversion to roots and the nuances of the local culture. This position can be viewed as an act of negotiating constantly, acceptable yet tight-rope stances of reconciliation between positions, between dichotomies, and between tradition and modernity. Maggie Peng (2012) in her short, yet animated and lively piece in an international magazine speaks of Malaysia in the quagmire of its cross-cultural modernity:

> *As this young nation continues to build at an ever rapid pace, the ambitious scale of current development describes the illusive process of the search for national identity …*
>
> *Already a city with many centers, new projects continue to tug and pull at the extents of KL.A walk through the city is an experience of polarization, contradiction an disjunction, moving through patchworks of iconic triumphs, bizarre*

> *urban conditions, and … all revealing the complex history and cultural mix that is intrinsically Malaysian.*
>
> *The unlikely mix of ingredients creates surprising urban landscapes and cultural conditions, almost by accident. Symbolism, iconography and forms are re-appropriated, given a new purpose in the process of creating Malaysia's national identity.*

Modernity is thus constantly characterised by the tensions of an internally-brewed and an external set of forces – whether cultural or social or economic – that collide and collude due to the pace of development in newly independent nations. Independence had brought a tide of optimism yet it has also cast a shadow of a tumultous time and tensions that can 'make' or 'break' a nation. With the disintegration of past socio-economic structures, and forces, there is a vacuum as the localities' traditions were often not yet matured enough to face the often rapid and momentous changes. In the context of Malaysia, the dynamics of identity oscillates between different poles of expressions and its attendant vocabularies.

The pace of development in a newly independent nation is often rapid and sudden. New ideas are not allowed the requisite time of reaching maturity and growth. Malaysia sits at the SouthEast Asian crossroads. Its position, throughout centuries, exposed it to a quagmire of forces and influences from all sources. As the nation underwent the throes of modernisation and the intersection of cultural identities, both national identity and regional inflections became entangled into a mixed bag of sorts.

The intersections and crucial junctures between modernity and tradition has manifested in multiple expressions and intersections between regionalism, national identity and localisation. Such tensions and conflations are critical in an increasingly homogenising world, as the forces of regionalism and search for identity represent signs of the assertion of the collective local consciousness of an urbanising and civic population. They also represent attempts at a resistance in the form of physical responses to the hegemony of global forces and a means to assert a measure of independence. In the case of Malaysia, such forms are emblemetic of a multicultural nation's perennial struggle to assert itself. Multiple forces confront a nation and the subsequent architectural and urban forms are but physical remnants of such dynamics of confrontations and constant tension. As such, developments arise partly from an anxious desire to depart from memories of a colonial past.

As Broadbent (1978) suggests that a building 'at any time, can be the signifier, signified or referent. A building exists as signifier in its site but as signified by photographs and diagrams.' In the Modernist and Post-Modernist eras of modernity, that a more inclusive language and urban-architectural form need to be pursued. It is the relationship between such language and its physical manifestation in structures, reflect the geneology of form which grow from the Asian traditions, and its historical-to-present time dynamics of global vs local powers which recall, amongst others its resilience despite the influence and impact of the Colonialism on local cultures. Such dichotomies and tensions are couched in structures. These forms are reflections of how a nation or culture resists yet absorb the impact of a global forces. During Colonial era, certain traditions have prevailed and instiutions become the cultural standard–bearers of memorable forms of urban design and architecture. Form then becomes a physical testament of the ability to synchronise competing agendas and interests, and ultimately the embodiment of is abiliy to syncretise cultures. Humanity's greatest achievements may perhaps be seen in terms of an era, or a time and hence an architecture of coexistence, which may lurk not in 21st century global cities, but in the fringes or even backwaters of what was once, Colonial outposts. Symbolic architecture – forms that reflect the perennial search for identity – is a recurring 'play' of the dominating forces, e.g. between the dominance and diffusion of forces in the form of cultural assertions and expressions of nations and races, in which their language can be different representations of stylistic shifts from one era or trajectory of Modernity to the next.

Identity is at times, formed and viewed as the degree of departure from convention, architects and urban designers are anxious to be judged according how much their departure and formal articulations can overthrow present convention or stereotypical forms. Their embrace and advocacy of certain styles must be seen as part of a Post-Modern concern of always creating something new and the reception of meaning that goes with it. Such forms must have the ability to communicate ideals and have a link with the modern world, while fulfilling the need to adapt to an increasingly universal audience or population. In the case of a post-colonial nation, such as Malaysia, such ambitions are intertwined with these of a diverse population and these challenges represent a continuous dynamic and dialectics, between a universal identity, and the need towards a rootedness in culture, tradition and place.

References

Broadbent, G. (1978). A plain man's guide to the theory of signs in architecture. *Architectural Design, 47*(7–8), 474–482.

Colquhoun, A. (1970 [1997]). Typology and design method. In K. Nesbitt (Ed.), *Theorising a new agenda for architectural theory.* New York: Princeton Architectural Press.

Colquhoun, A. (1989). Regionalism and technology. In A. Colquhoun (Ed.), *Modernity and the classical tradition: Architectural essays 1980–1987* (pp. 207–211). Cambridge, MA: MIT Press.

Correa, C. (2011, June 10/1964, June). Chandigarh: The assembly. *The Architectural Review.*

Evers, H.-D. (2000). Globalization, local knowledge, and the growth of ignorance: The epistemic construction of reality. *Asian Journal of Social Science, 28*(1), 13–22.

Gerlernter, M. (1995). *Sources of architectural form – A critical history of Western design theory.* New York: Manchester University Press.

Hagan, S. (1998). The good, the bad and the juggled: The new ethics of building materials. *Journal of Architecture, 3*(2), 107–115.

Jahn Kassim, P. S. (2004). *The bioclimatic skyscraper – A critical analysis of the theories and designs of Ken Yeang.* Unpublished PhD thesis 2004, University of Brighton.

Jones, P. (2011). *The sociology of architecture: Constructing identities.* Liverpool: Liverpool University Press.

Kahn, J. S. (2006). *Other Malays – Nationalism and cosmopolitanism in the modern Malay world* (p. 2). Singapore: NUS Press, National University Singapore.

Kassim, J., Shireen, P., Kadir, A., Anis, T., Latip, A., & Syala, N. (2017). *Architecture, identity and the city, - Issues and dichotomies of national identity in the Malaysian national palace, paper presentation, SUDLIC conference,* UTM Kuala Lumpur.

Othman, R., & Zainal-Abidin, Z. J. (2011). The importance of Islamic art in mosque interior. *Procedia Engineering, 20,* 105–109. https://doi.org/10.1016/j.proeng.2011.11.144.

Powell, R. (2000). *Singapore – Architecture of a global city*. Singapore: Archipelago Press.

Stern, R. (2009). *Architecture on the edge of post modernism*. New Haven: Yale University Press.

Watkin, D. (2000). Karl Frederich Schinkel. In *A history of western architecture* (3rd ed.). London: Laurence King Publishing.

Yat, M. L. (2013). *Architecture and urban form in Kuala Lumpur: Race and Chinese spaces in a postcolonial city*. London/New York: Routledge.

Yeang, K. (1984). Notes for a critical vernacular in contemporary Malaysian architecture. *UIA International Architect*, (6), 16–17. London.

Yeang, K. (1986). Landuse, climate and architectural form. In *Design for high-intensity development: Proceedings of the international conference on urban design*, The Aga Khan Programme for Islamic Architecture, USA, pp. 75–80.

Yeang, K. (1987). *Tropical urban regionalism: Building in a South East Asian city*. Singapore: Concept Media.

Yeang, K. (2016). Architecture and identity. *Architecture Malaysia, 28*(6), PAM (Malaysian Institute of Architects).

Index

© The Author(s) 2018
S. Jahn Kassim et al. (eds.), *Modernity, Nation and Urban-Architectural Form*,
https://doi.org/10.1007/978-3-319-66131-5

The manufacturer's authorised representative in the EU is Springer
Nature Customer Service Centre GmbH, Europaplatz 3, 69115 Heidelberg,
Germany. If you have any concerns regarding our products, please
contact ProductSafety@springernature.com

Printed and bound by CPI Group (UK) Ltd, Croydon, CR0 4YY
05/10/2026
02228138-0003